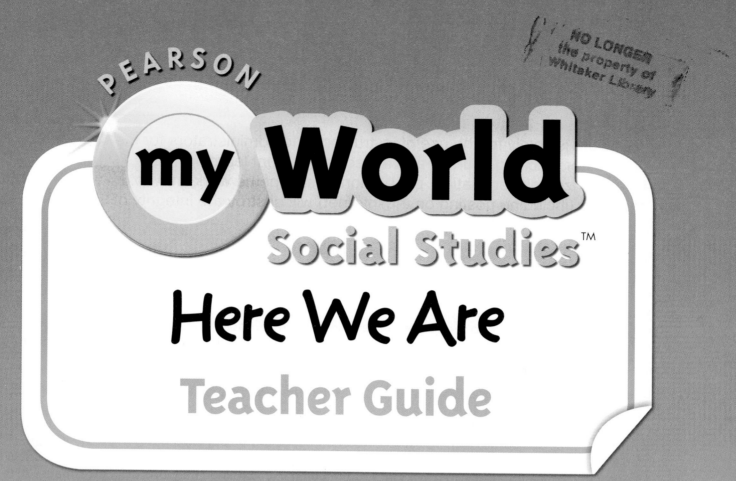

PEARSON

my World
Social Studies™
Here We Are
Teacher Guide

PEARSON

Boston, Massachusetts
Chandler, Arizona
Glenview, Illinois
New York, New York

Photography

Every effort has been made to secure permission and provide appropriate credit for photographic material. The publisher deeply regrets any omission and pledges to correct errors called to its attention in subsequent editions.

Unless otherwise acknowledged, all photographs are the property of Pearson Education, Inc.

Photo locators denoted as follows: Top (T), Center (C), Bottom (B), Left (L), Right (R), Background (Bkgd)

Front cover (TL) Albert de Bruijn, 2010/Shutterstock, (C) Ariel Skelley/Getty Images, (CR) Hemera/Thinkstock, (BL) JLP/Jose L. Pelaez/Corbis, (BL) Per-Anders Pettersson/Contributor/Getty Images News/Getty Images, (T) Susan Montgomery, 2010/Shutterstock; **iii** Jim Cummins; **iii** Linda Bennett; **xii** Grant Wiggins; **T12** Grant Wiggins; **T13** Authentic Education; **T16** Karen Wixson; **T20** Jim Cummins; **T24** Linda Bennett; **T25** Getty Images/AFP; **T29** Shutterstock/Monkey Business Images; **T33** Shutterstock/Rob Marmion; **T37** Shutterstock/Dmitriy Shironosov; **Back Cover** (TR) ©DK Images, (BL) Paper Boat Creative/Getty Images, (CC) Tom Tracy Photography/Alamy Images.

ISBN-13: 978-0-328-63964-9
ISBN-10: 0-328-63964-8
12   16

Program Consulting Authors

The Colonial Williamsburg Foundation
Williamsburg, VA

 Dr. Linda Bennett
Associate Dean,
Department of Learning,
 Teaching, & Curriculum
College of Education
University of Missouri
Columbia, MO

 Dr. Jim Cummins
Professor of Curriculum,
 Teaching, and Learning
Ontario Institute for
 Studies in Education
University of Toronto
Toronto, ON, Canada

 Dr. James B. Kracht
Byrne Chair for Student
 Success
Executive Associate Dean,
College of Education
 and Human
 Development
Texas A&M University
College Station, TX

 Dr. Alfred Tatum
Associate Professor,
 Director of the UIC
 Literacy, Language,
 and Culture Program
University of Illinois
 at Chicago
Chicago, IL

 Dr. William E. White
Vice President for
 Productions,
 Publications and
 Learning Ventures
The Colonial Williamsburg
 Foundation
Williamsburg, VA

Consultants and Reviewers

PROGRAM CONSULTANT

Dr. Grant Wiggins
Coauthor, *Understanding by Design*

ACADEMIC REVIEWERS

Bob Sandman
Adjunct Assistant Professor of
 Business and Economics,
Wilmington College–Cincinnati
 Branches
Blue Ash, OH

Jeanette Menendez
Reading Coach,
Doral Academy Elementary
Miami, FL

Kathy T. Glass
Differentiated Instruction
Glass Educational Consulting
Woodside, CA

Roberta Logan
African Studies Specialist Retired,
Boston Public Schools/Mission Hill
 School
Boston, MA

PROGRAM TEACHER REVIEWERS

Glenda Alford-Atkins
Eglin Elementary School
Eglin AFB, FL

Andrea Baerwald
Boise, ID

Ernest Andrew Brewer
Assistant Professor,
Florida Atlantic University
Jupiter, FL

Riley D. Browning
Gilbert Middle School
Gilbert, WV

Charity L. Carr
Stroudsburg Area School District
Stroudsburg, PA

Jane M. Davis
Marion County Public Schools
Ocala, FL

Stacy Ann Figueroa, MBA
Wyndham Lakes Elementary
Orlando, FL

LaBrenica Harris
John Herbert Phillips Academy
Birmingham, AL

Marianne Mack
Union Ridge Elementary
Ridgefield, WA

Emily L. Manigault
Richland School District #2
Columbia, SC

Marybeth A. McGuire
Warwick School Department
Warwick, RI

Laura Pahr
Holmes Elementary
Chicago, IL

Jennifer Palmer
Shady Hills Elementary
Spring Hill, FL

Diana Rizo
Miami-Dade County Public
 Schools/Miami Dade College
Miami, FL

Kyle Roach
Amherst Elementary,
 Knox County Schools
Knoxville, TN

Eretta Rose
MacMillan Elementary School
Montgomery, AL

Nancy Thornblad
Millard Public Schools
Omaha, NE

Jennifer Transue
Siegfried Elementary
Northampton, PA

Megan Zavernik
Howard-Suamico School District
Green Bay, WI

Dennise G. Zobel
Pittsford Schools–Allen Creek
Rochester, NY

CONTENTS

Program Overview xii

How to Use This Teacher Guide T8

Planning With the End in Mind T12

The Three Pillars of English Language Learning....... T16

Students as Digital Citizens T20

Building 21st Century Learning Environments T24

Reading in the Social Studies Classroom T28

**Differentiated Instruction and
Social Studies Content**........................... T32

Real Learning with Activities T36

Assessing Learning in Social Studies............... T40

Pacing Guide................................... T44

Correlation to the NCSSS....................... T46

Reading Programs Correlation T48

BALLOT BOX

Chapter 1 **My Family, My School**. 1
Chapter 2 **Everybody Works** 27
Chapter 3 **Where We Live** 49
Chapter 4 **Our Traditions**. 77
Chapter 5 **Life Then and Now** 101

My Family, My School

THE BIG ? How do people best cooperate?

	Flip Chart	Teacher Guide
my Story Spark	5	3
♫ "We Go to School"	6	4
Vocabulary Preview	7	4

Lesson 1
What makes a good citizen? 8 6

Lesson 2
What are rights? What are responsibilities? 10 8

Lesson 3
How do we get along with others? 12 10

◉ Reading Skills: Main Idea and Details 14 12

Lesson 4
What rules do we follow? 16 14

Lesson 5
Who are our leaders? 18 16

Lesson 6
How do we make decisions? 20 18

21C Collaboration and Creativity: Problem Solving 22 20

Lesson 7
What are our country's symbols? 24 22

Lesson 8
What are our country's monuments? 26 24

my Story Spark 28 26

Chapter 4

Our Traditions

How is culture shared?

	Flip Chart	Teacher Guide
my Story Spark	78	79
"Holidays Are Special Days"	79	80
Vocabulary Preview	80	80

Lesson 1
How are people alike and different? 81 82

⊙ Reading Skills: Compare and Contrast 83 84

Lesson 2
How are families alike and different? 85 86

Lesson 3
What is culture? 87 88

Lesson 4
How do we celebrate? 89 90

Lesson 5
What are national holidays? 91 92

Lesson 6
Who are American folk heroes? 93 94

Lesson 7
What are other cultures like? 95 96

21C Critical Thinking: Distinguish Fact From Fiction 97 98

my Story Spark 99 100

Chapter 5

Life Then and Now

How does life change throughout history?

	Flip Chart	Teacher Guide
my Story Spark	101	103
♫ "We Share History"	102	104
Vocabulary Preview	103	104

Lesson 1
What is my personal history? 104 106
◉ **Reading Skills:** Sequence 106 108

Lesson 2
How do we talk about time? 108 110

Lesson 3
How do we measure time? 110 112

Lesson 4
What is a timeline? 112 114

Lesson 5
How can we learn about history? 114 116
21c **Critical Thinking:** Use Illustrations 116 118

Lesson 6
Who are American heroes from the past? 118 120

Lesson 7
How have families changed? 120 122

Lesson 8
How has school changed? 122 124

Lesson 9
How have communities changed? 124 126

Lesson 10
How has technology changed? 126 128

my Story Book 128 130

Notes

The Journey Begins With Essential

myWorld Social Studies incorporates Backward Design, co-created by program author Grant Wiggins. The Backward Design process begins by asking an "Essential Question," with the goal of focusing on the desired understanding that students should acquire, and works backward to that understanding. Your students will be able to explore concepts, build knowledge, and transfer what they've learned beyond the classroom.

Why Essential Questions?

Each Essential Question provides a larger framework to guide students and help them see the big idea of each chapter. Woven throughout each lesson, activity, and assessment, the Essential Questions help students to

- connect to the content by activating prior knowledge and engaging them in each lesson

- experience social studies through meaningful hands-on activities

- transfer their knowledge to new learning situations that demonstrate true understanding

"We want students to understand . . . the goal is UNDERSTANDING, not superficial knowledge."

Grant Wiggins, *myWorld Social Studies* consultant

Questions

Active Reading

CONNECT

EXPERIENCE

Digital Presentations

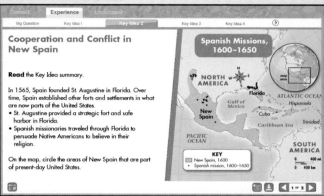

Cooperation and Conflict in New Spain

Read the Key Idea summary.

In 1565, Spain founded St. Augustine in Florida. Over time, Spain established other forts and settlements in what are now parts of the United States.
• St. Augustine provided a strategic fort and safe harbor in Florida.
• Spanish missionaries traveled through Florida to persuade Native Americans to believe in their religion.

On the map, circle the areas of New Spain that are part of present-day United States.

Spanish Missions, 1600–1650

THE BIG ?

UNDERSTAND

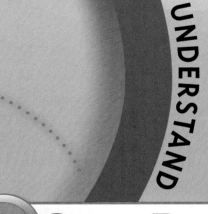

my Story Book

Mission San Luis
A Multicultural Community

Watch the myStory Video to learn more about the Mission San Luis built in Tallahassee, Florida.

myStory Video

**myStory Book
myWorld Activity**

ENDURING UNDERSTANDING

CONNECT

During the first phase of instruction, students are introduced to a Big Question and a myStory Video, both of which help them establish personal meaning and connect to the content in the chapter.

myStory Spark

The myStory Book writing strand in the program begins with a myStory Spark activity in which students record their initial ideas about the Big Question.

Chapter 4

U.S. Government

myStory Spark

Why do we have government?

Think about why leaders make rules. Then **write** about why are important.

Many people celebrate our government on Independence Day.

Chapter 3

Communities Build

myStory Spark

How does our past affect our present?

Describe something about your community that

The church at Mission San Luis

78

myStory Video

Students watch a video in which children their own age explore the Big Question and the key ideas they'll learn about in the chapter, or a character from the chapter comes to life in a graphic novel style animation. Print versions of both the "live student" and animated graphic novel videos are also included in the chapter opener of the Student Worktext.

Lesson 1 America's First Peoples
Lesson 2 Early Explorers
Lesson 3 Early Spanish Communities
Lesson 4 Early French Communities
Lesson 5 Early English Communities
Lesson 6 Creating a New Nation

Mission San Luis
A Multicultural Community

myStory Video

From about 1560 to 1690, there were more than 100 Spanish missions built throughout Florida. A mission is a settlement that has a church where religion is taught. One of the most famous missions is Mission San Luis. Located in Tallahassee, it is one of the last remaining mission sites today. "It's also the only place where both the Apalachee and the Spaniards lived together," says Grace. The Apalachee are Native Americans and [Spa]niards are people from Spain. "I love learning [ab]out other cultures," she adds. No one lives at the [mis]sion anymore, but it has been rebuilt. Visitors can [visit] the mission and watch people act out what life [was] like there hundreds of years ago.

Native Americans and
[Spa]niards shared this mission,"
[sh]e explains. At that
[time] Native Americans
[and] European settlers
[usual]ly did not live
[toget]her. Mission
[San] Luis was
[specia]l.

Grace was excited to visit one of the last remaining missions.

Lesson 1 Tensions With Britain
Lesson 2 The Colonists Rebel
Lesson 3 Declaring Independence
Lesson 4 On the Battlefield and at Home
Lesson 5 Winning Independence

Samuel Adams
Champion of Liberty

myStory Video

[The America]n Revolution was a war fought for liberty. It was [mar]ked greatness in a few ordinary people. George [Washington] known as a heroic general. Thomas Jefferson [is known fo]r writing the Declaration of Independence [and for] warning of a British invasion. However, [of all t]he battles of the revolution, one man in Boston [led a m]ovement that started the fight for liberty. He [fought] against the British, but the British called [him a d]angerous man in Massachusetts." His fellow [colonists calle]d him "the father of American independence." [That was Sa]muel Adams.

[As a young m]an, Samuel looked more like a poor student [than a futur]e revolutionary. After grammar school in his [home tow]n, Massachusetts, he attended Harvard [and gradu]ated at age seventeen.

[It wa]s not unusual to have such an early start [to an educa]tion. Adams's family hoped he would become [a minister. He] showed an interest only in politics. He loved to [debate a]bout how the colonies should be governed.

Samuel Adams speaking at Harvard College

EXPERIENCE

During the second phase of instruction, students actively engage in acquiring new knowledge and skills. This new knowledge helps them develop a deeper understanding of the Big Question, which they revisit at the end of each lesson.

Student Interactive Worktext

Students will love writing, drawing, circling, and underlining content in their own worktexts. The worktext format encourages greater interaction with the text and more active reading.

Lesson 1

America's First Peoples

Envision It!

Look at the picture. Write what natural resource was used to build these homes.

Every community has a history shaped by the people who first lived there. Your community is special ... past as well as its present.

Cultural Groups

Native Americans were the first people to settle in North America. There were many different Native American groups and they each had their own cultures and **customs,** or special ways of doing things.

The map shows the regions of North America where Native Americans lived. Each group used the natural resources in their region to meet their needs. Native Americans who lived in the Pacific Northwest caught fish from the Pacific Ocean. Those living on the Plains used the rich soil there for farming.

... two ways Native Americans used natural ... live.

Cherokee of the Southeast

Long ago, the Native American group called the Cherokee settled in the forests of the southeastern United States. The Cherokee settled in this area because of geography: rich soil, rivers, and trees.

The Cherokee first settled in North America more than 1,000 years ago. They were hunters and farmers. They ate meat, fruit, and vegetables. They used trees to build houses. They covered the wooden frames with mud from the nearby riverbanks. Later, the Cherokee built log homes that kept out the cold and snow in winter.

A famous Cherokee named Sequoyah (sih KWO uh) invented a system for writing the Cherokee language. Once people learned the 86 symbols, they could read and write the language.

2. ◉ **Main Idea and Details Describe** how the Cherokee used natural resources.

_____

_____

myworldsocialstudies.com ▶ Experience

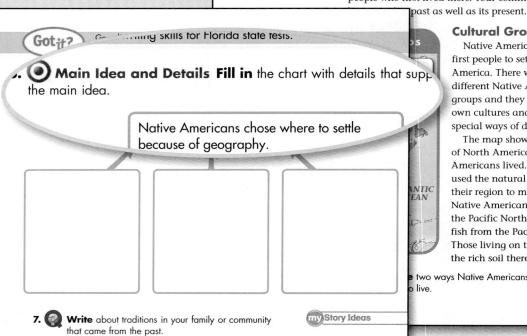

Got it? ... ng skills for Florida state tests.

. ◉ Main Idea and Details Fill in the chart with details that supp... the main idea.

Native Americans chose where to settle because of geography.

7. ❓ **Write** about traditions in your family or community that came from the past.

my Story Ideas

_____

_____

■ **Stop!** I need help with ....

❚❚ **Wait!** I have a question about ....

▶ **Go!** Now I know ....

myworldsocialstudies.com ▶ Experience ▶ Got it?   87

Target Reading Skills

The worktext enables students to practice important Target Reading Skills—essential skills they'll need when reading informational texts throughout their lives.

myStory Ideas

The myStory Book writing strand continues throughout the chapter. At the end of each lesson, students respond to a writing prompt labeled "myStory Ideas".

Got it? Go online to myworldsocialstudies.com to compare and contrast early French explorers.

5. ⊙ **Sequence Write** three main events of the lesson in order from first to last. For each event, **explain** why it was important.

Describe something unique about early French exploration.

my Story Ideas

Stop! I need help with

Digital Presentations

Every lesson includes a Digital Presentation that is whiteboard compatible and allows students to actively engage with the content.

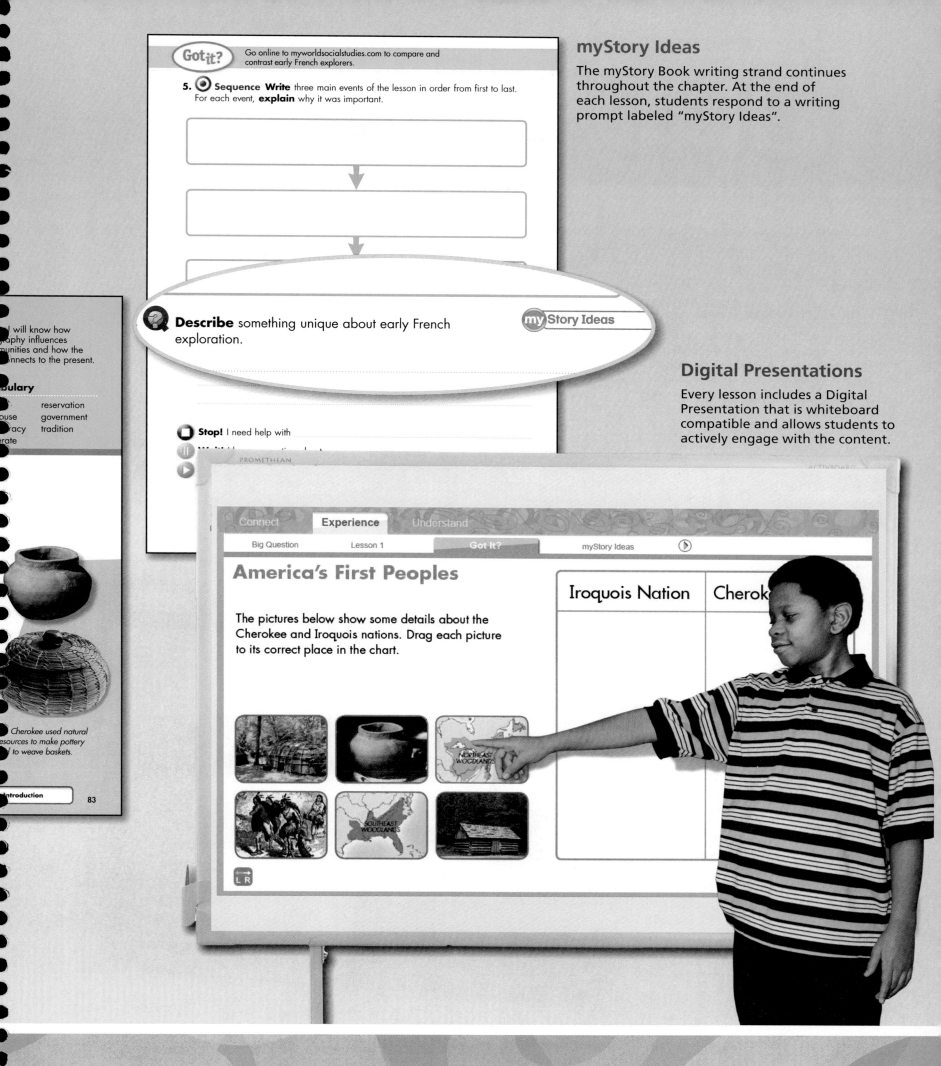

PROMETHEAN   ACTIVBOARD

Connect   **Experience**   Understand

Big Question   Lesson 1   **Got It?**   myStory Ideas

America's First Peoples

The pictures below show some details about the Cherokee and Iroquois nations. Drag each picture to its correct place in the chart.

Iroquois Nation	Cherok...

will know how geography influences communities and how the past connects to the present.

cabulary
to...	reservation
ghouse	government
f...acy	tradition
operate	

Cherokee used natural resources to make pottery and to weave baskets.

Introduction   83

UNDERSTAND

During the final phase of instruction, students actively demonstrate their understanding of the chapter content through a rich variety of assessment options.

myWorld Activities

Small group activities provide opportunities for students to demonstrate and transfer their understanding of the chapter content. Activities range from mapping, graphing, and role playing, to read-alouds and analyzing primary sources.

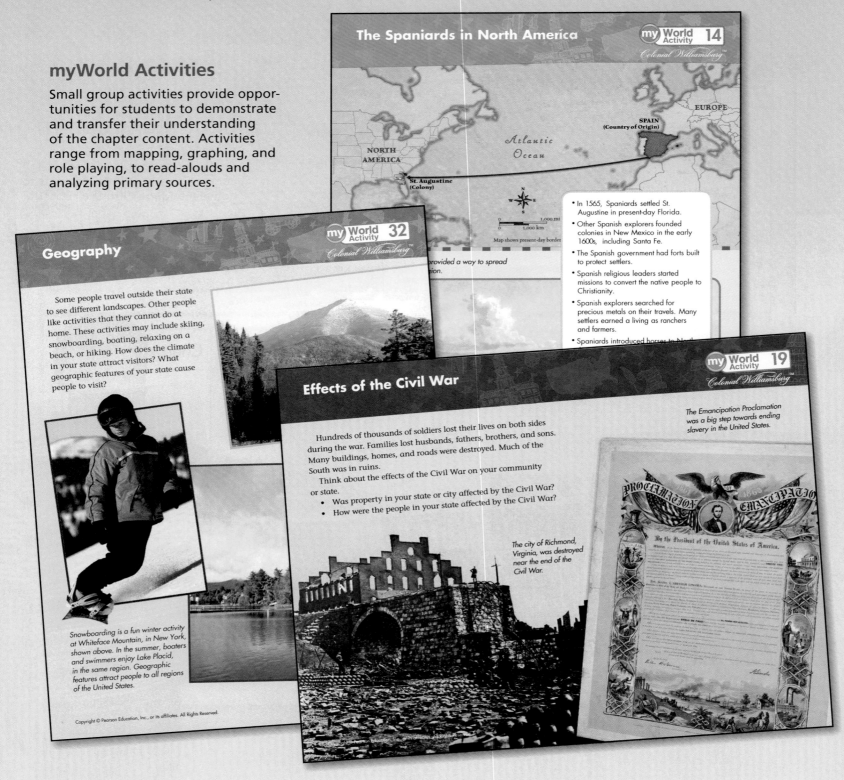

The Spaniards in North America

my World Activity 14
Colonial Williamsburg

EUROPE

SPAIN
(Country of Origin)

Atlantic Ocean

NORTH AMERICA

St. Augustine (Colony)

Map shows present-day borders

- In 1565, Spaniards settled St. Augustine in present-day Florida.
- Other Spanish explorers founded colonies in New Mexico in the early 1600s, including Santa Fe.
- The Spanish government had forts built to protect settlers.
- Spanish religious leaders started missions to convert the native people to Christianity.
- Spanish explorers searched for precious metals on their travels. Many settlers earned a living as ranchers and farmers.
- Spaniards introduced horses to North

Geography

my World Activity 32
Colonial Williamsburg

Some people travel outside their state to see different landscapes. Other people like activities that they cannot do at home. These activities may include skiing, snowboarding, boating, relaxing on a beach, or hiking. How does the climate in your state attract visitors? What geographic features of your state cause people to visit?

Snowboarding is a fun winter activity at Whiteface Mountain, in New York, shown above. In the summer, boaters and swimmers enjoy Lake Placid, in the same region. Geographic features attract people to all regions of the United States.

Copyright © Pearson Education, Inc., or its affiliates. All Rights Reserved.

Effects of the Civil War

my World Activity 19
Colonial Williamsburg

Hundreds of thousands of soldiers lost their lives on both sides during the war. Families lost husbands, fathers, brothers, and sons. Many buildings, homes, and roads were destroyed. Much of the South was in ruins.

Think about the effects of the Civil War on your community or state.
- Was property in your state or city affected by the Civil War?
- How were the people in your state affected by the Civil War?

The Emancipation Proclamation was a big step towards ending slavery in the United States.

The city of Richmond, Virginia, was destroyed near the end of the Civil War.

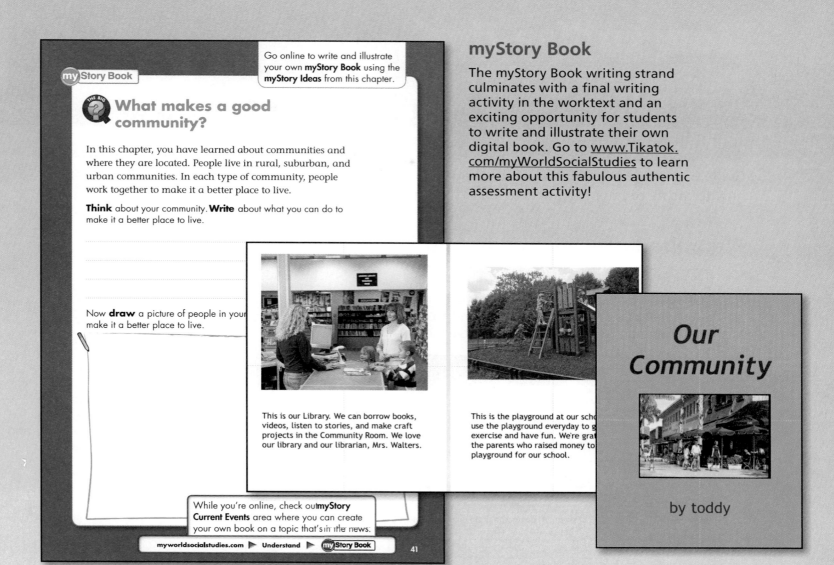

myStory Book

The myStory Book writing strand culminates with a final writing activity in the worktext and an exciting opportunity for students to write and illustrate their own digital book. Go to www.Tikatok. com/myWorldSocialStudies to learn more about this fabulous authentic assessment activity!

Assessment

Summative assessment is available for students to take online at myWorldSocialStudies.com. Or create your own test using the ExamView™, or use the ready-made Chapter Test Form A or B when you want an assessment of your students' learning.

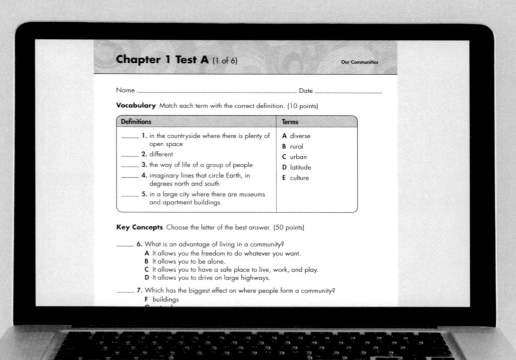

How to Use the Teacher Guide

Welcome to the myWorld Social Studies Teacher Guide. This guide provides quick information for how to use all of the program's resources during instruction. For more detailed Lesson Plans or to create your own customized lesson plans go to myworldsocialstudies.com.

Planning With the End in Mind:
Chapter Level Planning

The Planning With the End in Mind page for each chapter shows you at a glance the objectives and enduring understandings for each chapter as well as all of the print and digital resources available for teaching the chapter.

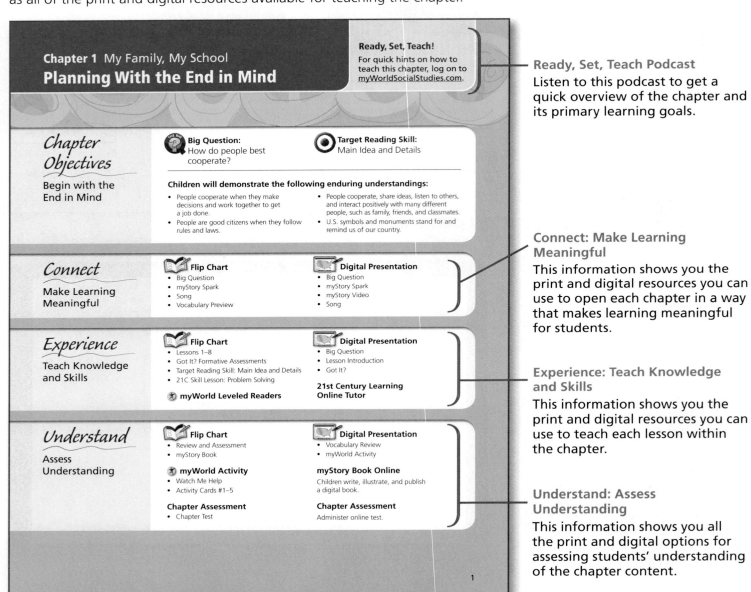

Ready, Set, Teach Podcast
Listen to this podcast to get a quick overview of the chapter and its primary learning goals.

Connect: Make Learning Meaningful
This information shows you the print and digital resources you can use to open each chapter in a way that makes learning meaningful for students.

Experience: Teach Knowledge and Skills
This information shows you the print and digital resources you can use to teach each lesson within the chapter.

Understand: Assess Understanding
This information shows you all the print and digital options for assessing students' understanding of the chapter content.

Lesson Plan Summaries

Lesson Plan Summaries for each lesson in the program provide you with a quick summary of the steps you can use to teach the lesson using both digital and print resources.

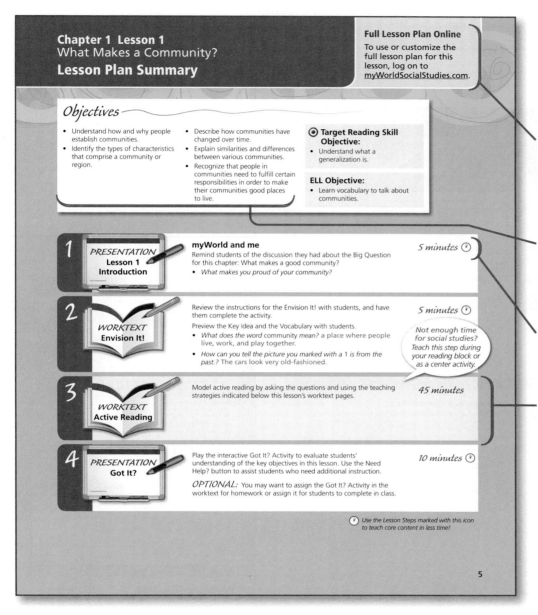

Complete Lesson Plans Online

Use the Online Lesson Planner to generate custom lesson plans. The Online Lesson Planner also provides links to all program resources at point of use.

Objectives

The Lesson Plan Summary includes learning objectives as well as Target Reading Skill Objectives and ELL objectives.

Pressed for Time?

A clock icon indicates lesson steps you can use to teach the essential ideas of the lesson in less time.

Lesson steps highlighted in blue can be taught during your reading block or independent reading time.

Active Reading Pages

These pages provide you with facsimiles of the Student Worktext pages with answers filled in.

Guided Reading

These pages also provide additional questions you can ask to help your students get the most from the informational text they're reading.

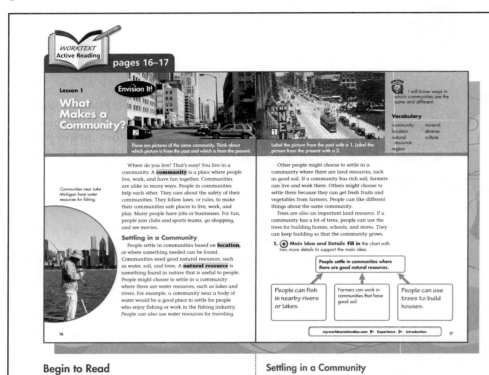

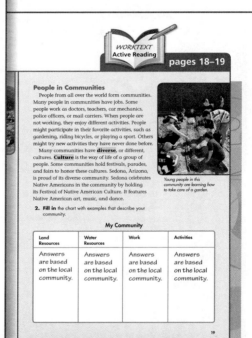

English Language Learner Notes
Provide suggestions for assisting English Language learners at various levels of English proficiency.

Differentiated Instruction Notes
Provide suggestions for how to modify the lesson for all the students in your classroom.

Chapter Review and Assessment Options

This page shows you all the options you have for assessing your students' understanding at the end of a chapter.

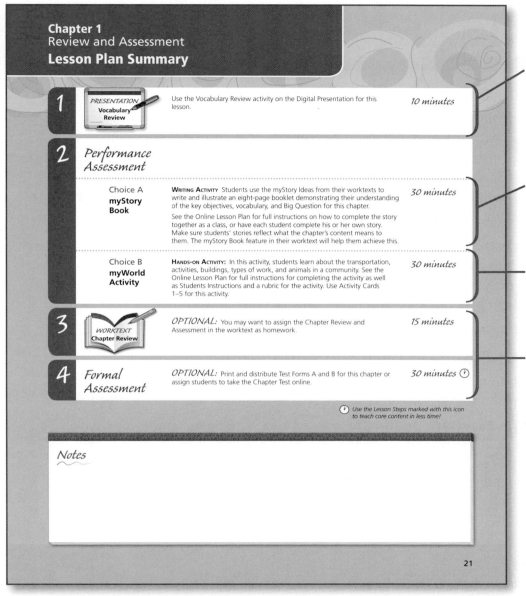

Chapter 1
Review and Assessment
Lesson Plan Summary

1 PRESENTATION Vocabulary Review — Use the Vocabulary Review activity on the Digital Presentation for this lesson. — *10 minutes*

2 *Performance Assessment*

Choice A **myStory Book** — **WRITING ACTIVITY** Students use the myStory Ideas from their worktexts to write and illustrate an eight-page booklet demonstrating their understanding of the key objectives, vocabulary, and Big Question for this chapter.

See the Online Lesson Plan for full instructions on how to complete the story together as a class, or have each student complete his or her own story. Make sure students' stories reflect what the chapter's content means to them. The myStory Book feature in their worktext will help them achieve this. — *30 minutes*

Choice B **myWorld Activity** — **HANDS-ON ACTIVITY:** In this activity, students learn about the transportation, activities, buildings, types of work, and animals in a community. See the Online Lesson Plan for full instructions for completing the activity as well as Students Instructions and a rubric for the activity. Use Activity Cards 1–5 for this activity. — *30 minutes*

3 WORKTEXT Chapter Review — *OPTIONAL:* You may want to assign the Chapter Review and Assessment in the worktext as homework. — *15 minutes*

4 *Formal Assessment* — *OPTIONAL:* Print and distribute Test Forms A and B for this chapter or assign students to take the Chapter Test online. — *30 minutes* ⏱

⏱ *Use the Lesson Steps marked with this icon to teach core content in less time!*

Notes

21

Digital Presentation

Use the Digital Presentation to review chapter vocabulary.

Performance Assessments

Choose from two highly engaging performance assessments.

MyStory Book

Students write and illustrate their own digital storybook using the writing and image prompts provided on each page.

myWorld Activity

Students engage in a variety of small group activities to demonstrate their understanding of the chapter content.

Worktext Review and Assessment and Formal Assessment

Use the worktext pages to help students review chapter content and assign Tests Forms A or B. Online testing is also an option at myworldsocialstudies.com

Grant Wiggins is the president of Authentic Education. He earned his Ed.D. from Harvard University and his B.A. from St. John's College. Dr. Wiggins consults with schools, districts, and state and national education departments on a variety of reform matters; organizes workshops; and develops resources on curricular change. He is also the coauthor, with Jay McTighe, of *Understanding by Design*, 2nd Edition, by Grant Wiggins & Jay McTighe © 2005 ASCD and *The Understanding by Design Handbook*, the award-winning materials on curriculum published by the Association for Supervision and Curriculum Development (ASCD).

Planning With the End in Mind

by Grant Wiggins,
co-author of *Understanding by Design*

What does it mean to plan with the end in mind? Planning with the end in mind is a method for planning curriculum, instruction, and assessment. Its goal is for students to achieve a deep understanding of important ideas. By planning your teaching with the end in mind, you can help your students break through and get it, not just for the test, but for life.

Planning with the end in mind provides a way to move from simply covering the curriculum to ensuring student understanding. The work of learning provides students with the opportunity to explore, test, verify, apply important concepts, and make sense of the content.

Steps to Planning With the End in Mind

In addition to backward design, teachers should make use of Big Ideas, Essential Questions, and Transfer to get the most out of planning with the end in mind.

Begin With Backward Design The use of a backward design process to develop instruction is key to planning with the end in mind. Rather than beginning the planning process with activities, materials, or textbook content, backward design starts by identifying the desired long-term results and appropriate assessment evidence. The following three steps help provide a basis for teachers to plan learning with the end in mind.

First, teachers should decide on their goals. What should students understand or be able to do?
- Consider what students should remember in the long term.
- Take state or national standards into account.
- Identify specific knowledge or skills students are expected to master.

Second, teachers should identify assessment evidence. How can students demonstrate their understanding of the skills and knowledge you identified as your goal?
- Design assessment, including performance or writing tasks as well as quizzes and tests.
- Create rubrics for each task.

Third, teachers should plan their instruction as a way to bring students to the desired understanding.

- Assess students' prior knowledge and use it to plan instruction.
- Use activities to accomplish goals.
- Regularly assess students' understanding and revise plans as needed.

Big Ideas, Big Questions When planning with the end in mind, teachers should use big ideas to give context and meaning to discrete facts and skills. What is a "big idea"? It is a powerful concept, theme, or issue that a student uses to make sense of otherwise disconnected content elements. Because big ideas are familiar and compelling, students readily connect their previous learning experiences to the new one.

Big ideas allow all students to participate in the learning, because everyone can share their ideas, values, and opinions and connect to content. Learning is thus about examining and informing students' various points of view—leading to new understanding.

One way of focusing in on a big idea is to use Essential Questions. Essential Questions are designed to challenge preconceived notions and force students to stretch their thinking, using course content to support and inform answers. In doing so, students discover meaning in the content and connections to their own lives. The use of big ideas and Essential Questions encourages students to not just

know something but understand why it matters and how it can be applied.

Transfer Knowledge and Skills The ultimate goal of education is to help students apply or "transfer" what they learn to new and unfamiliar situations. Transfer is about students being able to stretch the limits, use creativity, and tackle realistic challenges related to core content. Transfer ability means that students can adapt their learning to fit many different settings, issues, and problems—a key aim of schooling. The ability to transfer learning also helps students to succeed with state testing: Students often fail to apply prior learning to new readings, problems, or prompts on the test. When students show that they can transfer knowledge, skills, and understandings, it means they understand the connection between the classroom and the real world. It also means students are more prepared for the real work of the disciplines they study—whether as physicians, journalists, engineers, or artists.

The ultimate goal of education is to help students apply or "transfer" what they learn to new and unfamiliar situations.

The aim of Social Studies education must be to help students make sense of information about the world they live in and then act on it.

Goals for the Learning Experience

To help students fully master and transfer content, curriculum designers should work towards the following goals:

- Engage students in inquiry and application
- Promote the transfer of learning
- Provide a conceptual framework to help students make sense of discrete facts and skills
- Uncover and use the big ideas of the content
- Develop appropriate assessment methods to determine the degree of student understanding, knowledge, and skills
- Address misunderstandings or biases that interfere with learning
- Fold content standards and school mission into the design work

Achieving these goals requires backward planning, starting with the goals and working backward to what the students and you will actually do. Backward curriculum design lends purpose and conviction to every lesson, every activity, and every assignment.

Backward Planning and Social Studies Goals

The goal of planning with the end in mind is to help teachers move beyond superficial content coverage to plan for and cause in-depth student understanding. Understanding is about two crucial abilities: the ability to see connections and draw important inferences based on what you have learned, and the ability to transfer your learning to challenges beyond the classroom. The aim of Social Studies education must be to help students make sense of information about the world they live in and then act on it.

To help students reach that aim, you have to design backward from there instead of just designing backward from content mastery. The goal of school is not to be good at school. The goal of studying social studies is not just to master the book's content; the goal is to use this content as a means toward becoming more engaged citizens who can interact effectively with the world around them. Coursework must be designed and implemented backwards from those results.

Informed, effective citizens start as students capable of understanding connections in their world. This is why Essential Questions must be a cornerstone of teaching and assessment. The best questions signal the kinds of connections that need to be made to make content meaningful, and the kinds of thinking needed to more effectively transfer learning to new situations.

From Theory to Practice
Planning With the End in Mind in myWorld Social Studies

Student Worktext

- Each chapter is built around a Big Question, which is revisited in each lesson and chapter assessment.
- Each chapter begins with a song or myStory that introduces the topics presented in the chapter.
- Both the Big Question and the myStory help students make personal meaning of the chapter content.

Teacher Guide

- The planning page for each chapter highlights the enduring understandings you want students to demonstrate at the end of the chapter.

myStory Book

- Students write and illustrate their own digital book as an authentic assessment.
- Students demonstrate understanding of the chapter content.
- Students' writing reflects the personal meaning they've derived from the chapter content.

myWorld Activity

- Students work in small groups to demonstrate their understanding of chapter content.
- The activities demonstrate students' ability to transfer and apply their learning to new situations.

The Three Pillars of English Language Learning

by Dr. Jim Cummins, the University of Toronto

Dr. Cummins teaches in the Department of Curriculum, Teaching, and Learning of the Ontario Institute for Studies in Education at the University of Toronto. His research has focused on the education of bilingual students and the possibilities and pitfalls of technology in education. Dr. Cummins has written and presented many works on second-language learning and literacy development, including "Language and the Human Spirit" (TESOL Matters 13, December 2002–Feb 2003) and *The International Handbook of English Language Teaching* (Springer, 2007), co-edited with Chris Davison.

Teaching elementary social studies is as much about teaching new ideas and skills as it is about teaching language—new vocabulary, new terms, and new text structures abound in each new year of learning. Yet more teachers than ever before are working with students whose first language is not English. Students enter school from diverse backgrounds, and educators are sometimes overwhelmed by the challenge of meeting every student's needs.

Teachers of students who are English language learners will find that best teaching practices for those students are often the same as best teaching practices for all students. However, there are critical understandings that a teacher must possess, about language proficiency and about the foundations of teaching language, in order to successfully support English language learners on their journey through *myWorld Social Studies*.

Understanding Language Proficiency

In order to understand how English learners develop second-language literacy and verbal ability, we must distinguish among three different aspects of language proficiency.

Conversational fluency This dimension of proficiency represents the ability to carry on a conversation in face-to-face situations. Most native speakers of English have developed conversational fluency by age 5. This fluency involves the use of high-frequency words and simple grammatical constructions. English learners generally develop fluency in conversational English within a year or two of intensive exposure to the language in school or in their neighborhood environments.

Discrete language skills These skills reflect specific phonological, literacy, and grammatical knowledge that students can acquire in two ways—through direct instruction or through immersion in a literacy-rich and language-rich environment at home or in school. The discrete language skills acquired early include
- knowledge of the letters of the alphabet
- knowledge of the sounds represented by individual letters and combinations of letters
- the ability to decode written words

Children can learn these specific language skills concurrently with their development of basic English vocabulary and conversational fluency.

Academic language proficiency This dimension of proficiency includes the ability to interpret and produce increasingly complex language. As students progress through the grades, they encounter more

- low-frequency words, primarily from Greek and Latin sources
- complex syntax (for example, sentences in passive voice)
- abstract expressions

Acquiring academic language is challenging. Schools spend at least 12 years trying to teach all students the complex language associated with academic success.

It is hardly surprising that research has shown that English language learners, on average, require *at least* 5 years of exposure to academic English to catch up to native-speaker norms. Those who begin learning English in lower grades are fortunate to have a smaller vocabulary gap to bridge than their older counterparts.

Effective instruction for English language learners is built on three fundamental pillars.

Activate Prior Knowledge and Build Background

No learner is a blank slate. Each person's prior experience provides the foundation for interpreting new information. In reading, we construct meaning by bringing our prior knowledge of language and of the world to the text. The more we already know about the topic in the text, the more of the text we can understand. Our prior knowledge enables us to make inferences about the meaning of words and expressions that we may not have come across before.

Furthermore, the more we understand, the more new knowledge we can acquire. This expands our knowledge base (what cognitive psychologists call *schemata*, or

underlying patterns of concepts). Such comprehension, in turn, enables us to understand even more concepts and vocabulary.

It is more important to connect to students' prior knowledge because students may not realize what they already know. Their knowledge may not facilitate learning unless that knowledge is brought to consciousness. Teachers can use a variety of strategies to connect to students' prior experiences or activate their prior knowledge:

- Brainstorming
- Discussion
- Direct experience
- Dramatization
- Visual stimuli
- Student writing
- Drawing

When students don't already have knowledge about a topic, it is important to help them acquire that knowledge.

It is hardly surprising that research has repeatedly shown that English language learners, on average, require at least 5 years of exposure to academic English to catch up to native-speaker norms.

Successful Instruction for English Language Learners

Activate Prior Knowledge
——
Build Background

Access Content

Extend Language

> *We should constantly search for ways to link academic content with what students already know and what is familiar to them from their family or cultural experiences. This not only validates children's sense of identity, but it also makes the learning more meaningful.*

Access Content

How can teachers make academic English comprehensible for students who are still in the process of learning English?

We can *scaffold* students' learning by modifying the input itself. Here are a variety of ways of modifying the presentation of the academic content to students so that they can more effectively gain access to the meaning.

Using visuals Visuals enable students to "see" the basic concepts we are trying to teach much more effectively than if we rely only on words. Among the visuals we can use are

- pictures
- real objects
- vocabulary cards
- maps

Dramatization and acting out For beginning English learners, *Total Physical Response*, in which they follow commands such as "Turn around," can be highly effective. The meanings of words can be demonstrated through *gestures* and *pantomime*.

Language clarification This category of teaching methods includes language-oriented activities that clarify the meaning of new words and concepts.

Making personal and cultural connections We should constantly search for ways to link academic content with what students already know and what is familiar to them from their family or cultural experiences. This not only validates children's sense of identity, but it also makes the learning more meaningful.

Extend Language

An exploration of language is essential if students are to develop a curiosity about language and deepen their understanding of how words work. Students should become *language detectives* who investigate the mysteries of language and how it has been used throughout history to shape and change society.

When students know rules or conventions of how words are formed, it gives them an edge in extending vocabulary. It helps them figure out the meaning of words and how to form different parts of speech from words. The exploration of language can focus on meaning, form, or use.

Focus on meaning Categories that can be explored within a focus on meaning include

- native language equivalents or cognates
- synonyms, antonyms, and homonyms
- meaning of prefixes, roots, or suffixes

Focus on form Categories that can be explored within a focus on form include

- word families
- words with the same prefixes, roots, or suffixes
- grammatical patterns

Focus on use Categories that can be explored within a focus on use include

- general uses
- advertisements
- idioms
- proverbs
- puns and jokes

The Three Pillars

Establish a solid structure for the effective instruction of English language learners with the Three Pillars of English Language Learning:

- Activate Prior Knowledge and Build Background
- Access Content
- Extend Language

From Theory to Practice

Your Guide to English Language Learning in myWorld Social Studies

Student Worktext

- Colorful images convey key ideas contained in the text
- Boldfaced vocabulary with definitions at point of use

Digital Presentation

- As in the Student Worktext, colorful images convey key ideas contained in the text
- Extra Support at the bottom of each Digital Presentation provides Language Support

Teacher Guide

- ELL objectives for each lesson
- ELL notes on Active Reading pages provide suggestions for supporting English Language Learners at several levels of English proficiency.
- Support for Academic Vocabulary that appears in the text

Leveled Reader Lesson Plans

- Lesson plans for each leveled reader provide suggestions for supporting English Language Learners.

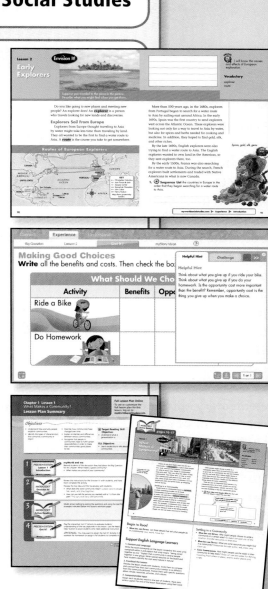

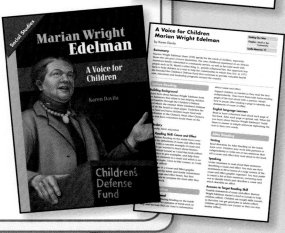

Students as Digital Citizens

by Linda B. Bennett

Linda B. Bennett serves as associate dean for educator preparation at the University of Missouri (MU) College of Education. She earned a doctorate of education from the University of Northern Colorado at Greeley prior to joining the MU College of Education in 1990. Throughout her MU career, she has served as the coordinator of elementary education, coordinator of social studies education, and co-director of graduate studies. Nationally, Bennett is the editor for *Social Studies and the Young Learner.*

From wireless communication tools to the virtual world of the Internet, technology has changed the lives of elementary students. They have access to technologies previous generations could not have imagined, and this access is integrated into their lives and their classrooms. Using electronic tools, inquisitive and creative students can investigate new knowledge, produce projects, and distribute their work to an extended audience. In social studies classes, students can explore their expanding world and make positive contributions as digital citizens.

Elementary Social Studies and Digital Citizenship

A digital citizen is any person who participates in society using modern communications technology, for example by writing a blog or making an online purchase. Elementary social studies teachers must teach their students to be good digital citizens, that is, to use the Internet and other technology responsibly, effectively, and safely. Students must learn the skills they need to be responsible citizens and make informed, ethical, and safe decisions while using technology. Learning to contribute in the digital world is now part of what students must learn in social studies.

Tips for Good Digital Citizens

Never... post personal, identifying information like your address or phone number.

Do not... write things that you would not be proud to put your name on.

Always... treat others with respect.

Do not... illegally copy material; always cite sources when referencing someone else's work.

Web 2.0 in the Classroom		
	What it is?	**What can I do with it**
Wiki	A Web site that allows users to create and edit content	Create a class wiki that students can edit to pool information and collaborate on projects.
Blog	A Web site made up of entries by one or more contributors; short for "weblog"	Have students post projects on a class blog to share their work with a broader audience and learn to be good digital citizens.

Web 2.0 is the "next generation" Internet, composed of Web-based services that facilitate interaction and collaboration.

Digital citizenship can be taught as part of an elementary social studies curriculum. A social studies class that uses technology effectively and teaches digital citizenship while doing so can help impart the skills students need to compete in a globally connected world and participate as digital citizens. Social studies gives teachers an opportunity to create student-centered assignments that engage students with technology beyond the walls of their classroom. Students studying social studies can use new tools to expand their world as digital citizens.

The challenge for teachers is to create student-centered classrooms that integrate technology and 21st century skills such as innovating, working in teams, or evaluating websites. Teachers need to develop experiences in which students use technology to communicate and collaborate with others in the classroom, school, community, and world.

Social Studies and Web 2.0 Tools

Web 2.0 tools such as blogs, podcasts, wikis, and social media can be useful to social studies teachers at all grade levels. Countless teachers have used Web 2.0 tools in the classroom to motivate students to have powerful learning experiences. They have used these social tools to create classroom environments that have made technology ubiquitous.

One innovative elementary teacher used Web 2.0 tools to set up a blog about a book the students were reading. Students used the blog to answer comprehension questions. To add excitement to the discussion, the teacher asked the author to respond to what the students wrote. With an authentic audience for students' ideas, they were more motivated to respond. The result was a detailed, rich discussion of the book.

Another example of using Web 2.0 tools to build an engaging learning experience comes from a middle school in North Carolina. While elementary teachers may not be able to duplicate this activity exactly, they could certainly adapt it to a level appropriate to their students. For this activity, the teacher developed a technology-infused project called Carbon Fighters. A class wiki explained expected outcomes, defined project roles, provided links to outside online resources, and tracked students' progress and participation.

In the introduction to the wiki, students described the problem of North Carolina's growing population, growing energy needs, and the impact of this growth on their state's environment. They then

Students must learn the skills they need to be responsible citizens and make informed, ethical, and safe decisions while using technology. Learning to contribute in the digital world is now part of what students must learn in social studies.

used the site to carry out a letter-writing campaign encouraging the governor to address this problem.

Students used online research tools and a collaborative online writing process to produce, revise, and present their letters. Using the wiki history feature, the teacher was able to track student contributions. Students were also able to use an online rubric to assess their own work.

In addition to Web 2.0 tools, myWorld Social Studies encourages the use of interactive whiteboard activities as a way to effectively integrate technology into the classroom. For example, students may come up to the whiteboard and fill out an interactive map.

Today's Elementary Social Studies Classroom

The highly effective teacher provides a learning environment that maximizes the use of tools such as the whiteboard to capture the interest of students to learn social studies content, and guides students to use digital media to communicate and collaborate effectively with the larger world. As life-long learners, elementary social studies teachers can be the leaders that guide students as citizens in the digital age.

From Theory to Practice
Your Guide to Digital Citizenship in myWorld Social Studies

Digital Presentation

- The program includes Digital Presentations for every chapter opener, lesson, skill lesson, and chapter closing lesson.
- Both teachers and students can access the presentations online.
- Teachers can "Click and Play" the Digital Presentations on a whiteboard or interactive whiteboard to help students engage in the chapter content.
- The presentation provides a rich variety of video, audio, and interactive experiences for students.
- The SupportPlus button at the bottom of the presentation provides extra support for language learners, challenge ideas, additional questions to stimulate discussion, and background notes.

Online Student Edition

- Online access to interactive student edition.
- Also available on DVD
- Provides audio and vocabulary support.

myStory Book

- An online digital book-building tool allows your students to use 21st century technology skills to write and illustrate their own 8-page book about the chapter they've just studied.
- Writing and image prompts on each page guide students in their writing.
- A glossary tool helps students use the key vocabulary from the chapter in their writing.

Building 21st Century Learning Environments

"Today's economy demands not only a high-level competence in the traditional academic disciplines, but also what might be called 21st century skills."

—*Time*, December 2006

An elementary school teacher leads an activity in which students come up to the front of the class and use an interactive whiteboard to answer questions about a map of their state. They use the whiteboard to drag the names of cities and towns to the correct locations, and to answer other questions. Pairs of students come up and collaborate while their classmates turn on computers and join a chat about the topic, reviewing their geography. They research maps on the Internet and integrate information from both the Internet and the live discussion to complete the activity. This 21st century teacher creates an integrated learning environment, allowing digital natives to use tools with which they are familiar to evaluate and create new information. Does this sound like your school?

In December 2006, *Time* published an article titled "How to Bring Our Schools Out of the 20th Century," which concluded that schools have not changed much in the last 100 years. The author argued, "Today's economy demands not only a high-level competence in the traditional academic disciplines, but also what might be called 21st century skills." What exactly are 21st century skills and how can educators ensure students are learning in 21st century environments?

The Partnership for 21st Century Schools (P21) has developed a unified vision for 21st century learning, as expressed in the graphic on the next page. Many school districts adopted this framework and have started integrating these skills into identified outcomes for student learning.

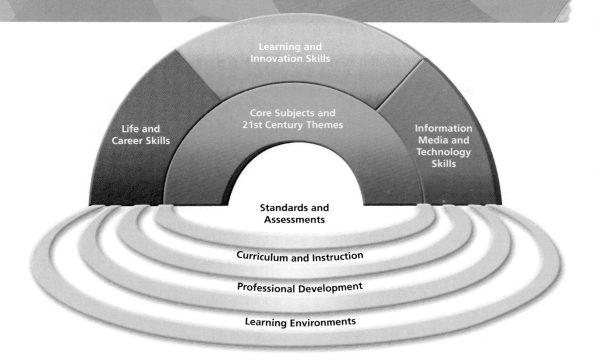

Life and
Career Skills

Learning and
Innovation Skills

Core Subjects and
21st Century Themes

Information
Media and
Technology
Skills

Standards and
Assessments

Curriculum and Instruction

Professional Development

Learning Environments

Understanding 21st Century Learning

Many educators require guidance translating the P21 vision, framework, and skills into classroom practice. As educators create 21st century learning environments, they must consider skills such as communication, collaboration, creation, information management and evaluation, as well as ethics and societal issues. These skills are not focused on technology, though it is a critical resource. It is important to begin developing 21st century skills in the elementary grades.

21st century creation skills Students must recognize that the ability to develop novel ideas after a careful process of synthesis and evaluation is far more important than simply consuming knowledge.

Tomorrow's students must also be able to fluidly move between creative formats. While text remains the primary vehicle for expressing thoughts, students must be comfortable with a range of multimedia products that are becoming common. Finally, students must embrace the idea

that work can be continually developed and revised by teams over time.

Communication skills 21st century students must be skilled communicators. Work is now driven by human interaction; the most successful members of any organization can leverage relationships to access information and to drive change.

Students must see communication as an opportunity to refine and revise their thinking. They must engage in both collaborative and competitive dialogue. They must understand different roles in complex networks of learners, respect multiple viewpoints, recognize that listening leads to productive conversations, and articulate a range of positions clearly.

Collaboration skills Digital tools have removed time and place as barriers to "teaming," so 21st century students must be skilled collaborators. Students require these skills to be successful in today's life and work environments. To prepare for this, students need experience collaborating across classrooms, schools, and communities. They must be equal partners in the creation of shared

Students must see communication as an opportunity to refine and revise their thinking.

> *Students of an earlier generation had access to a handful of sources while exploring new ideas; today's students have access to thousands of sources.*

documents and presentations—and have ample opportunities to create collective final products. Collaborative experiences help students learn task management skills that are prerequisites for successful participation in community and work activities driven by joint endeavors.

Information management and evaluation skills Perhaps the greatest challenge facing students sifting through content is to select what is truly useful. Students of an earlier generation had access to a handful of sources while exploring new ideas; today's students have access to thousands of sources.

Students must be effective managers and evaluators of information. They must quickly access content of value to their work and be able to judge the reliability of the sources that they have chosen to use. Students must synthesize information from a variety of primary and secondary sources to make predictions, validate information, and draw verifiable conclusions. Without information literacy, students will be ineffective information users.

Ethics and societal issues With a few mouse clicks, today's students may stumble upon inappropriate content or participate in potentially unsafe interactions. Students must learn to guard themselves and their identities while working in virtual environments. They must recognize and have an action plan for removing themselves from dangerous situations. Age-appropriate guidance, monitoring, and guidelines will assist students as they learn to take responsibility for their own behavior when using online resources.

Copyright infringement and plagiarism issues also arise in 21st century learning environments. Students and staff must understand and follow fair use guidelines when creating multimedia presentations, making copies, using student work, and downloading files.

21st Century Instruction

Use these strategies to bring 21st century instruction into your classroom.

Project-based learning Students who take ownership of their learning are more engaged and motivated than students with little control over their studies. Project-based learning allows teachers and students to develop standards-based units of study in which students show content mastery in meaningful ways. Educators evaluate mastery based on application of student learning to various authentic tasks. The project spans the unit of study and students demonstrate mastery by creating a product over the course of the project.

21st century assessment Some teachers are disinclined to design lessons emphasizing 21st century skills because they don't see these skills having a positive effect on standardized test scores. Testing ensures a measure of uniformity between the intended and implemented curriculum, but it can also control instruction.

Organizations are conducting research on 21st century assessments. Dr. Richard Hersh proposes that teachers redirect assessment toward feedback students can use to further their learning. He also favors assessments that involve simulation and guided practice with an emphasis on authentic applications and performance to demonstrate what students know.

Sound practices supported by the right tools Perhaps most important, 21st century learning must be focused on the development of deep understanding and the long-lasting acquisition of skills, rather than teaching how to use individual digital tools. Digital tools embraced today may be gone or antiquated by tomorrow. Instead, students should see tools within the context of individual skills—facilitating creation, collaboration, communication, and information management—and become adept at transferring skills from one context to another.

From Theory to Practice
Your Guide to 21st Century Learning in myWorld Social Studies

21st Century Learning Online Tutor

- Fun and interactive tutorials for students to use online include video and peer modeling of key skills.
- A checklist in the front of each Student Worktext enables students to track their own progress through the online tutorials.
- Students can work through the tutorials one-on-one at the computer or together on the whiteboard as a whole class.
- Includes tutorials for Target Reading Skills, Collaboration and Creativity Skills, Graph and Map Skills, Critical Thinking Skills and Media and Technology Skills as listed below.

The following skills are built into each component of myWorld Social Studies for students to learn, practice, and apply. Tutorials for each of these skills are available in the online 21st Century Skills Tutor.

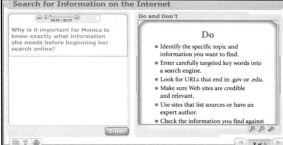

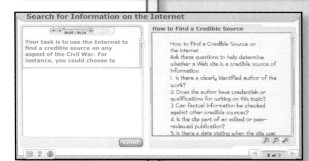

Target Reading Skills

- Main Idea and Details
- Classify and Categorize
- Draw Conclusions
- Compare and Contrast
- Summarize
- Cause and Effect
- Fact and Opinion
- Generalize
- Sequence

Collaboration and Creativity Skills

- Solve Problems
- Resolve Conflict
- Work in Cooperative Teams
- Generate New Ideas

Graph and Map Skills

- Interpret Graphs
- Interpret Timelines
- Interpret Physical Maps
- Interpret Cultural Data on Maps
- Create Charts
- Use Longitude and Latitude
- Interpret Economic Data on Maps

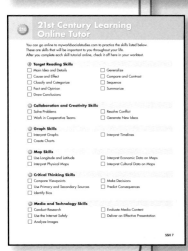

Critical Thinking Skills

- Compare Viewpoints
- Identify Bias
- Predict Consequences
- Use Primary and Secondary Sources
- Make Decisions

Media and Technology Skills

- Conduct Research
- Analyze Images
- Deliver an Effective Presentation
- Use the Internet Safely
- Evaluate Media Content

Reading in the Social Studies Classroom

Reading in the content areas presents a challenge for elementary school students. Young learners must make the switch from learning to read to reading to learn. Students need to be equipped with the correct strategies if they are to be successful readers in the content areas.

Social studies as a discipline is intimately connected to the use of literacy skills. In the elementary social studies classroom, a large portion of the information students are expected to learn comes from reading textbooks. Lengthy passages may be filled with unfamiliar schema and abstract concepts, expository text structures, specialized vocabulary, and various text features such as highlighted words, graphs, timelines, photos, and maps. The challenge for teachers in the elementary grades is to build not only their students' reading skills, but also their interest in more complicated types of reading materials. Explicit instruction in comprehension strategies and content-specific vocabulary within the context of social studies texts is necessary to help elementary school students develop competence in critical literacy skills.

Metacognition for Social Studies Reading

Research has consistently stated that metacognition plays an important role in reading. Learning metacognitive strategies can provide students with greater confidence and independence as readers in social studies. The goal is for metacognitive readers to be aware of what they understand, to know when their comprehension breaks down, and to apply specific strategies when they don't understand.

Comprehension strategies Teaching specific strategies can enhance students' comprehension of the social studies textbook. These strategies include pre-reading activities, such as activating relevant prior knowledge, previewing vocabulary, and surveying the text for clues about themes and main ideas. Helping students make personal connections supports comprehension by connecting what the reader already knows about a given topic with the new information offered in the text. Furthermore, previewing text for main ideas and concepts enables students to determine what they already know and what they will learn.

While reading, metacognitive readers apply strategies to identify the most

> **Teacher Reflection**
>
> *What are some of the challenges your students face when reading and comprehending social studies text?*
>
> *How can learning metacognitive strategies create more confident and independent readers?*

| Student recognizes breakdown in comprehension | → | Student applies specific reading strategies | → | Result: understanding |

important ideas and use a variety of strategies to achieve comprehension when it eludes them. For example, they may use graphic and semantic organizers such as concept maps and outlines. These visual structures are powerful comprehension tools because they offer concrete representations of abstract thinking processes.

Recognizing text structure Students need to understand that the texts they read in the content areas are not organized like stories. When students are aware of how authors structure their writing, they are better equipped to comprehend what they read. Elementary students need concrete experiences to assist them in differentiating content and structure. Teaching readers to recognize common academic and expository text structures can also improve their overall reading comprehension. Social studies textbooks are often organized according to chronological sequence, compare and contrast, concept and definition, description, or cause and effect.

Awareness of text structure also includes analyzing the physical presentation of a text, including text features and text divisions. Explicit instruction that includes teacher modeling and think alouds helps students become more strategic readers. Using a variety of graphic organizers that go hand in hand with each text structure supports the elementary reader.

Text-mapping, a graphic technique that emphasizes the prereading process, is one strategy that facilitates an in-depth look at the structure and features of a text. Students who can map or diagram a text's organization can read a text with specific questions in mind and better understand the author's message.

Building Vocabulary

Academic success also requires direct instruction in content-specific vocabulary. Students need a rich body of word knowledge to succeed in basic skill areas, but they also need a specialized vocabulary to learn from the social studies textbook and in the classroom.

Given the relative difficulty of social studies texts, teaching vocabulary is very

Cause and Effect Chart

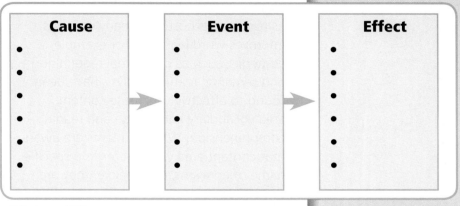

Venn Diagram

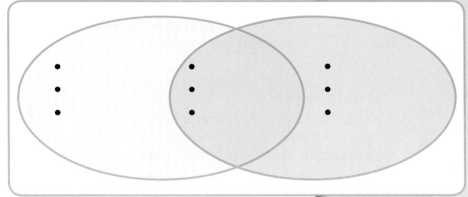

Word Web

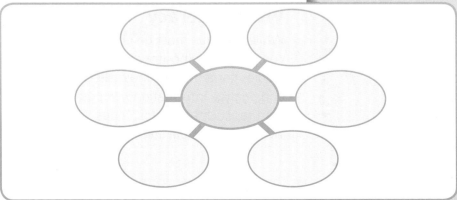

important. Vocabulary acquisition has been found to be a high predictor of reading comprehension. It is critical to teach vocabulary words through a variety of activities and at different times, not just once at the start of the lesson. The more students engage with words and make personal connections to their meanings, the more likely students are to recognize words in the text. Active engagement is key if students are to connect new vocabulary in a meaningful way.

Instruction that promotes active engagement with the vocabulary, as well as repeated exposure in many contexts, improves word learning. For example, strategies such as contextual redefinition and semantic feature analysis have been found to effectively increase content area vocabulary knowledge and reading comprehension. When students are aware that content area words refer to a specific name of an event, or principle, they are more likely to not only identify the words, but also build their long term vocabulary. Building these meaningful associations is critical to helping students remember key concepts and vocabulary.

Teacher Reflection

What strategies do you currently use in your classroom to help students develop an in-depth understanding of specialized vocabulary?

Visual Literacy

While students must be able to read and comprehend expository text to learn social studies content, they must also interpret and analyze information from graphic features such as photos, maps, and charts. This is called visual literacy.

Teachers can help students develop visual literacy by teaching specific skills. Merely asking students to pay attention to visual aids is not enough. Engaging students in specific tasks or asking specific higher order questions that require students to use and interact with the visuals increases the degree to which the visual improves comprehension. Three important ways to help students critically analyze visuals are to have students think about the way the visual aid was made, to have students make specific observations about details in the image, and to have students consider the photographer, chart designer, or author's purpose for including it.

Literacy and Social Studies Go Hand in Hand

Providing students with instruction in higher-level reading skills and content-specific vocabulary is critical in the social studies classroom. Focusing on metacognitive strategies encourages reader independence. Specifically, students become aware of their own mental processes as they read. Familiarity with text structure allows students to formulate questions and anticipate the author's purpose. Social studies textbooks include content-specific vocabulary that requires extended and explicit instruction followed by multiple opportunities to engage with the words and develop an in-depth and long term understanding of their meaning. Visual literacy skills must also be taught through creating tasks that use images and thinking critically about the purpose of the images.

From Theory to Practice
Your Guide to Reading Support in myWorld Social Studies

Student Worktext

- Introduces content-specific vocabulary at the beginning of each lesson
- Interactive format encourages self-monitoring throughout the lesson
- Includes extensive use of graphic organizers to help students recognize text structure and formulate notes and summaries
- Concludes each lesson with a Got It? formative assessment in which students self-assess their level of comprehension

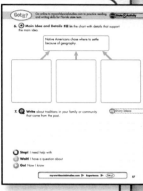

Target Reading Skills

- Each chapter focuses on one primary target reading comprehension skill, providing instruction, practice, and application.
- Target Reading Skills include all of the following:

Main Idea and Details	Fact and Opinion
Draw Conclusions	Generalize
Cause and Effect	Classify
Categorize	Sequence
Compare and Contrast	Summarize

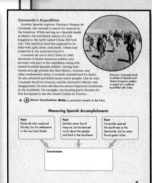

Words To Know

- Worksheet for each chapter
- Previews difficult vocabulary students will encounter within the Student Worktext

Teacher Guide

- Active Reading pages provide the teacher with additional questions they can ask for each page of the student worktext
- These questions help students comprehend the text, think critically about the text, and analyze visuals on the page.

Differentiated Instruction and Social Studies Content

Educators may improve student learning by incorporating innovative instructional strategies designed to meet students' varied needs. That is, they must personalize and differentiate instruction.

Do your students find social studies boring? Are you teaching and reteaching core content without an improvement in student test scores? Diverse student needs, experiences, and learning styles challenge today's teachers. Many factors play a role in student achievement: learning styles, students' interests, cultural backgrounds, economic backgrounds, and social issues. Educators may improve student learning by incorporating innovative instructional strategies designed to meet students' varied needs. That is, they must personalize and differentiate instruction.

What Is Differentiated Instruction?

Educators who differentiate instruction recognize students as individuals with individual learning needs. They realize that students learn at different rates and also in a variety of ways. Tracking is not synonymous with differentiated instruction. While some schools group students in a fixed situation at a certain level and consistently employ whole group instruction, differentiation implies varied approaches to learning within a heterogeneous class. Educators know that students differ in their readiness to learn, interests, experiences, and learning preferences. Teachers using differentiated instruction acknowledge these differences. They proactively plan instruction, practice, and assessment with this student-centered, personalized instructional approach.

Paths to Differentiated Instruction

In differentiating instruction, educators are mindful of the need to address state or district-mandated social studies standards while still taking into account the diverse needs of learners. To do so, educators can differentiate in three ways:

- **Content**—the skills, knowledge, and key ideas students learn and how they gain access to the information
- **Process**—the way in which students learn; what they do to actually grasp the content and make sense of it
- **Product**—how students demonstrate what they have learned after a unit of study or significant portion of learning

Differentiated Instruction
Includes
• Challenging and engaging tasks related to the content area
• Flexible teaching techniques oriented to various learning modalities and work habits
• Opportunities for students to demonstrate mastery in different ways
• Integration of standards
• Use of performance assessment
Leads to
• Increased academic learning
• Improved student self-efficacy
• Enhanced motivation

Differentiating instruction requires an emotionally safe learning environment, an appropriate level of challenge for each student, and at times an opportunity for students to choose a mode of learning that best fits their learning style and personal interests. Therefore, when differentiating, educators can prudently modify content, process, and/or product with regard to students' readiness levels, interests, and/or learning profiles in mind to address unit goals.

Differentiating to Respond to Learning Profiles To differentiate in response to how students learn best, educators can align teaching methods with students' learning styles and intelligence preferences. Howard Gardner's theory of Multiple Intelligences and the model of Learning Modalities address learning profiles. Both offer suggestions to help students learn by using preferences, strengths, and natural abilities. Gardner's theory states that individuals have preferences and assets that affect the speed and manner in which they acquire and process information. Students'

clarity of understanding when instruction engages their preferred modalities.

Using learning styles to personalize instruction helps to motivate students and can alleviate potentially stressful learning situations. At the end of a differentiated lesson, more students will have met the learning objectives if teachers are mindful to provide opportunities of instruction in a modality that resonates with each student.

Differentiating Social Studies Social studies integrates different modalities and intelligences through the varied nature of the skills required to analyze and interpret the content. Social studies curriculum incorporates maps, writing, reading, recording technologies, video, online geographic applications, role-playing, field trips, and more. Furthermore, varied social studies concepts—from politics to art to geography—can engage learners of every learning preference.

An Example from the Classroom The table on the next page shows examples for how an educator might differentiate to meet a standard that requires students to understand the functions of state governments in the United States. The entire unit of study would entail four or five other unit questions and associated lessons. The table shows samples of differentiation by content, process, and product, that appeal to learning style, interest, and readiness.

The content for this activity is divided into two parts. Part 1 requires students to read teacher-compiled assigned resources that are differentiated by readiness level. Teachers might initiate partner reading or adult assistance for those needing additional support with accessing the assigned material. In Part 2, students extend their acquisition of content by

Learning Modalities	
Visual	process information more completely by seeing
Auditory	understand more completely when information is given verbally
Kinesthetic/ Tactile	learn best with hands-on activities, including manipulatives

strengths influence how they understand and communicate ideas. Teachers can use these strengths as a bridge for students to cross into new and unfamiliar areas. The Learning Modalities theory focuses on sensory modes including sight, sound, and touch. Most students learn through a combination of modalities and gain

Gardner's Multiple Intelligences	
Visual-Spatial	learns through seeing
Logical-Mathematical	develops concepts with numbers and linear patterns
Musical-Rhythmic	learns best with hands-on activities, including manipulatives
Bodily-Kinesthetic	learns through tactile experiences and movement
Intrapersonal	has insights into own thinking
Interpersonal	interacts well with others
Naturalist	learns through outdoor and natural environments

Students are distinctive in their readiness to learn, interests, and learning styles and preferences. Students learn most effectively when educators consider ways to differentiate content, process, and product.

choosing their learning preference to access additional information.

The activity encourages teachers to differentiate process by collecting and creating graphic organizers that represent a range of readiness and learning preferences. Students record information on an organizer that suits their learning style, though teachers should help students select one that is also appropriately challenging. Next, students group themselves according to interest as they each address a role that state governments perform. They compile information as a group and present to the class.

Product represents a demonstration of understanding at the end of a significant segment of learning. The sample chart features one lesson guiding question, but the product students produce should be for a series of essential questions for an entire unit of study. This sample product shows differentiation by intelligence preference. In addition, teachers might have students write an essay, create a portfolio, or take a test to demonstrate understanding. It is important that teachers identify the format and also the expected criteria for a product. To do so, share with students a rubric or scoring guide and be sure to communicate expectations and steps for successful completion.

Summary

Students are distinctive in their readiness to learn, interests, and learning styles and preferences. Students learn most effectively when educators consider ways to differentiate content, process, and product. Students learn best when they make relevant connections between curriculum, individual interests, and previous learning experiences. Core curriculum dictates what content to teach, but differentiation enables educators to diversify instruction to meet a range of learning needs. Differentiating instruction provides pathways to an accessible social studies curriculum for all students.

What is the role of state governments in the United States?		
Content	**Process**	**Product**
Part 1 Assign individual students reading materials to address the guiding question: *What are the functions of a state government?*	**Graphic Organizers:** Using their resources, instruct students to record their responses to the guiding question on a prepared graphic organizer or one they create, such as: web; traditional; outline; bullets with subheadings; timeline or other sequence chart	Instruct students to choose one of the following ways to demonstrate understanding of all guiding questions in this unit: • PowerPoint or other technology presentation • Short story or journal entries • TV interview or play (with script) • Music lyrics put to song • Poster with art and writing
Part 2 Ask students to choose one of these three ways to access additional information to address the guiding question: *What are the functions of a state government?* • view a DVD entitled "Your State Government" • complete the "State Government" WebQuest • read additional resources about the jobs of state governments	**Interest Groups:** As a class, list the different roles of state governments. • Students arrange themselves into groups according to one role of interest to them. • Each group tackles a different role that state governments perform. • Groups collaborate to share information about their targeted role. • Groups decide on a way to display their information and present this information to the class. • Classmates add to their own graphic organizers as groups present.	Be sure to communicate expectations to students clearly and show them the format each project should take, the steps for completion, and a rubric for scoring.

From Theory to Practice
Your Guide to Differentiated Instruction in myWorld Social Studies

Teacher Guide

- Provides point-of-use suggestions for differentiating the instruction for each lesson
- Includes suggestions for all types of learners

Student Worktext

- Visual learners benefit from engaging photos, illustrations, maps, and charts
- Students with interpersonal learning preferences enjoy the myStory at the beginning of each chapter

Digital Presentation

- Gets students up out of their seats and more fully engaged in the content of each lesson
- Ideal for auditory and tactile learners

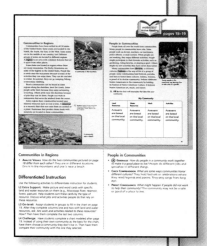

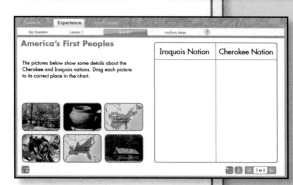

Real Learning With Activities

One of your most important and challenging responsibilities as a teacher is to create and execute activity-based learning experiences while ensuring that activities are high-quality and lead to real learning.

Teachers know that students learn best when they tackle real-world problems that spark their curiosity and relate to their lives. Teachers also understand their responsibility for teaching to high academic standards, helping students arrive at a deep understanding of content, and making sure students acquire the skills they will need to be successful in school and, later, at work. The challenge is to make lessons interesting and relevant for students, while making sure that real learning takes place.

Activity-Based Learning

One of your most important and challenging responsibilities as a teacher is to create and execute activity-based learning experiences while ensuring that activities are high quality and lead to real learning. Activity-based learning is a useful tool, but it is important to be sure that activities focus on real content and skills and not simply "making things."

It is also important to tailor activities to the different learning styles as much as possible. For example, imagine designing an activity to help teach students about the geography of their state. A teacher could best connect students with the content by allowing students to choose a form of the activity that best fits their learning style:

- Visual learners study maps in an atlas, or navigate interactive maps on a website.
- Auditory learners work in pairs to research and describe different places in the state to one another.
- Kinesthetic/tactile learners draw and label a map of the state.

After working alone or in groups, students working on each version of the activity come together in small groups to share what they have learned and prepare a group presentation to the class, a useful way to integrate cooperative learning into a differentiated activity.

Cooperative Learning

Cooperative learning is a strategy in which small groups of students work

Features of High-Quality Activities

Truly high-quality activities tend to have the following characteristics:

- Open-endedness—no obvious answers or solutions
- Intellectual challenge and interest
- In-depth exploration
- Student involvement in all aspects
- Encouraging teamwork and 100% participation

together on common tasks. Successful activity-based learning often depends on teaching cooperative learning. Groups of students share responsibility for setting goals, assessing learning, and facilitating learning. Students question and challenge each other, discuss their ideas, and internalize learning.

According to David Johnson and Roger Johnson (1999), there are five basic elements of successful small-group learning:

- *Positive interdependence:* Students feel responsible for their own and the group's effort.
- *Face-to-face interaction:* Students encourage and support one another; the environment encourages discussion and eye contact.
- *Individual and group accountability:* Each student is responsible for doing his or her part; the group is accountable for meeting its goal.
- *Group behaviors:* Group members learn by practicing interpersonal, social, and collaborative skills.
- *Group processing:* Group members analyze their own and the group's ability to work together.

- Leading to products that demonstrate mastery of important content and skills
- Application of a wide range of skills and knowledge
- Clear expectations
- Reliable measures of student performance
- Thoughtful use of technology

When implemented well, cooperative learning encourages achievement, active learning, discussion, confidence, and motivation. Collaboration skills such as verbalizing and justifying ideas, building consensus, disagreeing politely, and handling conflicts are increasingly valuable as more businesses organize employees into teams and task forces.

Teaching Collaborative Skills

You can help students learn the skills needed to work in groups by starting with short, structured lessons aimed at fostering taking turns, involving all students in the discussion, and clarifying the roles, rights, and responsibilities of group members. It may take time to develop a classroom community in which students respect one another, listen to one another, and feel safe enough to share their thoughts and feelings.

It is also important to establish guidelines governing how group members agree to work together. Students may not be used to working with others to complete tasks. Have groups discuss and develop guidelines that they will follow. See examples at the right.

Teachers should model positive interpersonal skills, have students practice the skills, and encourage students to reflect on how effectively they are performing the skills. After working in groups, students should engage in group-processing activities in which they discuss the interpersonal skills that influence their effectiveness in working together.

Assessing Activities

Individuals and groups must be made accountable for cooperative learning outcomes. You may choose performance assessments, group products, tests, or a combination of those things.

To accurately assess students' understanding, you must first make sure

Examples of team guidelines:

- *We always treat one another with respect.*

- *We always encourage new ideas.*

- *We always value all suggestions.*

- *We always explain our opinions to the team.*

- *We always make decisions as a team.*

that they understand the task at hand. It is also useful to create and use a rubric. Make sure this includes all the areas in which you wish to assess students, such as understanding of the necessary content, mastery of relevant skills, and follow-through in executing the assigned activity. Involving students in their own self-assessment can also be helpful.

Managing Class Activities

Teachers must tailor their instruction to provide remediation for students with gaps in their skills and to challenge students who have already achieved mastery. Here are some strategies to meet diverse needs.

- *Stations* are distinct areas where students work on different tasks simultaneously. Stations can be organized around ability levels so that every student can have review, challenge, and remediation at the appropriate level. The teacher may rotate to provide instruction and assistance.

- *Independent study* allows students to investigate a project independently with guidance and feedback from the teacher. Every student receives instruction at his or her own level. If a teacher notices that a small group of students needs instruction in a particular skill, he or she pulls the small group aside to provide the instruction. Whole-class instruction is less frequent.

- *Leveled instruction* is when a teacher gives an introductory lesson to the entire class, then provides varying access points for students to practice skills. For example, a teacher provides several assignments with different levels of difficulty. The student or teacher chooses an assignment. Students who choose levels that seem too difficult for them tend to rise to the occasion and accomplish more.

- *Choice board assignments* are written on cards hung on a board. Students choose an assignment from a particular row or area of the board. The rows and areas are organized around specific skills.

- *Individual contracts* allow teachers to give each student a list of tasks to complete. The tasks are based on the level and ability of each student. Throughout a defined period, students work with other students who need to work on the same skill or concept. Students like the independence and choice built into the system.

Activity-based learning allows students to engage in hands-on experiences that enrich their learning and spark their intellectual curiosity. By using effective planning, grouping, and assessment strategies, teachers can ensure students acquire a deep conceptual understanding of content, and that students are able to transfer and apply knowledge.

Student Roles within a Group	
Leader	Organizes the group, makes sure other members fulfill their roles
Supply Gatherer	Gathers any needed supplies for the project (books, art supplies, etc.)
Recorder	Writes or draws for the assigned project
Presenter	Presents the group's project to the class

From Theory to Practice
Your Guide to Activity-Based Learning in myWorld Social Studies

myWorld Activity

- An activity for each chapter includes five activity cards.
- Hands-on, minds-on activity for each chapter addresses a wide variety of learning styles.
- Provides a non-written performance assessment option for each chapter.
- Role playing and other small group activities appeal to students with diverse learning preferences and interests.
- Activities encourage collaboration and cooperation within small groups.

myWorld Activity: Step-by-Step Instructions for the Teacher

- Each activity includes complete instructions and tips for the teacher.
- Instructions include information about the activity's objectives, target skills, and learning styles.

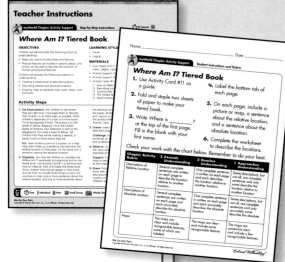

myWorld Activity: Instructions and Rubrics for the Students

- Each activity includes written instructions for students as well as a rubric to help them understand the quality of work expected.

myWorld Activity: Student Recording Sheet

- Each activity includes a recording sheet for students to use during the activity and to ensure that all students are involved and have a defined role in the activity.

Assessing Learning in Social Studies

Assessment should focus, guide, and support instruction. Teachers should make observations about students' strengths and weaknesses, analyze performance with respect to specific goals and criteria, and constantly assemble information from a variety of sources. Assessment must be used to identify goals and strategies, monitor progress, evaluate results, and improve performance.

Types of Assessment

Assessment takes a variety of formats. Traditional assessments focus on tests or written work such as essays. Performance assessments show learning in active and nontraditional formats. Alternative assessments range from metacognitive activities, such as journals, to student-generated assessments such as portfolios.

Formative assessment Formative assessment is often informal. It happens throughout the instructional process to monitor progress and provide feedback, allowing students to correct errors and encouraging teachers to modify their methods. It helps students understand what they are doing well, links to classroom learning, and provides input to adjust the learning process. Students must use formative assessments to self-assess, evaluate their progress, and accept responsibility for managing their learning. Teachers must help students understand the importance of this process and teach methods for reflection and self-evaluation.

Summative assessment Summative assessments are used to formally gauge student learning at particular points in time. They commonly occur at the end of chapters, units, or school terms to determine what students know. They can be used to track progress and reveal areas that need review. Tests and quizzes are the most common summative assessments.

Balancing assessments Proper use of assessment tools in the classroom will lead to greater learning. Incorporating a variety of assessments allows for a more fully developed picture of students' learning processes. The more information teachers have about students, the better they can judge teaching quality and student learning.

Reading-Based Assessment

As students progress into higher grades, the ability to read and analyze primary source documents to acquire knowledge and develop critical-thinking skills becomes increasingly important. Document analysis has also become an important assessment tool. Both the Advanced Placement examinations and many state-mandated tests incorporate document based questions. Writing tasks may ask students to think critically about sources, form opinions guided by a prompt, and present their analysis in an essay.

Teachers at the elementary level have a critical role to play in preparing their students for the types of document-based assessment they will see as they move into the higher grades, using reading-based assessments. These assessments are based on secondary sources at or near the students' reading level and could include selections from a textbook. They should focus on the skills students will need to analyze more complicated primary sources in the future. Students must learn to read a passage and ask

- Is the passage fact, opinion, or both?
- Does the passage show evidence of bias?
- Who wrote the passage?
- What can you discover about the author?
- What is the purpose of the passage?

Reading-based assessments should focus, guide, and support instruction. Teachers should make observations about students' strengths and weaknesses, analyze performance with respect to specific goals and criteria, and constantly assemble information from a variety of sources. Assessment must be used to identify goals and strategies, monitor progress, evaluate results, and improve performance.

Students need direct instruction in the use of reading passages to answer questions. They also need repeated opportunities to practice these skills both in class and independently. Teach students to understand reading passages by modeling a series of scaffolded questions that help students identify the passage's purpose. Begin by asking questions with concrete answers. These will form a basis for critical thinking. Consider these questions: *What kind of document is this? Who wrote it? Why was it written? Who is the intended audience?* The purpose of these questions is to help students identify relevant information contained in the document. The questions may also spark a class discussion or act as a focus for independent practice. Ultimately, students will evaluate documents on their own.

Rubrics

A rubric is a set of guidelines for assessing student work on a continuum of quality. Holistic rubrics give an overall impression of students' work. Analytic rubrics assign separate scores for distinct criteria. Rubrics are useful when assessing reasoning, composition, and evaluation skills.

Rubrics allow students to self-assess before submitting work. A clear definition of expectations helps students to perform

Assessment should focus, guide, and support instruction.

Chapter Activity Rubric	3 Exceeds Understanding	2 Reaches Understanding	1 Approaches Understanding
Paper Plate Mask	Many details are included and all are accurate.	Some details are included and all are accurate.	Some details are included and most are accurate.
Biography Worksheet	All elements of the biography are included. Additional details are added. Information is written in complete sentences and spelled correctly.	All elements of the biography are included. Information is written in complete sentences.	Some elements of the biography are included. Most information is written in complete sentences.
Living Timeline	The person was quickly put into the correct place on the timeline without help.	Some help was needed to put the person in the correct location on the timeline.	A great deal of help was needed to put the person in the correct place on the timeline.

A sample rubric

at the best of their ability. Students also begin to understand what areas they need to work on in order to improve.

Rubrics answer these questions:
- By what criteria will performance be judged?
- What are the elements of a quality performance?
- What does performance at each level look like?

Designing rubrics A strong rubric
- uses descriptive language, stating what each level of quality looks like. The best rubrics thus minimize value language ("Great work," "Poor job") or mere comparisons across levels ("not as thorough as a 3") to provide the most useful feedback.
- discriminates among performance levels validly—by the key features and difference in the levels of quality, not by what is easy to count or score.
- is general enough to enable inference to broad goals and state standards, but specific enough to enable useful feedback on a particular task.
- avoids combining independent criteria in the same descriptor. For example, "accuracy of facts" and "quality of the argument" are independent traits (i.e., facts may be accurate but reasoning poor and vice versa). This factor highlights the trade-off with holistic vs. analytic scoring: holistic is easier because it throws all the criteria together in one description; analytic is more work, but provides better feedback because each trait is scored separately.
- is based on specific work samples. The rubric summarizes the traits of samples of work at each level.

Rubrics reflect different aspects of performance In a complex performance, there are several simultaneous aims with distinct traits to consider. These include
- content vs. process
- quality of understanding vs. quality of the performance
- mechanics, organization, and facts vs. the style of student writing

Rubrics must address these different aspects of performance to ensure that the evaluation is valid and that the feedback is helpful and mindful of the trade-offs of time vs. accuracy. When constructing rubrics, consider IMPACT, WORK QUALITY, PROCESS, and CONTENT as different goals.

If you are new to rubrics, you may feel most comfortable starting with one holistic rubric or a rubric focusing on a single trait. Over time you may wish to have a set of rubrics related to the four categories above that you draw from over the course of a year. Rest assured the effort is worth it. Students will better understand what you are after, and the assessment process will actually be a key element of instruction instead of just a chore.

Indicator	Description
impact of performance	refers to the success of performance given the purposes, goals, and desired results
work quality and craftsmanship	refers to the overall polish, organization, and rigor of the work
adequacy of process/method/behavior	refers to the quality of the procedures and manner of presentation, prior to and during performance
validity of content	refers to the correctness of the ideas, skills, or materials used

From Theory to Practice
Your Guide to Assessment in myWorld Social Studies

Student Worktext

- Provides formative assessment for each lesson called Got it?

- Each chapter ends with a Review and Assessment, which includes a rich variety of question formats.

Digital Presentation

- Got it? formative assessment activities in the Digital Presentations allow you to monitor students' comprehension quickly and easily.

- Support Plus button in the Digital Presentations provides suggestions for reteaching or reframing content when students aren't getting it.

myWorld Activity and myStory Book

- Provide two great performance assessment options for each chapter

- myStoryBook provides an authentic assessment opportunity in which students create their own book which they can share with other students and the wider community.

Chapter Tests

- Ready-made test Forms A and B provide quick formal and summative assessment options.

- ExamView test banks on DVD allow you to create your own custom tests.

- Online testing available within your course at myworldsocialstudies.com

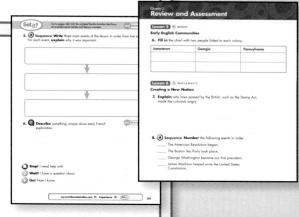

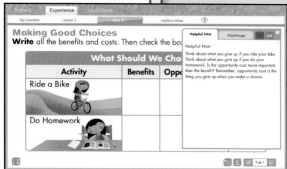

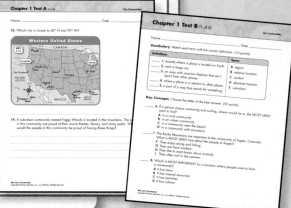

myWorld Social Studies Pacing Guide

Pearson's *myWorld Social Studies* offers a flexible, integrated approach to teaching elementary social studies. You will choose from an innovative menu of instructional strategies to build a curriculum and learning experiences that best meet your students' needs and your state's content requirements. Using your state standards as a guide, choose lessons and skills that meet your teaching needs.

The *myWorld Social Studies* program offers you a choice of three options to plan and teach your lessons. We recommend that you choose our **preferred** option, which uses a combination of digital whiteboard presentations and the print Worktext. This option takes advantage of the strengths of each format to create the most complete learning experience.

The **print** option is designed for teachers who prefer a print-only format or who do not have access to a digital whiteboard. This plan requires only the Worktext and other print materials available to you, but gives your students all they need to master social studies content and skills.

We understand that elementary teachers are expected to cover a great deal of content in a limited amount of classroom time, so we designed our **pressed for time** option for teachers facing a particularly busy curriculum. Like the preferred option, this includes elements from both the digital whiteboard presentations and the print Worktext, but focuses only on the most essential pieces, taking around half the time as the preferred option.

Option	What does it mean?
Preferred	• Uses digital whiteboard presentations and print Worktext • The two elements complement each other • Most complete option
Print	• Uses only print materials • For teachers who prefer print materials or for classrooms without digital whiteboards.
Pressed for Time	• Uses digital whiteboard presentations and print Worktext • Fits social studies into a packed curriculum • Includes only the most essential elements

Pacing Chart

Pacing Chart	Preferred	Print	Pressed for Time	
Chapter Opener				
Digital Presentation: Big Question	•		•	10 minutes
Digital Presentation: myStory Spark	•			10 minutes
Digital Presentation: myStory Video	•		•	10 minutes
Digital Presentation: Song	•			5 minutes
Worktext: myStory Spark		•		10 minutes
Worktext: Song		•		5 minutes
Worktext: Vocabulary Preview	•	•		10 minutes
Lesson				
Digital Presentation: Lesson Introduction	•		•	5 minutes
Worktext: Envision it!	•	•	•	5 minutes
Worktext: Active Reading	•	•		30 minutes
Worktext: Got it?		•		10 minutes
Digital Presentation: Got it?	•		•	10 minutes
Digital Presentation: myStory Ideas	•			10 minutes
Skill Lesson				
Digital Presentation: Target Reading Skill Lesson	•		•	15 minutes
Worktext: Target Reading Skill Lesson		•		20 minutes
Digital Presentation: 21st Century Skill Lesson	•		•	15 minutes
Worktext: 21st Century Skill Lesson		•		20 minutes
Chapter Review				
Worktext: Review and Assessment		•		15 minutes
Digital Presentation: Vocabulary Review	•		•	10 minutes
myWorld Activity	•	•		30 minutes
myStory Book	•	•		30 minutes

Use this chart to help plan your lessons. Activities highlighted in light blue refer to digital presentations. Activities in beige use the Worktext. Green activities can use either digital presentations or the Worktext.

Correlation to the National Curriculum Standards for Social Studies

The *myWorld Social Studies* program is correlated to the themes of social studies found in the National Curriculum Standards for Social Studies. These themes were developed by the National Council for the Social Studies to address overall curriculum design.

A description of each theme is drawn from the curriculum standards book published by the National Council for the Social Studies in 2010.

Theme Title	Theme Description	Chapter	Big Question
Theme I: Culture	Social studies programs should include experiences that provide for the study of culture and cultural diversity.	4	How is culture shared?
Theme II: Time, Continuity, and Change	Social studies programs should include experiences that provide for the study of the past and its legacy.	5	How does life change throughout history?
Theme III: People, Places, and Environments	Social studies programs should include experiences that provide for the study of people, places, and environments.	3	What is the world like?
Theme IV: Individual Identity and Development	Social studies programs should include experiences that provide for the study of individual development and identity.	4	How is culture shared?
Theme V: Individuals, Groups, and Institutions	Social studies programs should include experiences that provide for the study of interactions among individuals, groups, and institutions.	1	How do people best cooperate?

Theme Title	Theme Description	Chapter	Big Question
Theme VI: Power, Authority, and Governance	Social studies programs should include experiences that provide for the study of how people create, interact with, and change structures of power, authority, and governance.	1	How do people best cooperate?
Theme VII: Production, Distribution, and Consumption	Social studies programs should include experiences that provide for the study of how people organize for the production, distribution, and consumption of goods and services.	2	How do people get what they need?
Theme VIII: Science, Technology, and Society	Social studies programs should include experiences that provide for the study of relationships among science, technology, and society.	3	What is the world like?
Theme IX: Global Connections	Social studies programs should include experiences that provide for the study of global connections and interdependence.	4	How is culture shared?
Theme X: Civic Ideals and Practices	Social studies programs should include experiences that provide for the study of the ideals, principles, and practices of citizenship in a democratic republic.	4	How is culture shared?

Correlating myWorld Social Studies to Your Reading Program

The **myWorld Social Studies** program teaches reading as well as social studies content. Each chapter in the program highlights a key reading skill, such as drawing conclusions. To help you integrate social studies lessons more effectively into your curriculum, this correlation matches the reading skill in each **myWorld Social Studies** chapter with similar skills highlighted in several popular reading programs.

Pearson myWorld Social Studies Target Reading Skills	Scott Foresman Reading Street ©2011	Scott Foresman Reading Street ©2008	Houghton Mifflin Harcourt Journeys ©2011	
Chapter 1				
⊙ **Main Idea and Details**	Unit K.2 Look at Us Week 3 Unit K.3 Changes All Around Us Week 6 Unit K.5 Going Places Week 5 Unit K.6 Putting It Together Week 3	**Volume K.2 Animals Live Here** Week 3 Time for Science **Volume K.3 Watch Me Change** Week 6 Time for Science **Volume K.5 Going Places** Week 5 Time for Social Studies **Volume K.6 Building Our Homes** Week 3 Time for Science	Unit 1 Friendly Faces Lesson 1 Unit 2 Show and Tell Lesson 8 Unit 6 Look at Us Lesson 29	
Chapter 2				
⊙ **Cause and Effect**	Unit K.3 Changes All Around Us Week 3 Unit K.4 Let's Go Exploring Week 2 Unit K.5 Going Places Week 2	**Volume K.3 Watch Me Change** Week 3 Time for Social Studies **Volume K.4 Let's Explore** Week 2 Time for Social Studies **Volume K.5 Going Places** Week 2 Time for Science	Unit 3 Outside My Door Lesson 14 Unit 4 Let's Find Out Lesson 19 Unit 6 Look at Us Lesson 26	
Chapter 3				
⊙ **Classify and Categorize**	Unit K.1 All Together Now Week 4 Week 6 Unit K.4 Let's Go Exploring Week 5	**Volume K.1 All Together Now** Week 4 Time for Social Studies Week 6 Time for Science **Volume K.4 Let's Explore** Week 5 Time for Science		

Pearson myWorld Social Studies Target Reading Skills	Macmillan McGraw-Hill Treasures ©2011	Harcourt School Storytown ©2008	Good Habits, Great Readers ©2012
Chapter 1			
◉ **Main Idea and Details**	Unit 6 Neighborhood **Week 1** Our Neighborhood **Week 2** People and Places Unit 7 Weather **Week 1** Kinds of Weather	Unit 5 Whatever the Weather Lesson 13 Lesson 14 **Unit 8 Jobs People Do** Lesson 22 Lesson 23 **Unit 9 Animals All Around** Lesson 25 Lesson 26 Lesson 27	**Unit 3 Great Readers Use What They Know** Week 1 Making Connections **Unit 5 Great Readers Read to Learn** Week 1 Learning Information from Nonfiction Week 2 Learning Information From Nonfiction
Chapter 2			
◉ **Cause and Effect**	Unit 10 I Know a Lot! **Week 2** Art All Around		**Unit 7 Great Readers Think Critically About Books** Week 1 Responding to Characters
Chapter 3			
◉ **Classify and Categorize**	Unit 3 Transportation **Week 2** Traveling Far and Near Unit 5 Animals **Week 2** How Animals Change and Grow Unit 9 Amazing Creatures **Week 1** Interesting Insects		**Unit 2 Great Readers Make Sense of Text** Week 3 Problem-Solving Unfamiliar Words

Pearson myWorld Social Studies Target Reading Skills	Scott Foresman Reading Street ©2011	Scott Foresman Reading Street ©2008	Houghton Mifflin Harcourt Journeys ©2011	
Chapter 4				
◉ **Compare and Contrast**	Unit K.2 Look at Us Week 1 Unit K.3 Changes All Around Us Week 1 Unit K.5 Going Places Week 3 Unit K.6 Putting It Together Week 1	**Volume K.2 Animals Live Here** Week 1 Time for Science **Volume K.3 Watch Me Change** Week 1 Time for Science **Volume K.5 Going Places** Week 3 Time for Social Studies **Volume K.6 Building Our Homes** Week 1 Time for Science	Unit 2 Show and Tell Lesson 6 Unit 3 Outside My Door Lesson 11 Unit 6 Look at Us Lesson 27	
Chapter 5				
◉ **Sequence**	Unit K.1 All Together Now Week 3 Unit K.2 Look at Us Week 5 Unit K.4 Let's Go Exploring Week 1 Week 3	**Volume K.1 All Together Now** Week 3 Time for Social Studies **Volume K.2 Animals Live Here** Week 5 Time for Science **Volume K.4 Let's Explore** Week 1 Time for Social Studies Week 3 Time for Science	Unit 1 Friendly Faces Lesson 5 Unit 3 Outside My Door Lesson 15 Unit 5 Growing and Changing Lesson 23	

Pearson myWorld Social Studies Target Reading Skills	Macmillan McGraw-Hill Treasures ©2011	Harcourt School Storytown ©2008	Good Habits, Great Readers ©2012
Chapter 4			
◉ **Compare and Contrast**	**Unit 2 Friends** **Week 2** What is a Friend? **Unit 9 Amazing Creatures** **Week 2** The Amazing Ocean		**Unit 4 Great Readers Understand How Stories Work** Week 4 Identifying and Using Text Features
Chapter 5			
◉ **Sequence**	**Unit 4 Food** **Week 1** Where Food Comes From **Unit 8 Plants** **Week 1** How Trees Grow	**Unit 3 Friends at School** Lesson 7 Lesson 8 **Unit 4 On the Farm** Lesson 12 **Unit 6 Let's Play** Lesson 18	**Unit 1 Great Readers See Themselves as Readers** Week 2 Choosing Books Week 3 Knowing Yourself as a Readers **Unit 2 Great Readers Make Sense of Text** Week 2 Asking Questions Week 4 Summarizing and Retelling

Notes

Ready, Set, Teach!
For quick hints on how to teach this chapter, log on to myWorldSocialStudies.com.

Chapter Objectives

Begin with the End in Mind

 Big Question:
How do people best cooperate?

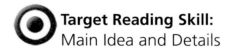 **Target Reading Skill:**
Main Idea and Details

Children will demonstrate the following enduring understandings:

- People cooperate when they make decisions and work together to get a job done.
- People are good citizens when they follow rules and laws.

- People cooperate, share ideas, listen to others, and interact positively with many different people, such as family, friends, and classmates.
- U.S. symbols and monuments stand for and remind us of our country.

Connect

Make Learning Meaningful

 Flip Chart
- Big Question
- myStory Spark
- Song
- Vocabulary Preview

 Digital Presentation
- Big Question
- myStory Spark
- myStory Video
- Song

Experience

Teach Knowledge and Skills

 Flip Chart
- Lessons 1–8
- Got It? Formative Assessments
- Target Reading Skill: Main Idea and Details
- 21C Skill Lesson: Problem Solving

 **myWorld Leveled Readers**

 Digital Presentation
- Big Question
- Lesson Introduction
- Got It?

**21st Century Learning
Online Tutor**

Understand

Assess Understanding

 Flip Chart
- Review and Assessment
- myStory Book

 **myWorld Activity**
- Watch Me Help
- Activity Cards #1–5

Chapter Assessment
- Chapter Test

 Digital Presentation
- Vocabulary Review
- myWorld Activity

myStory Book Online

Children write, illustrate, and publish a digital book.

Chapter Assessment

Administer online test.

Full Lesson Plan Online

To use or customize the full lesson plan for this lesson, log on to myWorldSocialStudies.com.

Objectives

- Establish meaning.
- Make meaningful connections to personal experiences.
- Use prior knowledge to gain understanding.

◉ Target Reading Skill Objective:
- Identify main idea and details.

ELL Objective:
- Use different strategies to explore new vocabulary.

1

PRESENTATION
Chapter 1 Introduction

Use the Big Question Activity to introduce the chapter's main idea.
- myStory Spark
- myStory Video
- Song

🔲 Click on the Extra Support button for helpful hints and vocabulary help.

30 minutes 🕐

Introduce this chapter using the Digital Presentation or the Flip Chart.

2

FLIP CHART
Active Reading

Use the Big Question to introduce the chapter's main idea.
- *How do you cooperate with family members at home?*
- *How do you cooperate with classmates in school?*

myStory Spark
- *What do you work on with friends?*

Song
- *What do you do in school each day?*
- *How do you and your classmates work together?*

Vocabulary Preview
- *What is one rule you follow?*

45 minutes

Not enough time for social studies? Teach these steps during your reading block or as a center activity.

3

LEVELED READER ☆

Use these Leveled Readers as you work through the chapter.
- On Level: *George Washington*
- Advanced: *George Washington: Our First President*

🕐 *Use the lesson steps marked with this icon to teach core content in less time!*

The Big Question

- **ACADEMIC VOCABULARY** *To cooperate means to work together. How do you cooperate when it is time to go to school?* Possible answer: I eat my breakfast instead of playing.
- **ANALYZE VISUALS** *How are the children cooperating, or working together?* They are working together to hold up an American flag.
- **MAKE CONNECTIONS** *How do you cooperate with your family?* help with dinner, listen to my parents

myStory Spark

- **ANALYZE VISUALS** *What are these children doing?* working together
- **MAKE CONNECTIONS** *How do you work together with your friends?* do projects together, help clean up

Differentiated Instruction

Use the following ideas to differentiate instruction for the myStory Spark:

L2 Extra Support: Help children decide on the focus for their drawing by recalling highlights from the class discussion.

L3 On-level: Have children write a simple label for their picture that explains what they are working on together, such as *share, take turns, draw, count.*

L4 Challenge: Encourage children to write a sentence caption for their pictures.

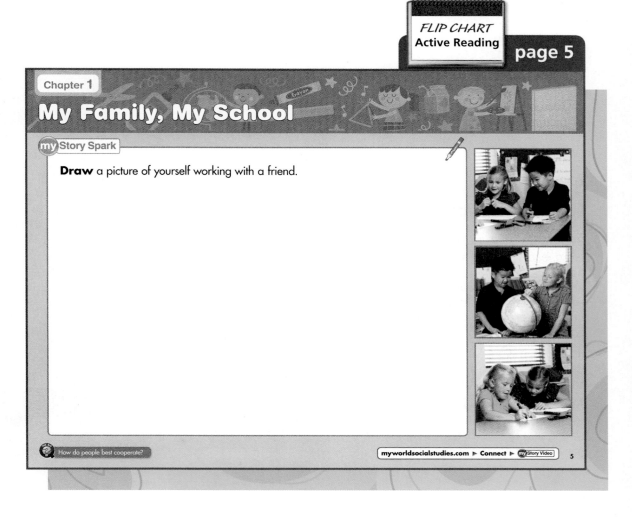

Song

- ◉ **MAIN IDEA AND DETAILS** *What are things children do each day in school?* learn, read, write, spell, work, play

- **ANALYZE VISUALS** *What do the pictures show?* children at school

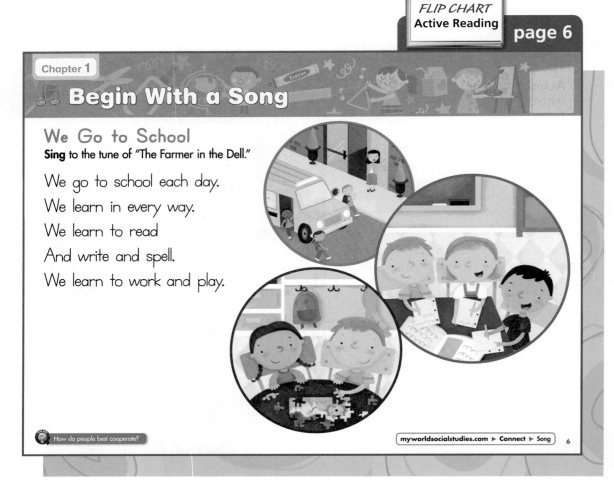

Vocabulary

- **ANALYZE VISUALS** *What does the picture show?* children arriving at school

Support English Language Learners

Beginning LOW/HIGH Point to the word *leader*. Say the word slowly and have children echo you. Use gestures and say: *I am the leader of our class.* Have children point to leaders pictured on the page.

Intermediate LOW Encourage children to use each word in a simple sentence. If necessary, provide sentence frames, such as: *One rule I follow is ____.*

Advanced HIGH Have children take turns giving a definition and have the class guess the word. For example: *It is the place where we learn (school).*

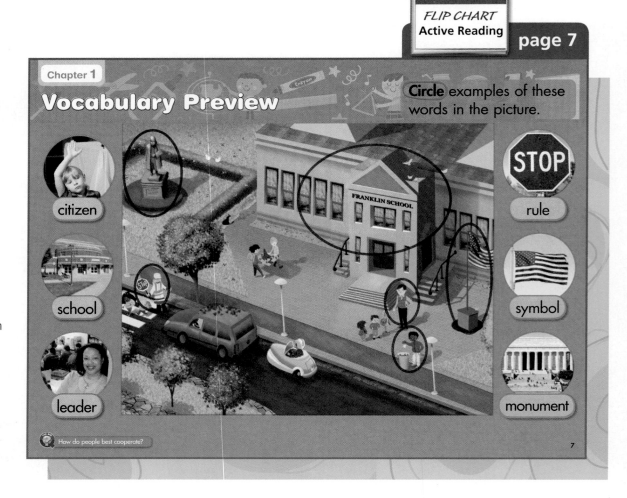

Chapter 1 Lesson 1
What makes a good citizen?
Lesson Plan Summary

Full Lesson Plan Online

To use or customize the full lesson plan for this lesson, log on to myWorldSocialStudies.com.

Objectives

- Identify that good citizenship includes individual responsibility and patriotism.
- Demonstrate that a good citizen takes turns, cooperates, respects others, and shares.

⊙ **Target Reading Skill Objective:**
- Identify main idea and details.

ELL Objective:
- Describe and role-play ways to be good citizens.

1
PRESENTATION
Lesson 1 Introduction

myWorld and Me
Remind children of the discussion they had about the Big Question for this chapter: How do people best cooperate?
- *How do you work with other people to do things?*

5 minutes ⏱

2
FLIP CHART
Student Activity Worksheets

Introduce the Lesson Vocabulary words: *citizen, parade, recycle,* and *cooperate.* Point to pictures on the lesson pages as you explain the meaning of each word. Then ask:
- *What are some ways you can cooperate?* help others, share, listen when others talk

Hand out the Vocabulary Worksheet, page 2. Help children complete it.

5 minutes ⏱

Not enough time for social studies? Teach this step during your reading block or as a center activity.

3
FLIP CHART
Active Reading

Model active reading by asking the questions and using the teaching strategies indicated next to this lesson's Flip Chart pages.

30 minutes

4
PRESENTATION
Got It?

Play the interactive Got It? activity to evaluate children's understanding of the key objectives in this lesson. Use the Extra Support button to assist children who need additional instruction.

OPTIONAL: You may want to assign the Got It? Activity Worksheet for homework or have children complete it in class.

10 minutes ⏱

⏱ *Use the Lesson Steps marked with this icon to teach core content in less time!*

Begin to Read

- **MAIN IDEA AND DETAILS** *Tell how these children show characteristics of being good citizens.* They are taking part in a parade to honor our country. They are helping each other. They are recycling and taking care of Earth.

Support English Language Learners

1. Content and Language
Paraphrase the objectives for this lesson. Explain each one to children. Encourage children to say the objectives in their own words.

2. Frontload the Lesson
Preview the lesson by looking at the pictures. Encourage children to say what the people are doing in each picture.

3. Comprehensible Input
Demonstrate ways of being a good citizen, and then invite children to role-play how they are good citizens.

- **SUMMARIZE** *How can you show that you are a good citizen in school?* Possible answers: work together and share toys, recycle paper and cans, feed the class pet

Differentiated Instruction

Use the following ideas to differentiate instruction.

L2 Extra Support: Have volunteers take turns acting out one of the pictures. Have the class use a simple sentence to describe the action. For example: *She feeds the fish.*

L3 On-level: Ask children to draw and label a picture showing another way that they can be good citizens. Have them work in pairs to write one or two word labels for each other's work.

L4 Challenge: Invite children to make an accordion book that shows examples of good citizenship.

Lesson 1
What makes a good citizen?

I can help. I can take turns.

 How do people best cooperate?

myworldsocialstudies.com ▸ Experience ▸ Introduction   8

Lesson 1
What makes a good citizen?

Tell how these children are good citizens.

Possible answers: Children may say the children show they are good citizens by waving our country's flag, sharing and taking turns, helping to recycle, helping with classroom jobs.

How do people best cooperate?

myworldsocialstudies.com ▸ Experience ▸ (Got it?)   9

Full Lesson Plan Online

To use or customize the full lesson plan for this lesson, log on to myWorldSocialStudies.com.

Objectives

- Describe roles and responsibilities children have with their family, at school, and in the community.
- Identify personal rights, such as the right to food, clothing, shelter, and the right to go to school.

⊙ Target Reading Skill Objective:
- Identify main idea and details.

ELL Objective:
- Understand the difference between a right and a responsibility.

---

1 PRESENTATION Lesson 2 Introduction

myWorld and Me
Remind children of the discussion they had about the Big Question for this chapter: How do people best cooperate?
- *What responsibilities do you have at home and in school?*

5 minutes ⓥ

---

2 FLIP CHART Student Activity Worksheets

Introduce the Lesson Vocabulary words: *rights, responsibility, home,* and *school*. Point to pictures on the lesson as you explain the meaning of each word. Then ask:
- *What is a right you have?* to have food to eat, clothing to wear, to be able to go to school
- *What is a responsibility you have?* keeping my room clean, taking care of a pet, learning at school

Hand out the Vocabulary Worksheet, page 4. Help children complete it.

5 minutes ⓥ

Not enough time for social studies? Teach this step during your reading block or as a center activity.

---

3 FLIP CHART Active Reading

Model active reading by asking the questions and using the teaching strategies indicated next to this lesson's Flip Chart pages.

30 minutes

---

4 PRESENTATION Got It?

Play the interactive Got It? activity to evaluate children's understanding of the key objectives in this lesson. Use the Extra Support button to assist children who need additional instruction.

OPTIONAL: You may want to assign the Got It? Activity Worksheet for homework or have children complete it in class.

10 minutes ⓥ

ⓥ *Use the Lesson Steps marked with this icon to teach core content in less time!*

Begin to Read

- ⊙ **MAIN IDEA AND DETAILS** *What rights do these children have?* living in a home, going to school

Support English Language Learners

1. Content and Language
Write the words *responsibilities* and *rights* on the board. Point to the words as you read aloud the objectives for the lesson. Have children restate the objectives in their own words.

2. Frontload the Lesson
Preview the pictures. Have children predict the lesson content.

3. Comprehensible Input
Have volunteers take turns acting out and describing the rights and responsibilities of the children in the photographs.

- **MAKE CONNECTIONS** *What are responsibilities you have at home?* Possible answers: picking up toys, doing homework
- **MAKE CONNECTIONS** *What are responsibilities you have in school?* Possible answers: trying our best, working with classmates

Differentiated Instruction

Use the following ideas to differentiate instruction.

L2 Extra Support: Have children cut out and sort magazine pictures of rights and responsibilities, or have them choose from pictures you have selected and paste them on the Activity Worksheet.

L3 On-level: Have children find and sort magazine pictures as they describe each right and responsibility and then paste pictures on the Activity Worksheet page.

L4 Challenge: Ask children to draw and label a picture that shows responsibilities they have at home and at school.

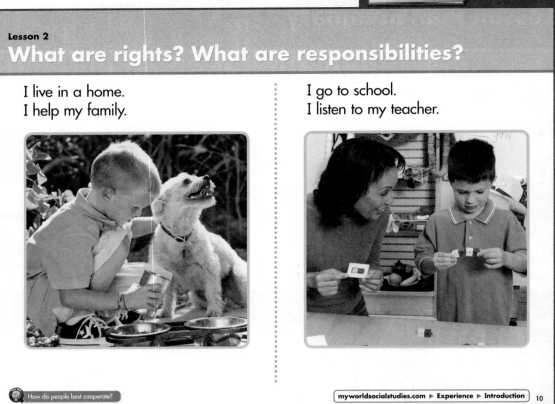

FLIP CHART
Active Reading
page 10

Lesson 2
What are rights? What are responsibilities?

I live in a home.
I help my family.

I go to school.
I listen to my teacher.

How do people best cooperate?   myworldsocialstudies.com ▶ Experience ▶ Introduction   10

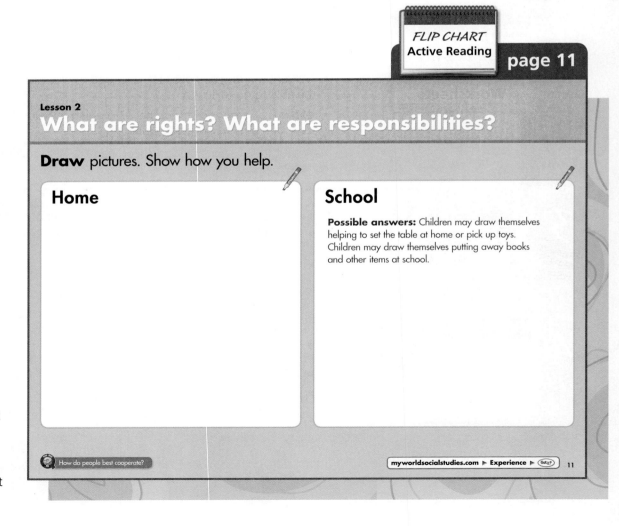

FLIP CHART
Active Reading
page 11

Lesson 2
What are rights? What are responsibilities?

Draw pictures. Show how you help.

Home

School

Possible answers: Children may draw themselves helping to set the table at home or pick up toys. Children may draw themselves putting away books and other items at school.

How do people best cooperate?   myworldsocialstudies.com ▶ Experience ▶ Got it?   11

Full Lesson Plan Online

To use or customize the full lesson plan for this lesson, log on to myWorldSocialStudies.com.

Objectives

- Explain how cooperating with others helps to get a job done.
- Identify conflicts and ways to solve them.
- Explain how working with others helps to resolve conflicts.

⊙ **Target Reading Skill Objective:**
- Identify main idea and details.

ELL Objective:
- Describe problems and solutions.

1
PRESENTATION
Lesson 3 Introduction

myWorld and Me

Remind children of the discussion they had about the Big Question for this chapter: How do people best cooperate?

- *What do you do to get along with others?*

5 minutes ⊘

2
FLIP CHART
Student Activity Worksheets

Introduce the Lesson Vocabulary words: *problem, conflict,* and *solution.* Point to pictures on the lesson pages as you explain the meaning of each word. Then ask:

- *What is a problem you could have?* wanting the same thing as someone else, not being able to do something you want to do

- *What would be a solution to the problem?* take turns, do something else

Hand out the Vocabulary Worksheet, page 6. Help children complete it.

5 minutes ⊘

> *Not enough time for social studies? Teach this step during your reading block or as a center activity.*

3
PRESENTATION
Active Reading

Model active reading by asking the questions and using the teaching strategies indicated next to this lesson's Flip Chart pages.

30 minutes

4
PRESENTATION
Got It?

Play the interactive Got It? activity to evaluate children's understanding of the key objectives in this lesson. Use the Extra Support button to assist children who need additional instruction.

OPTIONAL: You may want to assign the Got It? Activity Worksheet for homework or have children complete it in class.

10 minutes ⊘

⊘ *Use the Lesson Steps marked with this icon to teach core content in less time!*

Begin to Read

- **Analyze Visuals** *What is the problem?* They all want to use the swing.

- ⊙ **Main Idea and Details** *How do these friends solve the problem?* They take turns on the swing.

Support English Language Learners

1. Content and Language

Explain each objective on page 9 of this guide. Have children restate the objectives in their own words.

2. Frontload the Lesson

Draw a problem and solution chart on the board. Fill it in with problems and solutions the children describe.

3. Comprehensible Input

Role-play a problem and solution scenario with volunteers. Have children guess the problem and solution. represented. Repeat the activity.

- **Analyze Visuals** *What problem are these two children having?* They want to read the same book.

- **Analyze Visuals** *How can they can solve the problem?* take turns

Differentiated Instruction

Use the following ideas to differentiate the activity on page 13.

L2 Extra Support: Before they draw, have children describe the problem shown in the picture and discuss possible solutions.

L3 On-level: Have children complete the activity on page 13 individually or with a partner.

L4 Challenge: On a separate page, have children draw a picture of a problem and an associated solution. Help them write a caption for each one.

Lesson 3
How do we get along with others?

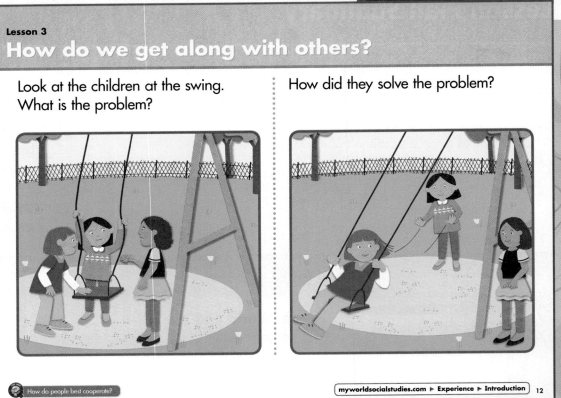

Look at the children at the swing. What is the problem?

How did they solve the problem?

How do people best cooperate?   myworldsocialstudies.com ▸ Experience ▸ Introduction   12

Lesson 3
How do we get along with others?

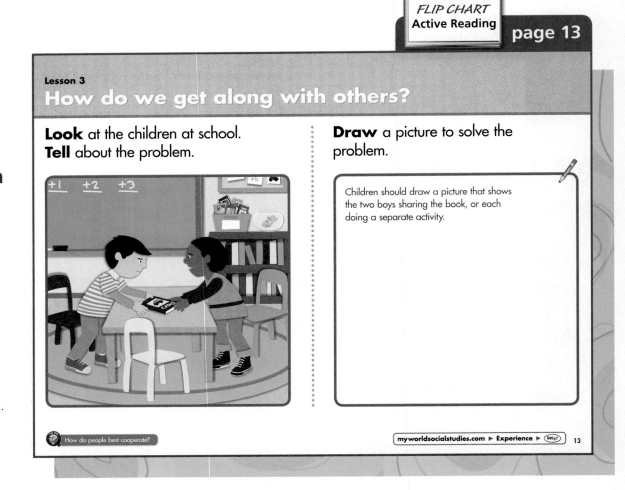

Look at the children at school. **Tell** about the problem.

Draw a picture to solve the problem.

> Children should draw a picture that shows the two boys sharing the book, or each doing a separate activity.

How do people best cooperate?   myworldsocialstudies.com ▸ Experience ▸   13

Full Lesson Plan Online

To use or customize the full lesson plan for this lesson, log on to myWorldSocialStudies.com.

Objectives

- Identify the main idea and retell key details of a text with prompting and support.

1

FLIP CHART
Teach the Skill

Main Idea and Details

20 minutes

Before reading, invite children to tell what is happening in each picture. Then read the explanation for main idea and details. Next, read the first sentence and track the print using your finger or a pointer. Invite a volunteer to point to the picture that illustrates the main idea. Then read each detail sentence and have children point to the picture that matches it.

2

FLIP CHART
Try It

Model active reading by asking the questions and using the teaching strategies indicated next to this lesson's Flip Chart pages.

15 minutes

3

PRESENTATION
Digital Presentation

Review the skill with children using the Digital Presentation. Click on the Extra Support button for helpful hints and vocabulary help.

15 minutes

Differentiated Instruction

Use the following ideas to differentiate instruction when discussing finding the main idea and details on the activity page.

L1 Special Needs Invite children to act out or use gestures to reinforce the details of each picture.

L2 Extra Support Ask: *How does Lin take care of Barker?* Have volunteers complete this sentence: *Lin takes care of Barker by* _____ feeding him, walking him, washing him

L3 On-level Provide four pieces of paper to each child. On the first piece, ask the child to draw a picture that supports the sentence *I go to school.* Then have children draw three detail pictures that show activities they do in school.

L4 Challenge Invite children to take turns telling the main idea of a favorite story, then retelling details that support it.

FLIP CHART
Active Reading

page 14

Reading Skills: Main Idea and Details

The main idea tells what a story is about. The details tell more about the main idea.

<u>Anna and Ben go to school.</u>
They help each other read.
They share toys.
They clean up, too.

main idea

detail   **detail**   **detail**

myworldsocialstudies.com ▶ Experience ▶ Skills   14

FLIP CHART
Active Reading

page 15

Reading Skills: Main Idea and Details

(Try it!)

Underline the main idea.

<u>Lin takes care of Barker.</u>
She gives him a bath.
She feeds him.
Lin takes Barker for a walk, too.

Write "d" under the details.

main idea   d

d   d

myworldsocialstudies.com ▶ Experience ▶ Skills   15

Lesson Plan Summary

Full Lesson Plan Online

To use or customize the full lesson plan for this lesson, log on to myWorldSocialStudies.com.

Objectives

- Explain why there are rules and laws.
- Identify rules to follow at home, at school, and in the community.
- Describe how laws keep people safe.
- Understand that there are consequences for not following rules and laws.

⦿ Target Reading Skill Objective:
- Identify main idea and details.

ELL Objective:
- Learn to talk about the meaning of and reasons for rules.

---

1 **PRESENTATION** Lesson 4 Introduction

myWorld and Me
Remind children of the discussion they had about the Big Question for this chapter: How do people best cooperate?
- *What rules do you follow at home, at school, and in your community?*

5 minutes ⏱

---

2 **FLIP CHART** Student Activity Worksheets

Introduce the Lesson Vocabulary words: *home, school, community,* and *playground*. Point to pictures on the lesson pages as you explain the meaning of each word. Then ask:
- *What is a rule you follow at home?* Possible answers: clean up toys; wash my hands before eating
- *A law is a rule we follow in our community. What is a law you follow in your community?* Possible answers: cross at a crosswalk; throw trash in a trash can

Hand out the Vocabulary Worksheet, page 9. Help children complete it.

5 minutes ⏱

Not enough time for social studies? Teach this step during your reading block or as a center activity.

---

3 **FLIP CHART** Active Reading

Model active reading by asking the questions and using the teaching strategies indicated next to this lesson's Flip Chart pages.

30 minutes

---

4 **PRESENTATION** Got It?

Play the interactive Got It? activity to evaluate children's understanding of the key objectives in this lesson. Use the Extra Support button to assist children who need additional instruction.

OPTIONAL: You may want to assign the Got It? Activity Worksheet for homework or have children complete it in class.

10 minutes ⏱

⏱ *Use the Lesson Steps marked with this icon to teach core content in less time!*

Begin to Read

- ⊙ **Main Idea and Details** *What rules do you follow?* Possible answers: wash hands before eating, raise hand before talking, cross at a crosswalk

- **Make Connections** *Why is it important to follow rules?* because rules keep us safe

Support English Language Learners

1. Content and Language
Display the photographs on the Flip Chart page as you read aloud the lesson objectives. Then have children restate the objectives in their own words.

2. Frontload the Lesson
Preview the lesson by looking at the pictures. Have children describe what the people in the photos are doing.

3. Comprehensible Input
Display the Flip Chart photographs. Ask: *What rules are the children following? Why are the children following rules?*

- **Analyze Visuals** *What rules are being followed?* Possible answers: throwing trash where it belongs, wearing a bike helmet

- **Draw Conclusions** *What might happen if someone doesn't follow a rule?* Possible answer: They could get hurt.

Differentiated Instruction

Use the following ideas to differentiate instruction for this lesson.

L2 Extra Support: Ask children which rules they follow. Record them on chart paper using words and drawings.

L3 On-level: Write *Home, School,* and *Community* on three separate pieces of chart paper and post them on the wall or on tables. Have children circulate around the room and draw pictures on each paper to illustrate rules and laws they follow.

L4 Challenge: Help children write and illustrate rules and laws they follow on sentence strips.

Lesson 4
What rules do we follow?

Good citizens follow rules.

home   **school**   **community**

How do people best cooperate?   myworldsocialstudies.com ▶ Experience ▶ Introduction   16

Lesson 4
What rules do we follow?

Circle people who follow rules.

How do people best cooperate?   myworldsocialstudies.com ▶ Experience ▶ Got it?   17

Full Lesson Plan Online

To use or customize the full lesson plan for this lesson, log on to myWorldSocialStudies.com.

Objectives

- Identify leaders at home, at school, and in the community.
- Describe how leaders help people at home, at school, and in the community.

⊙ **Target Reading Skill Objective:**
- Identify main idea and details.

ELL Objective:
- Use different strategies to access vocabulary about leaders.

1
PRESENTATION
Lesson 1 Introduction

myWorld and Me
Remind children of the discussion they had about the Big Question for this chapter: How do people best cooperate?
- *Who can help when you have a problem at home?*

5 minutes ⊙

2
FLIP CHART
Student Activity Worksheets

Introduce the Lesson Vocabulary words: *leaders* and *help*. Point to pictures on the lesson pages and use gestures as you explain the meaning of each word. Then ask:
- *Who are leaders at school? What do they do to help you?* Teachers help you learn.

Hand out the Vocabulary Worksheet, page 9. Help children complete it.

5 minutes ⊙

Not enough time for social studies? Teach this step during your reading block or as a center activity.

3
FLIP CHART
Active Reading

Model active reading by asking the questions and using the teaching strategies indicated next to this lesson's Flip Chart pages.

30 minutes

4
PRESENTATION
Got It?

Play the interactive Got It? activity to evaluate children's understanding of the key objectives in this lesson. Use the Extra Support button to assist children who need additional instruction.

OPTIONAL: You may want to assign the Got It? Activity Worksheet for homework or have children complete it in class.

10 minutes ⊙

⊙ *Use the Lesson Steps marked with this icon to teach core content in less time!*

Begin to Read

- **ANALYZE VISUALS** *What leader might help us learn how to ride a bike?* Possible answers: mom, dad
- ⦿ **MAIN IDEA AND DETAILS** *What are some ways leaders help us?* Possible answers: They help us learn and keep us safe.

Support English Language Learners

1. Content and Language

Read aloud the objectives for this lesson. Have children look at the Flip Chart and restate the objectives.

2. Frontload the Lesson

Preview the lesson pictures. Have children tell what they know about each person and how the person helps them.

3. Comprehensible Input

Point to each leader pictured, and role-play how that leader helps children.

- **PREDICT** *What could happen if children don't listen to the crossing guard?* They could get hurt.
- **MAKE CONNECTIONS** *What is one law that the crossing guard helps us remember?* to cross at a crosswalk

Differentiated Instruction

Use the following ideas to differentiate instruction for this lesson.

L2 Extra Support: Point to the first picture and say: *This is a teacher. A teacher helps me learn.* Have children echo you. Repeat the routine with the other pictures.

L3 On-level: Have children brainstorm the names of leaders. Encourage them to tell how each leader helps them.

L4 Challenge: Invite children to make up riddles about leaders who help them.

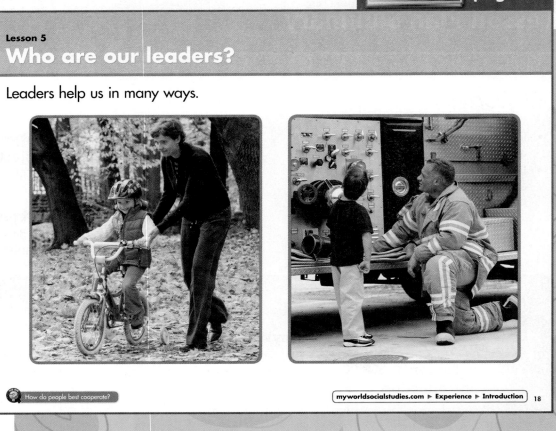

Lesson 5
Who are our leaders?

Leaders help us in many ways.

How do people best cooperate? myworldsocialstudies.com ▶ Experience ▶ Introduction 18

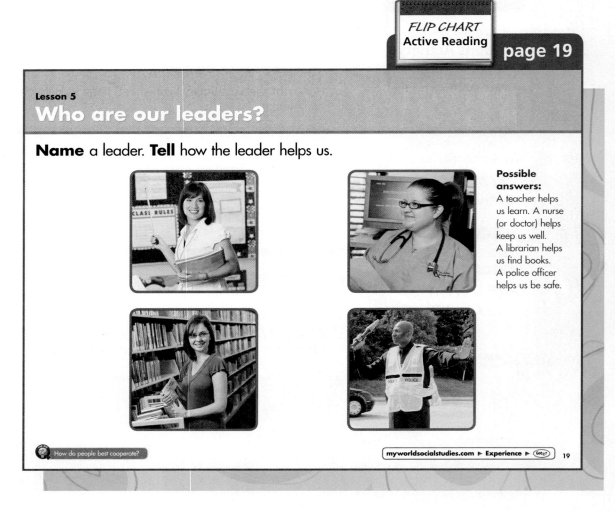

Lesson 5
Who are our leaders?

Name a leader. **Tell** how the leader helps us.

Possible answers: A teacher helps us learn. A nurse (or doctor) helps keep us well. A librarian helps us find books. A police officer helps us be safe.

How do people best cooperate? myworldsocialstudies.com ▶ Experience ▶ Got it? 19

Full Lesson Plan Online

To use or customize the full lesson plan for this lesson, log on to myWorldSocialStudies.com.

Objectives

- Describe steps in making a decision.
- Identify different ways that groups make decisions.
- Explain voting as a way to make a decision.
- Identify the consequences of decision making.
- Participate in problem solving.

◉ **Target Reading Skill Objective:**
- Identify main idea and details.

ELL Objective:
- Use different strategies to describe how to make decisions.

1
PRESENTATION
Lesson 1 Introduction

myWorld and Me
Remind children of the discussion they had about the Big Question for this chapter: How do people best cooperate?
- *How do you make decisions that are fair for everyone?*

5 minutes ⊙

2
FLIP CHART
Student Activity Worksheets

Introduce the Lesson Vocabulary words: *vote* and *discuss*. Point to pictures on the lesson pages and explain the meaning of each word. Then ask:
- *What are ways to show how you vote?* a show of hands, in writing, going to stand in a certain place
- *How do you make decisions with friends?* vote, discuss, take turns making decisions, play rock, paper, scissors

Hand out the Vocabulary Worksheet, page 13. Help children complete it.

5 minutes ⊙

Not enough time for social studies? Teach this step during your reading block or as a center activity.

3
FLIP CHART
Active Reading

Model active reading by asking the questions and using the teaching strategies indicated next to this lesson's Flip Chart pages.

30 minutes

4
PRESENTATION
Got It?

Play the interactive Got It? activity to evaluate children's understanding of the key objectives in this lesson. Use the Extra Support button to assist children who need additional instruction.

OPTIONAL: You may want to assign the Got It? Activity Worksheet for homework or have children complete it in class.

10 minutes ⊙

⊙ *Use the Lesson Steps marked with this icon to teach core content in less time!*

Begin to Read

- ⊙ **MAIN IDEA AND DETAILS** *What are two ways we make decisions?* Possible answers: voting, talking

- **ANALYZE VISUALS** *What are the mother and son doing?* thinking and talking about what they would like to do

Support English Language Learners

1. Content and Language
Paraphrase the objectives for this lesson. Then have children restate them in their own words.

2. Frontload the Lesson
Invite children to share personal experiences of how they make decisions at home and in school.

3. Comprehensible Input
Role-play the way decisions are being made on the lesson page. Then invite children to act out and describe ways they make decisions.

- **ASK QUESTIONS** *What could you ask a friend before deciding what to do together?* Possible answer: Do you like puzzles?

- **DRAW CONCLUSIONS** *What happens after a vote is taken?* A decision is made, then everyone does what is decided.

Differentiated Instruction

Use the following ideas to differentiate instruction for this lesson.

L2 Extra Support: Discuss decisions children make every day, such as what to have for breakfast, what to wear, what activity to play. Discuss how they make their final decision.

L3 On-level: Ask children to draw two pictures that show different ways to make a decision. Have them explain how they arrived at their final choice.

L4 Challenge: Invite children to act out or share with the class their answer to the guiding question: *How do we make good decisions with friends?*

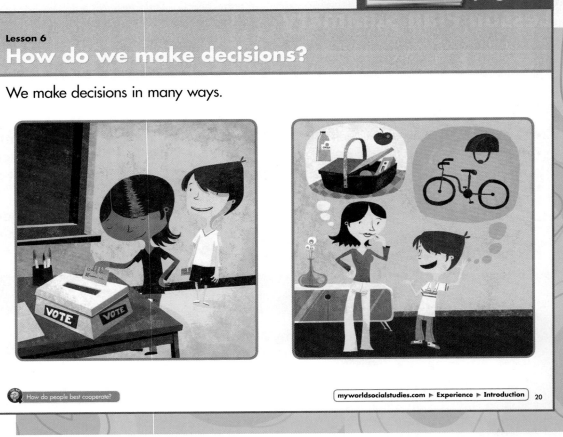

FLIP CHART
Active Reading
page 20

Lesson 6
How do we make decisions?

We make decisions in many ways.

How do people best cooperate?   myworldsocialstudies.com ▶ Experience ▶ Introduction   20

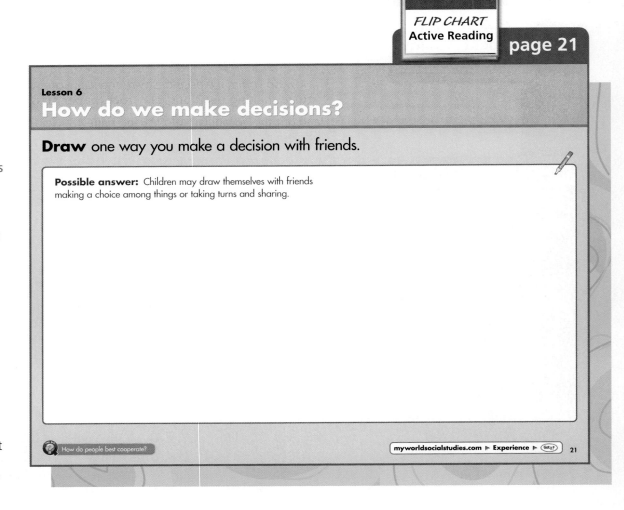

FLIP CHART
Active Reading
page 21

Lesson 6
How do we make decisions?

Draw one way you make a decision with friends.

> **Possible answer:** Children may draw themselves with friends making a choice among things or taking turns and sharing.

How do people best cooperate?   myworldsocialstudies.com ▶ Experience ▶ Got it?   21

Full Lesson Plan Online

To use or customize the full lesson plan for this lesson, log on to myWorldSocialStudies.com.

Objectives

- Demonstrate that conflicts among friends can be resolved in ways that are consistent with being a good citizen.
- Identify a problem.

- Think of ways to solve a problem.
- Decide the best way to solve a problem.
- Participate in problem solving.

1 FLIP CHART
Teach the Skill

Problem Solving

Have children look at the large picture on the left and encourage them to describe the problem. Then ask them to look closely at the rest of the pictures and tell how these children want to solve the problem. Lead a discussion about all the solutions before having children vote on their first choice for a way to solve the problem. Then invite children to describe ways they have solved problems.

20 minutes

2 FLIP CHART
Try It

Model active reading by asking the questions and using the teaching strategies indicated next to this lesson's Flip Chart pages.

15 minutes

3 PRESENTATION
Digital Presentation

Review the skill with children using the Digital Presentation.

Click on the Extra Support button for helpful hints and vocabulary help.

15 minutes

Differentiated Instruction

Use the following ideas to differentiate instruction for this lesson.

L1 Special Needs As you provide examples of problems and solutions, use gestures and simple sentences to illustrate them.

L2 Extra Support Show magazine, clip art, or other pictures of people frowning. For each picture, ask: *Why is this person frowning or sad?* Encourage them to state the problem using a complete sentence. Discuss possible solutions.

L3 On-level Invite children to draw a picture of a problem they have had. Then have them use another piece of paper to draw a solution.

L4 Challenge Divide the class into two groups. Invite one group to role-play a problem while the other group role-plays a solution. Then have the groups switch roles.

21C Collaboration and Creativity: Problem Solving

1. Name the problem.

2. Think of ways to solve it.

3. Decide the best way to solve the problem.

myworldsocialstudies.com ▶ Experience ▶ Skills 22

21C Collaboration and Creativity: Problem Solving

Try it!

1. Name the problem.

2. Circle the best way to solve the problem.

Answers will vary.

myworldsocialstudies.com ▶ Experience ▶ Skills 23

Chapter 1 Lesson 7
What are our country's symbols?
Lesson Plan Summary

Full Lesson Plan Online

To use or customize the full lesson plan for this lesson, log on to myWorldSocialStudies.com.

Objectives

- Identify important symbols that stand for our country.
- Describe why we have symbols.

⊙ **Target Reading Skill Objective:**
- Identify main idea and details.

ELL Objective:
- Describe symbols and what they stand for.

---

1 PRESENTATION
Lesson 7 Introduction

myWorld and Me

Remind children of the discussion they had about the Big Question for this chapter: How do people best cooperate?
- *What is the U.S. flag?*

5 minutes ⏱

---

2 FLIP CHART
Student Activity Worksheets

Introduce the Lesson Vocabulary words: *eagle, flag, statue,* and *symbol.* Point to pictures on the lesson pages as you explain the meaning of each word. Then ask:
- *What is a symbol that stands for our country?* the U.S. flag, the bald eagle, the Statue of Liberty

Hand out the Vocabulary Worksheet, page 16. Help children complete it.

5 minutes ⏱

Not enough time for social studies? Teach this step during your reading block or as a center activity.

---

3 FLIP CHART
Active Reading

Model active reading by asking the questions and using the teaching strategies indicated next to this lesson's Flip Chart pages.

30 minutes

---

4 PRESENTATION
Got It?

Play the interactive Got It? activity to evaluate children's understanding of the key objectives in this lesson. Use the Extra Support button to assist children who need additional instruction.

OPTIONAL: You may want to assign the Got It? Activity Worksheet for homework or have children complete it in class.

10 minutes ⏱

⏱ *Use the Lesson Steps marked with this icon to teach core content in less time!*

Begin to Read

- **DRAW CONCLUSIONS** *Why are symbols important?* Possible answer: They help us remember important things.

Support English Language Learners

1. Content and Language
Read aloud the objectives for this lesson. Encourage children to restate them in their own words.

2. Frontload the Lesson
Preview the lesson pictures. Invite children to tell about the pictures.

3. Comprehensible Input
Point to the American flag. Ask: *What is this? Why is it important? What does it stand for?*

- **ANALYZE VISUALS** *What do you see in each picture?* a statue, a bear, a flag, a flag, and a bird
- ⦿ **MAIN IDEA AND DETAILS** *What are some symbols of our country?* the Statue of Liberty, the American flag, and the bald eagle

Differentiated Instruction

Use the following ideas to differentiate instruction for this lesson.

L2 Extra Support: Have children point to each U.S. symbol and complete statements such as *This symbol is ...*

L3 On-level: Display pictures of our country's symbols from the text. Have children point to each symbol and say a simple sentence about each one.

L4 Challenge: Have children cut out magazine pictures of U.S. symbols, glue them to index cards, and write a label. Then have them tell something about each symbol from personal experience or from what they have learned.

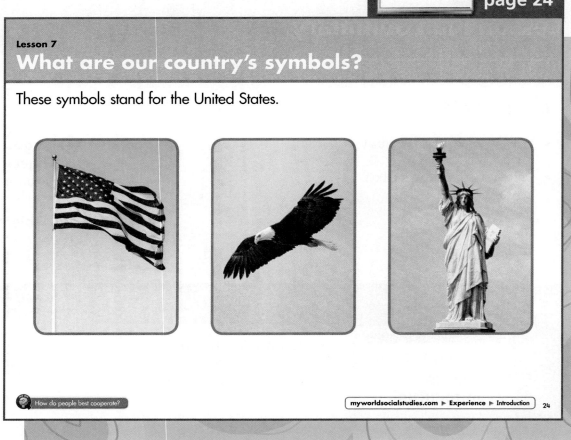

Lesson 7
What are our country's symbols?

These symbols stand for the United States.

How do people best cooperate?   myworldsocialstudies.com ▶ Experience ▶ Introduction 24

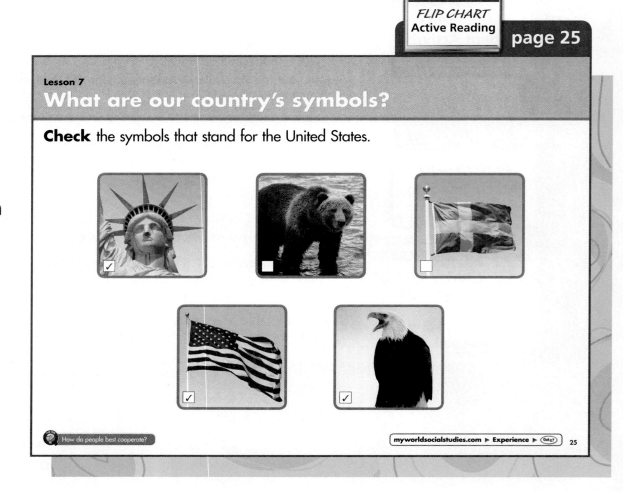

Lesson 7
What are our country's symbols?

Check the symbols that stand for the United States.

How do people best cooperate?   myworldsocialstudies.com ▶ Experience ▶ Got it? 25

Chapter 1 Lesson 8
What are our country's monuments?
Lesson Plan Summary

Full Lesson Plan Online

To use or customize the full lesson plan for this lesson, log on to myWorldSocialStudies.com.

Objectives

- Explain the meaning and importance of U.S. symbols.
- Explain why U.S. monuments and buildings are important.
- Identify where the president of the United States lives and works.

⊙ **Target Reading Skill Objective:**
- Identify main idea and details.

ELL Objective:
- Use different strategies to explore new vocabulary.

1

PRESENTATION
Lesson 8 Introduction

myWorld and Me

Remind children of the discussion they had about the Big Question for this chapter: How do people best cooperate?

- *What do you think about when you see your home?*
- *What other buildings can make us think about something special?*

5 minutes ⊙

2

FLIP CHART
Student Activity Worksheets

Introduce the Lesson Vocabulary words: *monument, important, president,* and *remind*. Point to pictures on the lesson pages as you explain the meaning of each word. Then ask:

- *What do we call the leader of the United States?* the president.

Hand out the Vocabulary Worksheet, page 18. Help children complete it.

5 minutes ⊙

Not enough time for social studies? Teach this step during your reading block or as a center activity.

3

FLIP CHART
Active Reading

Model active reading by asking the questions and using the teaching strategies indicated next to this lesson's Flip Chart pages.

30 minutes

4

PRESENTATION
Got It?

Play the interactive Got It? activity to evaluate children's understanding of the key objectives in this lesson. Use the Extra Support button to assist children who need additional instruction.

OPTIONAL: You may want to assign the Got It? Activity Worksheet for homework or have children complete it in class.

10 minutes ⊙

⊙ *Use the Lesson Steps marked with this icon to teach core content in less time!*

Begin to Read

- **MAIN IDEA AND DETAILS** *What are some of our country's monuments?* the Lincoln Memorial, the Washington Monument, the White House

Support English Language Learners

1. Content and Language
Display the photographs on the Flip Chart page. Read aloud the lesson objectives for this lesson. Encourage children to use the pictures and words to restate the objectives.

2. Frontload the Lesson
Invite children to tell what they know about each photograph. Record the information on the board.

3. Comprehensible Input
Display pictures of monuments and buildings. Have children brainstorm what they know about the pictures.

- **MAKE CONNECTIONS** *What does the president of the United States do at the White House?* The president lives and works there.

Differentiated Instruction

Use the following ideas to differentiate instruction for this lesson.

L2 Extra Support: Display pictures of the president and the White House. Have children identify and describe each picture.

L3 On-level: Ask children to tell what they know about the president, the White House, and Washington, D.C.

L4 Challenge: Distribute outline maps of the United States to children. Have them draw a circle around Washington D.C.

FLIP CHART
Active Reading

page 26

Lesson 8

What are our country's monuments?

These monuments remind us of important people.

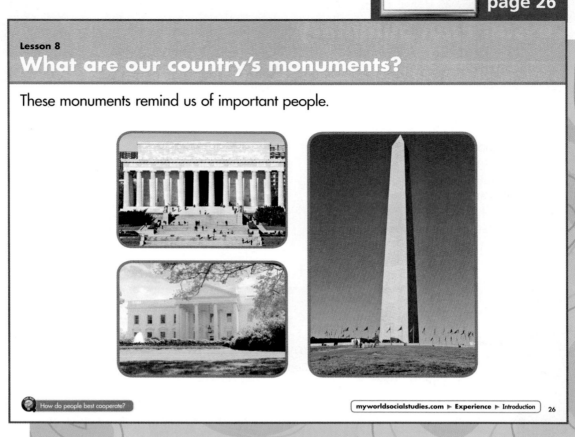

How do people best cooperate?   myworldsocialstudies.com ▶ Experience ▶ Introduction   26

FLIP CHART
Active Reading

page 27

Lesson 8

What are our country's monuments?

Circle the place where our president lives and works.

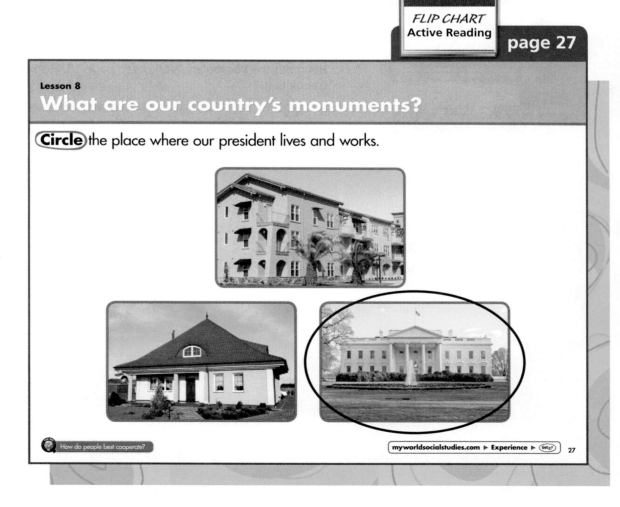

How do people best cooperate?   myworldsocialstudies.com ▶ Experience ▶ Got it?   27

1 PRESENTATION Vocabulary Review

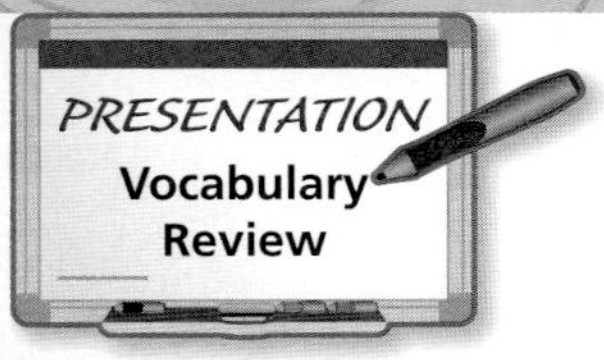

Use the Vocabulary Review game on the Digital Presentation for this lesson.

10 minutes ⏱

2 *Performance Assessment*

Choice A
myStory Book

WRITING ACTIVITY Children write and illustrate an eight-page booklet demonstrating their understanding of the key objectives, vocabulary, and Big Question for this chapter.

See the Online Lesson Plan for full instructions on how to complete the story together as a class, or have each child complete his or her own story. Make sure children's stories reflect what the chapter's content means to them.

30 minutes

Choice B
myWorld Activity

HANDS-ON ACTIVITY: Watch Me Help In this activity children demonstrate ways they help at home, in the classroom, on the playground, in the neighborhood, and at the park. See the Online Lesson Plan for full instructions for completing the activity. Use Activity Cards 1–5 for this activity.

30 minutes

3 *Formal Assessment*

OPTIONAL: You can assign the chapter Review and Assessment Student Activity Worksheets or use the Chapter Test and track scores online.

30 minutes ⏱

⏱ Use the Lesson Steps marked with this icon to teach core content in less time!

Notes

 Big Question

1. Ask children to think back to all the ways people cooperate and work together in this chapter.
2. Call on children to share what they remember.
3. Discuss with children how working together and cooperating with others makes our home, school, community, and country a better place to live.

myWorld and Me

1. Have children think about ways people work together to do a job.
2. Encourage children to recall ways they cooperate with family members or friends to accomplish a task.

myStory Book

1. Explain to children that they will now have the opportunity to create a story about what they learned in this chapter.
2. Have children choose their own words and select the images they think are best for the story.
3. Explain that prompts will guide them through the writing of the story.

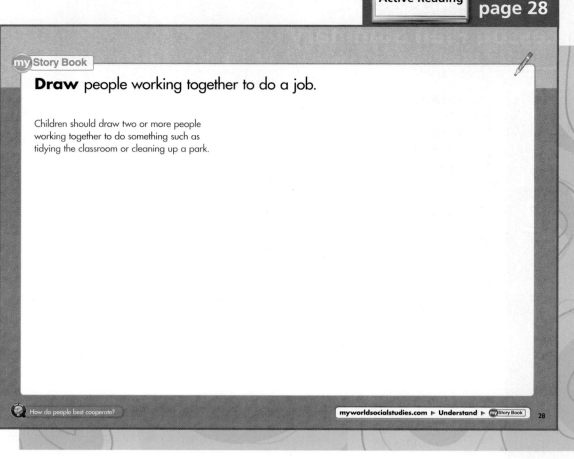

Draw people working together to do a job.

Children should draw two or more people working together to do something such as tidying the classroom or cleaning up a park.

How do people best cooperate?   myworldsocialstudies.com ▶ Understand ▶ my Story Book   28

Planning With the End in Mind

Ready, Set, Teach!
For quick hints on how to teach this chapter, log on to myWorldSocialStudies.com.

Chapter Objectives

Begin With the End in Mind

 Big Question:
How do people get what they need?

 Target Reading Skill:
Cause and Effect

Children will demonstrate the following enduring understandings:

- People make choices about needs and wants.
- People do many kinds of work making goods or providing services.
- People use money to buy and sell.

- People buy things because they cannot make everything themselves.
- People sell things because others want to buy them.

Connect

Make Learning Meaningful

 Flip Chart
- Big Question
- myStory Spark
- Song
- Vocabulary Preview

 Digital Presentation
- Big Question
- myStory Spark
- myStory Video
- Song

Experience

Teach Knowledge and Skills

 Flip Chart
- Lessons 1–6
- Got It? Formative Assessments
- Target Reading Skill: Cause and Effect
- 21C Skill Lesson: Listening and Speaking

 Digital Presentation
- Big Question
- Lesson Introduction
- Got It?

myWorld Leveled Readers

21st Century Learning Online Tutor

Understand

Assess Understanding

 Flip Chart
- Review and Assessment
- myStory Book

myWorld Activity
- Let's Go Shopping
- Activity Cards #6–10

Chapter Assessment
- Chapter Test

 Digital Presentation
- Vocabulary Review
- myWorld Activity

myStory Book Online

Children write, illustrate, and publish a digital book.

Chapter Assessment

Administer online test.

Full Lesson Plan Online
To use or customize the full lesson plan for this lesson, log on to myWorldSocialStudies.com.

Objectives

- Establish meaning.
- Make meaningful connections to personal experiences.
- Use prior knowledge to gain understanding.

⊙ **Target Reading Skill Objective:**
- Identify cause and effect.

ELL Objective:
- Use different strategies to explore new vocabulary.

1

PRESENTATION
Chapter 2 Introduction

Use the Big Question Activity to introduce the chapter's main idea.
- myStory Spark
- myStory Video
- Song
- 📋 Click on the Extra Support button for helpful hints and vocabulary help.

30 minutes ⊘

Introduce this chapter using the Digital Presentation or the Flip Chart.

2

FLIP CHART
Active Reading

Use the Big Question to introduce the chapter's main idea.
- *How does your family get what they need?*

myStory Spark
- *What jobs do you do at home?*

Song
- *What kind of work would you like to do?*

Vocabulary Preview
- *What can you buy with money?*

45 minutes

Not enough time for social studies? Teach these steps during your reading block or as a center activity.

3

LEVELED READER

Use these Leveled Readers as you work through the chapter.
- On Level: *Steve Jobs*
- Advanced: *Steve Jobs and the Computer Business*

⊘ *Use the lesson steps marked with this icon to teach core content in less time!*

The Big Question

- **ANALYZE VISUALS** *What kind of work is the family doing?* They are picking ripe tomatoes.

- **MAKE CONNECTIONS** *What kind of work do you do to help your family?* Sample responses: help prepare a meal, pick fruit and vegetables in the garden

Chapter 2

Everybody Works

How do **people** get what they need?

myworldsocialstudies.com ▶ Connect ▶ 🅱 Big Question 29

myStory Spark

- **SUMMARIZE** *What job do you like to do at home? Why?* Answers will vary, but children should describe valid jobs and valid reasons why they like doing them.

Differentiated Instruction

Use the following activities to differentiate instruction.

L2 Extra Support: Point to each picture and say a simple sentence. For example: *She makes her bed.* Then ask children about a job they do at home. Encourage them to say a simple sentence about the job and act it out.

L3 On-level: Have children draw a picture of a job they do and write a one or two word label for it.

L4 Challenge: Have children draw a picture of a job they do and write a sentence caption. Provide help, when necessary.

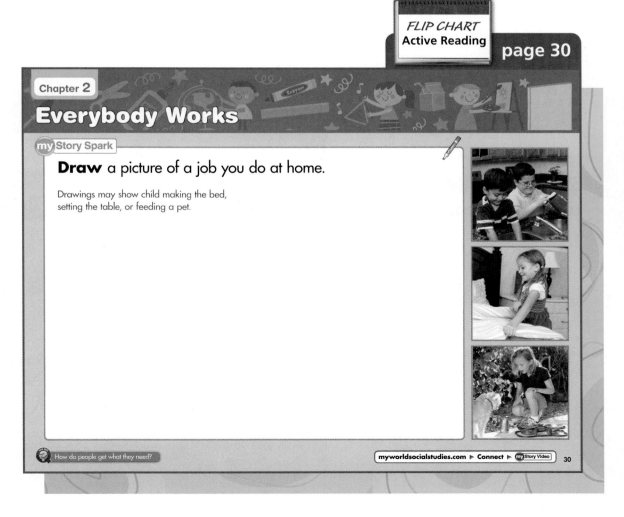

Chapter 2

Everybody Works

🅼 Story Spark

Draw a picture of a job you do at home.

Drawings may show child making the bed, setting the table, or feeding a pet.

How do people get what they need?   myworldsocialstudies.com ▶ Connect ▶ 🅼 Story Video 30

Song

- ◉ **CAUSE AND EFFECT** *If you weren't feeling well, which worker would you go to?* a doctor

- **MAKE CONNECTIONS** *What kind of work would you like to do when you grow up?* Encourage children to think of other kinds of work not mentioned in the song.

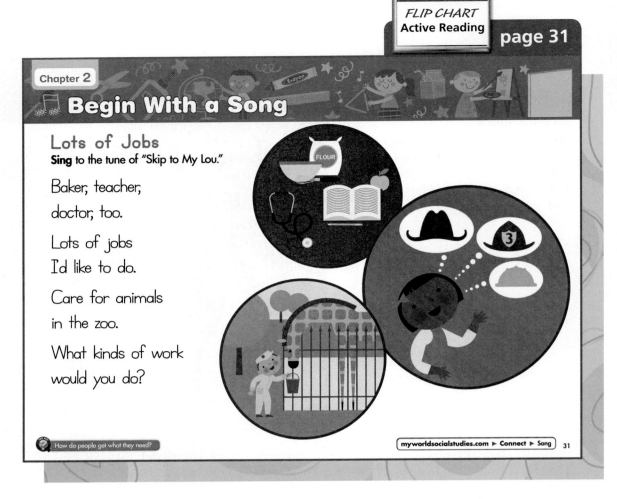

Vocabulary

- **ANALYZE VISUALS** *What kind of service is the police officer providing?* directing traffic

Support English Language Learners

Beginning LOW/HIGH Create illustrated flash cards using the vocabulary words. Point to a word such as *money* and to the picture of money. Say the word slowly and have children echo you.

Intermediate LOW Point to a word and its corresponding picture and explain its meaning. Encourage children to use the word in a simple sentence.

Advanced LOW/HIGH Invite children to name each worker on the page and describe the job he or she is doing. Encourage children to use the vocabulary words in complete sentences.

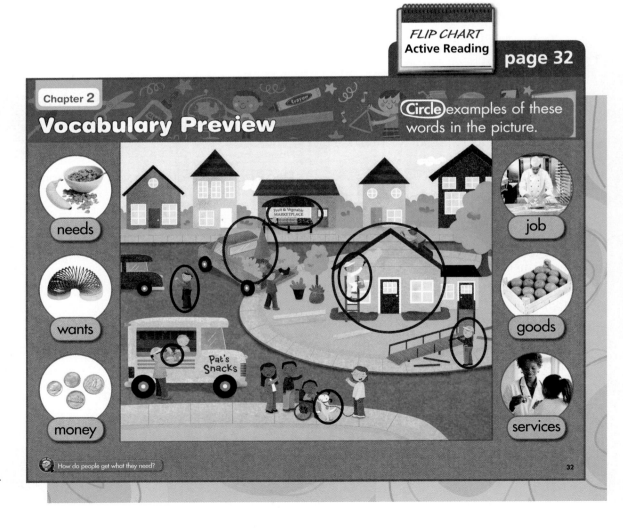

Full Lesson Plan Online

To use or customize the full lesson plan for this lesson, log on to myWorldSocialStudies.com.

Objectives

- Define the basic human needs for food, shelter, and clothing.
- Identify the difference between basic need and wants.
- Differentiate between needs and wants within the family, at school, and in the community.

⊙ **Target Reading Skill Objective:**
- Identify cause and effect.

ELL Objective:
- Use role-playing to learn about the difference between needs and wants.

---

1 *PRESENTATION* **Lesson 1 Introduction**

myWorld and me

Remind children of the discussion they had about the Big Question for this chapter: How do people get what they need?

- *What do you and your family need to live?*

5 minutes ⊘

---

2 *FLIP CHART* **Student Activity Worksheets**

Introduce the Lesson Vocabulary words: *needs, wants, clothing, food,* and *shelter*. Point to pictures on the lesson pages as you explain the meaning of each word. Then ask:

- *What are* needs? things we must have to live: food, clothing, shelter

Hand out the Vocabulary Worksheet, page 24. Help children complete it.

5 minutes ⊘

Not enough time for social studies? Teach this step during your reading block or as a center activity.

---

3 *FLIP CHART* **Active Reading**

Model active reading by asking the questions and using the teaching strategies indicated next to this lesson's Flip Chart pages.

30 minutes

---

4 *PRESENTATION* **Got It?**

Play the interactive Got It? activity to evaluate children's understanding of the key objectives in this lesson. Use the Extra Support button to assist children who need additional instruction.

OPTIONAL: You may want to assign the Got It? Activity Worksheet for homework or have children complete it in class.

10 minutes ⊘

⊘ *Use the Lesson Steps marked with this icon to teach core content in less time!*

Begin to Read

- ⦿ **CAUSE AND EFFECT** *What would happen if you didn't have enough food to eat?* We would be hungry.

Support English Language Learners

1. Content and Language
Paraphrase the learning objectives for this lesson. Have children use the pictures in the Flip Chart as prompts for restating the objectives in their own words.

2. Frontload the Lesson
Preview the lesson vocabulary and take a picture walk through the text. Encourage children to describe each image. Then have them make illustrated flash cards with pictures of different objects. After the lesson, have children write either *N* or *W* on each card.

3. Comprehensible Input
Have children role-play using things they need and want. Encourage children to guess whether each item is a need or a want.

Begin to Read

- **ANALYZE VISUALS** Which pictures show needs? the jeans, the sandwich and the apple

Differentiated Instruction

Use the following ideas when discussing needs and wants.

L2 Extra Support: Pantomime using items that are needs and wants. For example, pretend to put on and button a coat. When children guess the item correctly, have them pantomime and say: *I need a coat.* Continue the routine with other needs and wants.

L3 On-level: Have children cut out magazine pictures of needs and wants. Invite them to take turns sorting the pictures into two categories.

L4 Challenge: Invite pairs of children to draw pictures that show needs and wants they have at home, at school, and in the community. Encourage them to write a caption for each picture.

32

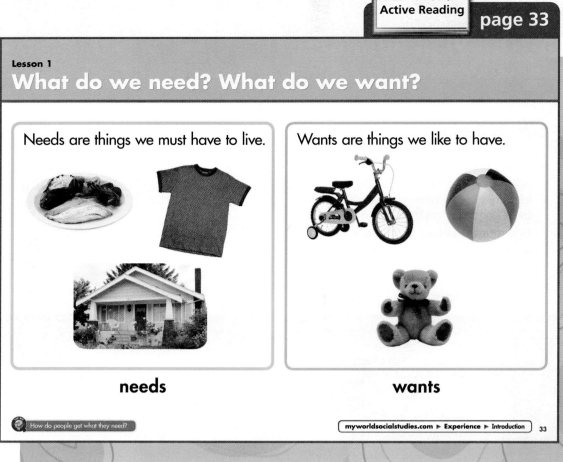

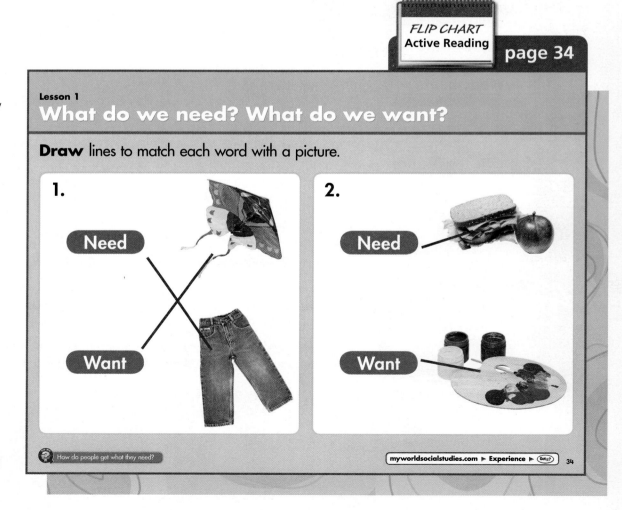

Chapter 2 Lesson 2
How do we get what we need or want?
Lesson Plan Summary

Full Lesson Plan Online

To use or customize the full lesson plan for this lesson, log on to myWorldSocialStudies.com.

Objectives

- Identify how people meet their basic needs of food, clothing, and shelter.
- Explain that people can get their needs and wants through trade.

- Explain that people use money to buy things they need and want.
- Compare and contrast the roles of buyer and seller.

⊙ **Target Reading Skill Objective:**
- Identify cause and effect.

ELL Objective:
- Learn strategies to access vocabulary about trading and buying.

1
PRESENTATION
Lesson 2 Introduction

myWorld and me
Remind children of the discussion they had about the Big Question for this chapter: How do people get what they need?
- *Have you ever traded something with a friend?*

5 minutes Ⓥ

2
FLIP CHART
Student Activity Worksheets

Introduce the Lesson Vocabulary words: *buy, sell,* and *trade.* Point to pictures on the lesson pages as you explain the meaning of each word. Then ask:
- *What does your family use to buy food at the store?* money
- *What do you call it when you and a friend switch snacks?* trade

Hand out the Vocabulary Worksheet, page 26. Help children complete it.

5 minutes Ⓥ

Not enough time for social studies? Teach this step during your reading block or as a center activity.

3
FLIP CHART
Active Reading

Model active reading by asking the questions and using the teaching strategies indicated next to this lesson's Flip Chart pages.

30 minutes

4
PRESENTATION
Got It?

Play the interactive Got It? activity to evaluate children's understanding of the key objectives in this lesson. Use the Extra Support button to assist children who need additional instruction.

OPTIONAL: You may want to assign the Got It? Activity Worksheet for homework or have children complete it in class.

10 minutes Ⓥ

Ⓥ *Use the Lesson Steps marked with this icon to teach core content in less time!*

Begin to Read

- ◉ **CAUSE AND EFFECT** *Why is the girl selling lemonade?* to earn money

Support English Language Learners

1. Content and Language
Paraphrase the objectives on page 33 of this guide. Display illustrated flash cards with the words *trade, buy,* and *sell*. Encourage children to hold up the flash cards as they restate the objectives in their own words.

2. Frontload the Lesson
Preview the lesson title and pictures. Invite children to predict what they will learn about in the lesson. Encourage them to share experiences of trading and buying.

3. Comprehensible Input
Invite a volunteer to role-play trading toys with you. Say: *We can trade our toys.* Then use money to role-play buying a toy. Say: *I use money to buy this toy.*

Begin to Read

- **DRAW CONCLUSIONS** *How do families get money to buy what they need?* They work to earn money.

Differentiated Instruction

Use the following activities to differentiate instruction when discussing buying, selling, and trading.

L2 Extra Support: Display pictures of people trading items, buying them, and selling them. Point to each picture and say: *People trade.* Or: *People buy and sell.* Hold up the pictures and have children say what is happening in each one.

L3 On-level: Invite pairs to role-play scenarios that involve trading, buying, and selling. Have the class guess what the children are doing.

L4 Challenge: Set up a classroom store with books, toys, games, and play money. Have children practice trading, buying, and selling items. Modify the items and money, as needed.

Lesson 2
How do we get what we need or want?

We can trade.   We can buy and sell.

How do people get what they need? | myworldsocialstudies.com ▶ Experience ▶ Introduction | 35

Lesson 2
How do we get what we need or want?

Finish the drawing. **Show** how they trade or sell.

Drawings may show a book being traded for a ball, or a book being exchanged for money.

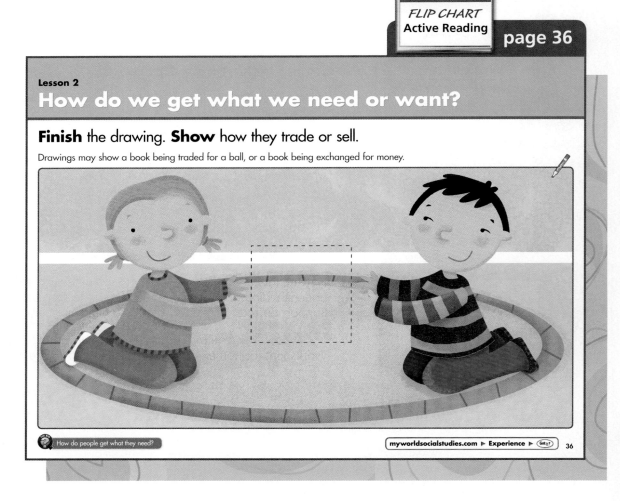

How do people get what they need? | myworldsocialstudies.com ▶ Experience ▶ (Get It?) | 36

Full Lesson Plan Online

To use or customize the full lesson plan for this lesson, log on to myWorldSocialStudies.com.

Objectives

- Give examples of how money is used to purchase goods and services.
- Identify the various forms of U.S. money, bills and coins.

⊙ **Target Reading Skill Objective:**
- Identify cause and effect.

ELL Objective:
- Use cooperative activities to learn about buying and selling.

---

1 PRESENTATION
Lesson 3
Introduction

myWorld and me

Remind children of the discussion they had about the Big Question for this chapter: How do people get what they need?

- *What do people use to buy things?*

5 minutes ⏱

---

2 FLIP CHART
Student Activity
Worksheets

Introduce the Lesson Vocabulary words: *money, coins, bills,* and *spend.* Point to pictures on the lesson as you explain the meaning of each word. Then ask:

- *What can you buy with money?* Sample responses: stuffed animal, action figure, toy, book

Hand out the Vocabulary Worksheet, page 28. Help children complete it.

5 minutes ⏱

Not enough time for social studies? Teach this step during your reading block or as a center activity.

---

3 FLIP CHART
Active Reading

Model active reading by asking the questions and using the teaching strategies indicated next to this lesson's Flip Chart pages.

30 minutes

---

4 PRESENTATION
Got It?

Play the interactive Got It? activity to evaluate children's understanding of the key objectives in this lesson. Use the Extra Support button to assist children who need additional instruction.

OPTIONAL: You may want to assign the Got It? Activity Worksheet for homework or have children complete it in class.

10 minutes ⏱

⏱ *Use the Lesson Steps marked with this icon to teach core content in less time!*

Begin to Read

- **ANALYZE VISUALS** *What does money look like?* paper bills and coins of different sizes and colors

Support English Language Learners

1. Content and Language
Display different kinds of goods and play money. Read aloud the objectives for this lesson. Have children restate them in their own words using the money and goods as prompts.

2. Frontload the Lesson
Preview the lesson by looking at the visuals. Ask children if they know the names of the paper bill and coins pictured on the page. Then ask them what the children are buying and selling in the picture.

3. Comprehensible Input
Using play money, have children role-play buying and selling lemonade. Have them identify the coins and bills as they buy and sell.

Begin to Read

- ◉ **CAUSE AND EFFECT** *What is one way people get things they need?* They use money to buy them.

Differentiated Instruction

Use the following activities when discussing how we use money.

L2 Extra Support: Show children that money comes in different forms. Help them sort play money into piles according to its value.

L3 On-level: Invite children to draw pictures of items they want to buy. Underneath the pictures, ask them to draw the money they would use to buy the items, or affix prepared money labels.

L4 Challenge: Put price tags on classroom items using sticky notes. Invite children to buy and sell these items using the correct amount of play money.

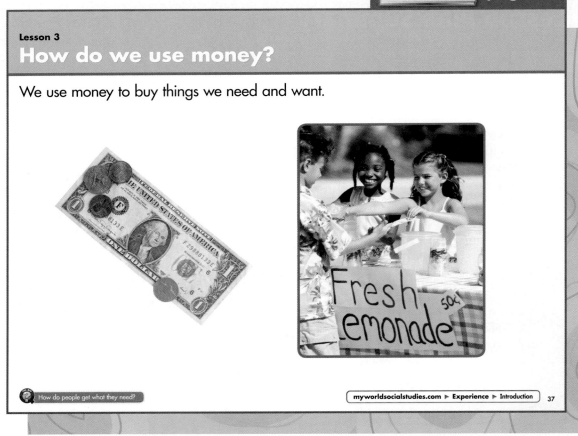

Lesson 3
How do we use money?

We use money to buy things we need and want.

How do people get what they need? myworldsocialstudies.com ▶ Experience ▶ Introduction 37

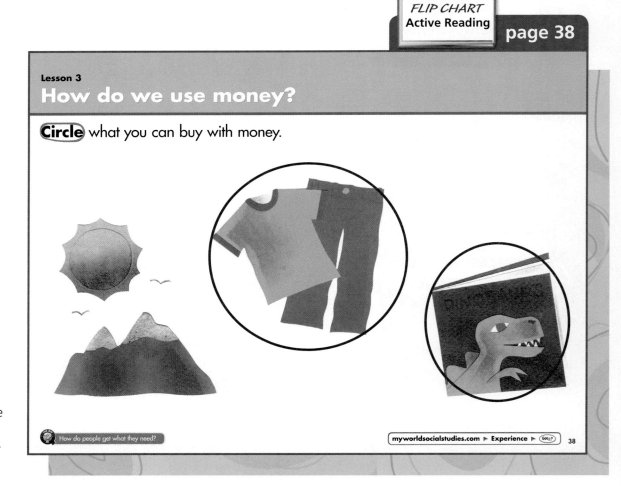

Lesson 3
How do we use money?

Circle what you can buy with money.

How do people get what they need? myworldsocialstudies.com ▶ Experience ▶ Got it? 38

Full Lesson Plan Online

To use or customize the full lesson plan for this lesson, log on to myWorldSocialStudies.com.

Objectives

- Communicate effectively when relating experiences and retelling stories.
- Use complete sentences when speaking.

- Describe different kinds of jobs that people do and the tools or equipment used.

1

FLIP CHART
Teach the Skill

Listening and Speaking

Invite children to identify each worker and say a sentence about what he or she does. Encourage them to speak slowly and clearly. Then have children choose a picture of a job they would like to do when they grow up. Invite children to take turns describing the job using complete sentences.

20 minutes

2

FLIP CHART
Try It

Model active reading by asking the questions and using the teaching strategies indicated next to this lesson's Flip Chart pages.

15 minutes

3

PRESENTATION
Digital Presentation

Review the skill with children using the Digital Presentation.

Click on the Extra Support button for helpful hints and vocabulary help.

15 minutes

Differentiated Instruction

Use the following ideas to differentiate instruction for the activity page.

L1 Special Needs: After children identify the item they would like to buy, help them frame a sentence naming the item. Encourage them to tell why they want it in another sentence.

L2 Extra Support: Have children use this sentence frame to describe something they would buy. *I want to buy_____ because _____.* Model saying the sentence with fluency, then have children repeat after you.

L3 On-level: Have children draw a picture of something they want to buy, then help then write a sentence caption for their picture. Have them read or recite the sentence with fluency to a classmate.

L4 Challenge: After children draw a picture, tell them to give two reasons they want to buy the item they chose. You may also ask children to write about the reasons if they can.

21c Collaboration and Creativity: Listening and Speaking

Look and listen when a friend speaks. **Talk** clearly when you speak.

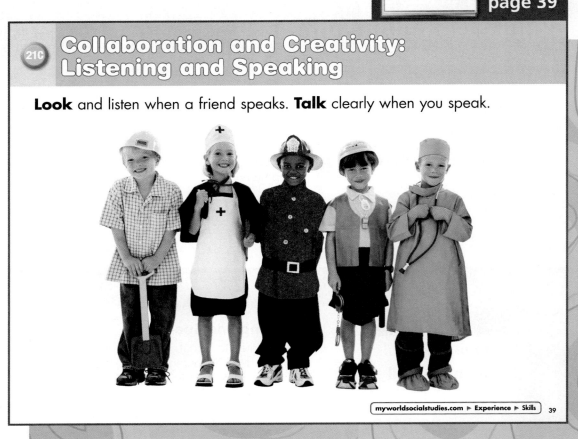

myworldsocialstudies.com ▶ Experience ▶ Skills 39

21c Collaboration and Creativity: Listening and Speaking

Try it!

Draw something you would like to buy. **Tell** a friend why. Then **listen** to your friend.

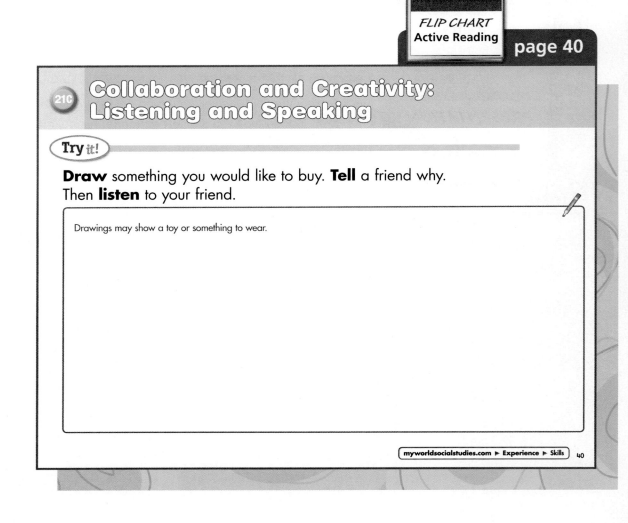

Drawings may show a toy or something to wear.

myworldsocialstudies.com ▶ Experience ▶ Skills 40

Full Lesson Plan Online

To use or customize the full lesson plan for this lesson, log on to myWorldSocialStudies.com.

Objectives

- Explain why people have jobs.
- Identify the variety of jobs people do in their home, schools, and communities.

- Describe the roles of helpers and leaders in the school and community.
- Describe the tools, equipment, and resources that workers use.

⊙ **Target Reading Skill Objective:**
- Identify cause and effect.

ELL Objective:
- Learn strategies to access vocabulary about workers and the tools they use.

1

PRESENTATION
Lesson 4 Introduction

myWorld and me

Remind children of the discussion they had about the Big Question for this chapter: How do people get what they need?

- *What jobs do people in your family do?*

5 minutes ⏱

2

FLIP CHART
Student Activity Worksheets

Introduce the Lesson Vocabulary words: *work, jobs, helper,* and *worker.* Point to pictures as you explain the meaning of each word. Then ask:

- *What jobs do you do at home?* Sample responses: feed the dog, make my bed
- *What jobs do you do in class?* Sample responses: help pass out papers, clean up after snack time.

Hand out the Vocabulary Worksheet, page 31. Help children complete it.

5 minutes ⏱

Not enough time for social studies? Teach this step during your reading block or as a center activity.

3

FLIP CHART
Active Reading

Model active reading by asking the questions and using the teaching strategies indicated next to this lesson's Flip Chart pages.

30 minutes

4

PRESENTATION
Got It?

Play the interactive Got It? activity to evaluate children's understanding of the key objectives in this lesson. Use the Extra Support button to assist children who need additional instruction.

OPTIONAL: You may want to assign the Got It! Activity Worksheet for homework or have children complete it in class.

10 minutes ⏱

⏱ *Use the Lesson Steps marked with this icon to teach core content in less time!*

Begin to Read

- ⊙ CAUSE AND EFFECT *Why does a letter carrier work?* to earn money to buy things

Support English Language Learners

1. Content and Language
Display pictures of workers and the tools they use at home, at school, and in the community. Paraphrase the objectives on page 39 of this guide. Then have children restate them using the pictures as prompts.

2. Frontload the Lesson
Preview the pictures and ask children what tools the people are using, such as rubber gloves, a ladle, a mailbag. Encourage them to tell why these tools are important.

3. Comprehensible Input
Have children take turns role-playing what each worker on the page is doing while the class guesses the action.

Begin to Read

- DRAW CONCLUSIONS *What tools and equipment does a firefighter need?* helmet, hose, special clothing, truck

Differentiated Instruction

Use the following activities when discussing the jobs people do.

L2 Extra Support: After children match the worker and tools, have them complete this sentence frame: *A _____ uses a _____ to _____. A cook uses a spoon to serve soup.*

L3 On-level: Have children cut out magazine pictures of workers and glue them onto cards. On separate cards, have them draw the tools each worker uses. Mix up the cards and have pairs of children match workers and tools.

L4 Challenge: Invite volunteers to make up clues about different workers and their tools. Allow the class to guess the worker.

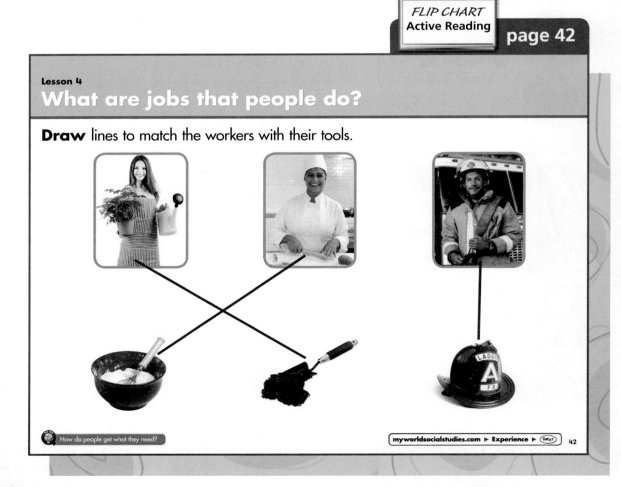

Lesson 4
What are jobs that people do?

People do many kinds of jobs.

home   school   community

How do people get what they need?   myworldsocialstudies.com ▸ Experience ▸ Introduction   41

Lesson 4
What are jobs that people do?

Draw lines to match the workers with their tools.

How do people get what they need?   myworldsocialstudies.com ▸ Experience ▸   42

Chapter 2 Target Reading Skill
Cause and Effect
Skill Lesson Plan Summary

Full Lesson Plan Online
To use or customize the full lesson plan for this lesson, log on to myWorldSocialStudies.com.

Objectives

- Identify cause and effect.
- Make a connection between two ideas or visuals with prompting and support.

1

FLIP CHART
Teach the Skill

Cause and Effect

20 minutes

Before reading, ask children what is happening in each picture. Record their responses on chart paper. For example: *A girl rakes leaves for a neighbor. She gets money for doing the job.* Explain that the girl makes something happen by raking the leaves and the effect, or what happens is that she gets paid. Present other cause and effect relationships children are familiar with and help them identify the relationship between the two. For example, point out that when they water the class plants (the cause), the plants grow healthy (the effect).

2

FLIP CHART
Try It

Model active reading by asking the questions and using the teaching strategies indicated next to this lesson's Flip Chart page.

15 minutes

3

PRESENTATION
Digital Presentation

Review the skill with children using the Digital Presentation.
Click on the Extra Support button for helpful hints and vocabulary help.

15 minutes

Differentiated Instruction

Use the following ideas when discussing cause and effect.

L1 Special Needs: Provide support by acting out and describing what is happening in each picture. For example: *The cat pushes the vase. It breaks.* Show an authentic cause and effect situation with something in the classroom like a stapler falling.

L2 Extra Support: Ask: *Why did the vase tip over? What happened to the vase?* Have children use complete sentences to tell about the vase.

L3 On-level: Show other pictures that have cause and effect relationships. Invite children to take turns identifying which one is the cause and which one is the effect.

L4 Challenge: Have children fold a piece of paper in half. Ask them to draw a cause and effect scenario and label their pictures.

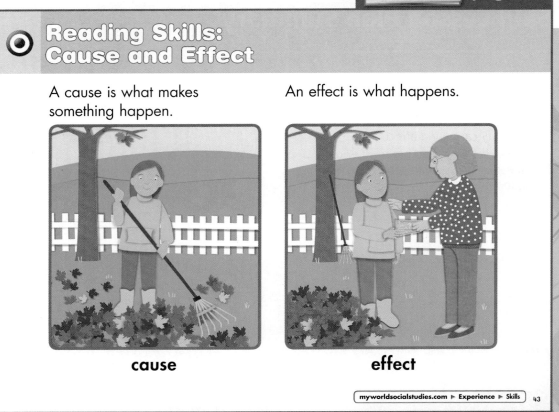

Reading Skills: Cause and Effect

A cause is what makes something happen.

An effect is what happens.

cause

effect

myworldsocialstudies.com ▶ Experience ▶ Skills 43

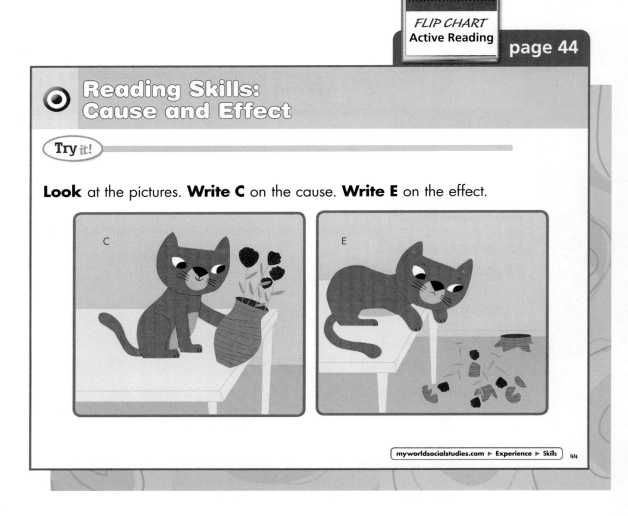

Reading Skills: Cause and Effect

Try it!

Look at the pictures. **Write C** on the cause. **Write E** on the effect.

C

E

myworldsocialstudies.com ▶ Experience ▶ Skills 44

Full Lesson Plan Online

To use or customize the full lesson plan for this lesson, log on to myWorldSocialStudies.com.

Objectives

- Recognize that there is a limit to money and goods.
- Explain that people must make choices because they cannot have everything they want.

- Explain that when you choose one thing, you give up something else.
- Identify examples of scarcity such as limited money, time, or goods.
- Analyze why people save money.

⊙ **Target Reading Skill Objective:**
- Identify cause and effect.

ELL Objective:
- Learn vocabulary to role-play making choices.

1
PRESENTATION
Lesson 5 Introduction

myWorld and Me
Remind children of the discussion they had about the Big Question for this chapter: How do people get what they need?
- *If you could have either an action figure or a stuffed animal, which would you pick?*

5 minutes ⊙

2
FLIP CHART
Student Activity Worksheets

Introduce the Lesson Vocabulary words: *save, spend, choose,* and *choice.* Point to pictures as you explain the meaning of each word. Then ask:
- *Where could you put money to save it?* bank, piggy bank
- *If you had $5.00, would you spend it or save it?* Sample responses: spend it; save it to buy a game that costs more than $5.00

Hand out the Vocabulary Worksheet, page 34. Help children complete it.

5 minutes ⊙

Not enough time for social studies? Teach this step during your reading block or as a center activity.

3
FLIP CHART
Active Reading

Model active reading by asking the questions and using the teaching strategies indicated next to this lesson's Flip Chart pages.

30 minutes

4
PRESENTATION
Got It?

Play the interactive Got It? activity to evaluate children's understanding of the key objectives in this lesson. Use the Extra Support button to assist children who need additional instruction.

OPTIONAL: You may want to assign the Got It! Activity Worksheet for homework or have children complete it in class.

10 minutes ⊙

⊙ *Use the Lesson Steps marked with this icon to teach core content in less time!*

43

Begin to Read

- ⊙ **CAUSE AND EFFECT** *What happens when you can choose only one thing?* You give up something else.

Support English Language Learners

1. Content and Language

Paraphrase the objectives for this lesson. Then encourage children to restate the objectives in their own words, using the pictures on the Flip Chart pages as prompts.

2. Frontload the Lesson

Preview the lesson by reading the title and looking at the visuals. Encourage children to share experiences of times when they have made choices.

3. Comprehensible Input

Display pictures of different kinds of goods. Have children role-play making choices using the pictures as prompts.

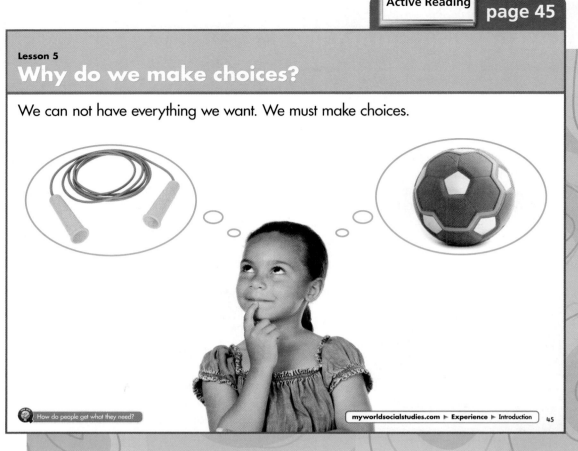

Lesson 5
Why do we make choices?

We can not have everything we want. We must make choices.

How do people get what they need?   myworldsocialstudies.com ▶ Experience ▶ Introduction   45

Begin to Read

- **DRAW CONCLUSIONS** *What do people need to do in order to buy things?* They work to earn money.

Differentiated Instruction

Use the following ideas when discussing why we make choices.

L2 Extra Support: After children identify each item on the Flip Chart page, have them use a complete sentence to tell what they chose.

L3 On-level: Ask children to draw pictures of two things they would like to buy. Then have them choose one, and say why they chose it.

L4 Challenge: Ask children to draw two items they would like to buy. Have them describe one item they could buy right now and one item they would need to save up money to buy. Have them tell why they made those choices.

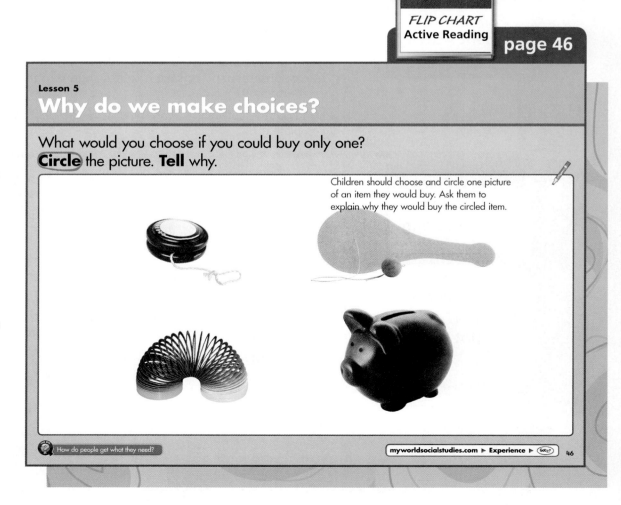

Lesson 5
Why do we make choices?

What would you choose if you could buy only one?
Circle the picture. **Tell** why.

Children should choose and circle one picture of an item they would buy. Ask them to explain why they would buy the circled item.

How do people get what they need?   myworldsocialstudies.com ▶ Experience ▶ Got it?   46

Full Lesson Plan Online

To use or customize the full lesson plan for this lesson, log on to myWorldSocialStudies.com.

Objectives

- Explain that goods are things that people make or grow.
- Explain that services are actions provided by people such as doctors, teachers, and cab drivers.

- Give examples of goods and services at home, at school, and in the community.
- Identify workers as producers of goods or providers of services.

◉ **Target Reading Skill Objective:**
- Identify cause and effect.

ELL Objective:
- Use new vocabulary and cooperative activities to talk about goods and services.

**1 PRESENTATION
Lesson 6
Introduction**

myWorld and Me
Remind children of the discussion they had about the Big Question for this chapter: How do people get what they need?
- *Does your family grow anything in a garden?*

5 minutes ⏱

**2 FLIP CHART
Student Activity
Worksheets**

Introduce the Lesson Vocabulary words: *grow, make, goods,* and *services.* Point to pictures as you explain the meaning of each word. Then ask:
- *What* goods *do you use each day?* Sample responses: food or clothing items
- *What workers provide a* service? Sample responses: teacher, doctor, firefighter

Hand out the Vocabulary Worksheet, page 36. Help children complete it.

5 minutes ⏱

Not enough time for social studies? Teach this step during your reading block or as a center activity.

**3 FLIP CHART
Active Reading**

Model active reading by asking the questions and using the teaching strategies indicated next to this lesson's Flip Chart pages.

30 minutes

**4 PRESENTATION
Got It?**

Play the interactive Got It? activity to evaluate children's understanding of the key objectives in this lesson. Use the Extra Support button to assist children who need additional instruction.

OPTIONAL: You may want to assign the Got It? Activity Worksheet for homework or have children complete it in class.

10 minutes ⏱

⏱ *Use the Lesson Steps marked with this icon to teach core content in less time!*

Begin to Read

- ⊙ **CAUSE AND EFFECT** *What happens to the goods that workers grow or make?* People buy them.

Support English Language Learners

1. Content and Language
Point to Flip Chart pages 47 and 48 as you paraphrase the objectives on page 45 of this guide. Encourage children to point to the visuals as they restate the objectives in their own words.

2. Frontload the Lesson
Preview the lesson vocabulary and pictures. Encourage children to share what they know about goods and services and record this information on a KWL chart in the *K* column.

3. Comprehensible Input
Display pictures of people providing goods and services. Act out what each person is doing. Encourage children to tell whether the worker provides a good or a service. Use prompts such as: *Who is this worker? What does this person provide? Where does this person work?*

Begin to Read

- **DRAW CONCLUSIONS** *How does the person working in the garden earn money?* She sells tomatoes.

Differentiated Instruction

Use the following activities when discussing goods and services. Display children's work on a bulletin board, under the headings *Goods* and *Services.*

L2 Extra Support: After children identify each worker in the lesson, encourage them to dictate a short sentence that describes whether this worker produces goods or provides a service.

L3 On-level: Ask children to draw two pictures that show a good and a service. Have them label their pictures.

L4 Challenge: Provide children with index cards. Have children identify other goods and services they see around the school. Ask them to draw a picture and write a label for each one.

Lesson 6
What are goods and services?

Goods are things people grow or make.

Services are work people do to help others.

How do people get what they need?

myworldsocialstudies.com ▶ Experience ▶ Introduction 47

Lesson 6
What are goods and services?

Write G on pictures that show goods.
Write S on pictures that show services.

G

S

G

S

How do people get what they need?

myworldsocialstudies.com ▶ Experience ▶ Got it? 48

Chapter 2
Review and Assessment
Lesson Plan Summary

1

PRESENTATION
Vocabulary Review

Use the Vocabulary Review activity on the Digital Presentation for this lesson.

10 minutes ⏱

2

Performance Assessment

Choice A
myStory Book

Writing Activity Children write and illustrate an eight-page booklet demonstrating their understanding of the key objectives, vocabulary, and Big Question for this chapter.

See the Online Lesson Plan for full instructions on how to complete the story together as a class, or have each child complete his or her own story. Make sure children's stories reflect what the chapter's content means to them.

30 minutes

Choice B
myWorld Activity

Hands-on Activity: Let's Go Shopping In this activity children set up a store in the classroom and demonstrate how to buy, sell, trade, save, and produce goods. See the Online Lesson Plan for full instructions for completing the activity. Use Activity Cards 6–10.

30 minutes

3

Formal Assessment

OPTIONAL: You can assign the chapter Review and Assessment Student Activity Worksheets or use the Chapter Test and track scores online.

30 minutes ⏱

⏱ *Use the Lesson Steps marked with this icon to teach core content in less time!*

Notes

Big Question

1. Ask children to recall what they have learned about how people get what they need and want.
2. Call on children to share what they remember.
3. Discuss with children the choices people make about meeting their needs and wants, including what kind of work to do.

myWorld and Me

1. Have children think about jobs they like to do.
2. Encourage children to recall what they have made or done for other people.

myStory Book

1. Explain to children that they will now have the opportunity to create a story about what they learned in this chapter.
2. Have children choose their own words and select images they think are best for the story.
3. Explain that prompts will guide them through the writing of the story.

myStory Book

Draw a picture of a job you would like. Show what you would make or do for others.

Drawings may show a doctor examining a patient, a cook preparing food, or a farmer planting a crop.

How do people get what they need?

myworldsocialstudies.com ▶ Understand ▶ myStory Book   49

Planning With the End in Mind

Ready, Set, Teach!
For quick hints on how to teach this chapter, log on to myWorldSocialStudies.com.

Chapter Objectives

Begin With the End in Mind

 Big Question:
What is the world like?

 Target Reading Skill:
Classify and Categorize

Children will demonstrate the following enduring understandings:

- Maps and globes are simple representations of places on Earth.
- The world is made up of landforms and bodies of water.
- The weather and seasons affect what people wear and do.

- Physical features are located in specific places and words can be used to describe the locations of human and physical features.
- People use the world's natural resources to satisfy basic needs.

Connect

Make Learning Meaningful

 Flip Chart
- Big Question
- myStory Spark
- Song
- Vocabulary Preview

 Digital Presentation
- Big Question
- myStory Spark
- myStory Video
- Song

Experience

Teach Knowledge and Skills

 Flip Chart
- Lessons 1–9
- Got It? Formative Assessments
- Target Reading Skill: Classify and Categorize
- 21C Skill Lesson: Map Skills

 myWorld Leveled Readers

 Digital Presentation
- Big Question
- Lesson Introduction
- Got It?

21st Century Learning Online Tutor

Understand

Assess Understanding

 Flip Chart
- Review and Assessment
- myStory Book

 myWorld Activity
- Our World
- Activity Cards #11–15

Chapter Assessment
- Chapter Test

Digital Presentation
- Vocabulary Review
- myWorld Activity

myStory Book Online
Children write, illustrate, and publish a digital book.

Chapter Assessment
Administer online test.

Full Lesson Plan Online

To use or customize the full lesson plan for this lesson, log on to myWorldSocialStudies.com.

Objectives

- Establish meaning.
- Make meaningful connections to personal experiences.
- Use prior knowledge to gain understanding.

⊙ Target Reading Skill Objective:
- Classify and categorize.

ELL Objective:
- Use different strategies to explore new vocabulary.

1

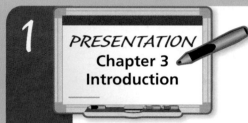

PRESENTATION
Chapter 3 Introduction

Use the Big Question Activity to introduce the chapter's main idea.
- myStory Spark
- myStory Video
- Song

📋 Click on the Extra Support button for helpful hints and vocabulary help.

30 minutes ⓥ

Introduce this chapter using the Digital Presentation or the Flip Chart.

2

FLIP CHART
Active Reading

Use the Big Question to introduce the chapter's main idea.
- *What is the weather like where you live?*

myStory Spark
- *What do you see outside the window?*

Song
- *Do you do any of these activities?*

Vocabulary Preview
- *Do you ever go to a lake with your family?*
- *Do you ever go to the beach?*

45 minutes

Not enough time for social studies? Teach these steps during your reading block or as a center activity.

3

LEVELED READER

Use these Leveled Readers as you work through the chapter.
- On Level: *Mish Michaels*
- Advanced: *Mish Michaels, Weather Chaser*

ⓥ *Use the lesson steps marked with this icon to teach core content in less time!*

The Big Question

- **ANALYZE VISUALS** *What is this family doing?* They are riding in a boat on a body of water, such as a river or a lake.
- **MAKE CONNECTIONS** *What would you do with your family where you live?* Possible answers: play in a park, go to a museum, swim in the ocean.

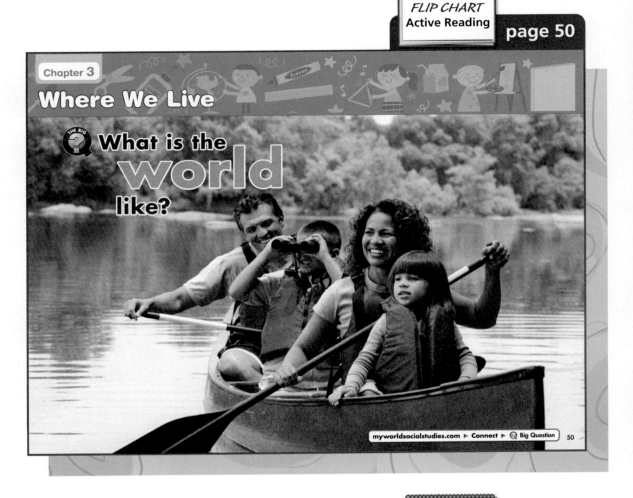

Chapter 3

Where We Live

What is the world like?

myworldsocialstudies.com ▸ Connect ▸ Big Question 50

myStory Spark

- **VISUALIZE** *What is one thing you see out of your window at home?* houses, driveway *What is one thing you see out of the window at school?* playground, buildings

Differentiated Instruction

Use the following ideas and activities to differentiate instruction.

L2 Extra Support: Take a picture walk through the chapter and have children describe the pictures. Then have them draw something near the school.

L3 On-level: Have children draw a picture of something they can see out a classroom window. Ask them to say a sentence that describes it and record it underneath their picture.

L4 Challenge: Invite children to draw pictures of nearby places, then write accompanying sentences.

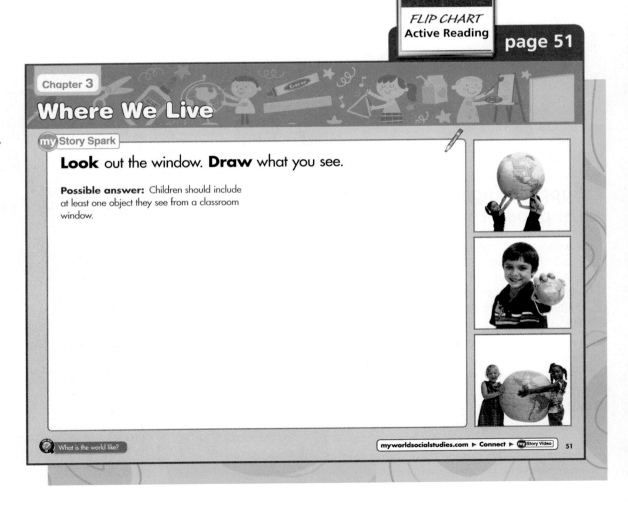

Chapter 3

Where We Live

my Story Spark

Look out the window. **Draw** what you see.

Possible answer: Children should include at least one object they see from a classroom window.

What is the world like? myworldsocialstudies.com ▸ Connect ▸ myStory Video 51

Song

- **SUMMARIZE** *What is the song about?* Children may say that it is about what people do in their community.
- **ANALYZE VISUALS** *What buildings are found in this community?* houses, stores
- **ANALYZE VISUALS** *What are the children doing in this community?* They are riding bikes, playing with pets, and having a picnic.

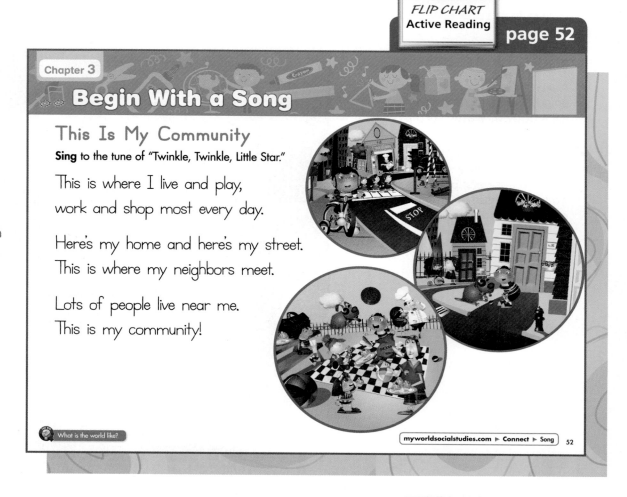

Vocabulary

- **ANALYZE VISUALS** *What are the father and daughter doing?* looking at a map, pointing at something they see

Support English Language Learners

Beginning LOW/HIGH Point to a vocabulary word such as *map* and the picture of a map. Say the word slowly and have children echo you. Then have children complete this sentence frame. *This is a ___. (map)*

Intermediate LOW Have children point to a word and its corresponding picture. Encourage children to use it in a simple sentence.

Advanced HIGH Display a physical map. Point to different landforms and bodies of water and ask children to identify them. Encourage them to use each word in a complete sentence.

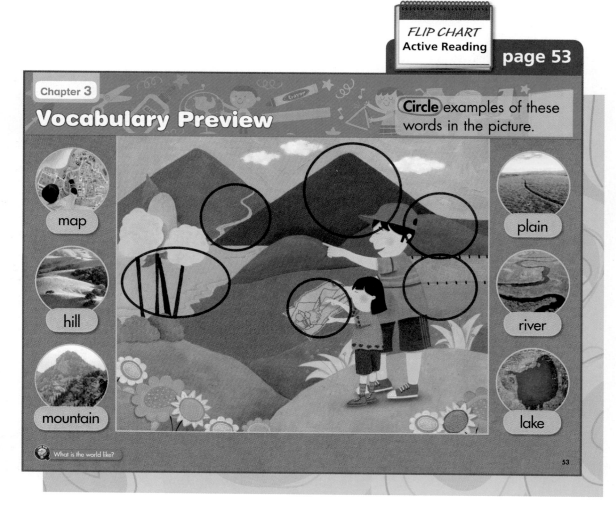

Chapter 3 Lesson 1
Where do we live?
Lesson Plan Summary

Full Lesson Plan Online
To use or customize the full lesson plan for this lesson, log on to myWorldSocialStudies.com.

Objectives

- Recognize that there is an exact address for most places.
- Identify places and personal connections at home, at school, and in the neighborhood.
- Identify unique physical and human characteristics of places they study.

- Recite from memory their own phone number, street address, city or town, and the state in which they live.

⊙ **Target Reading Skill Objective:**
- Classify and categorize.

ELL Objective:
- Learn strategies to access vocabulary about where children live.

---

1 PRESENTATION
Lesson 1 Introduction

myWorld and Me
Remind children of the discussion they had about the Big Question for this chapter: What is the world like?
- *What is your neighborhood like?*

5 minutes ⊙

2
FLIP CHART
Student Activity Worksheets

Introduce the Lesson Vocabulary words: *neighborhood, live, work,* and *address.* Point to pictures on the lesson pages as you explain the meaning of each word. Then ask:
- *What are some activities you do in your neighborhood?* Possible answers: go to school, go to the park, play in my yard

Hand out the Vocabulary Worksheet, page 42. Help children complete it.

5 minutes ⊙

Not enough time for social studies? Teach this step during your reading block or as a center activity.

---

3 FLIP CHART
Active Reading

Model active reading by asking the questions and using the teaching strategies indicated next to this lesson's Flip Chart pages.

30 minutes

4
PRESENTATION
Got It?

Play the interactive Got It? activity to evaluate children's understanding of the key objectives in this lesson. Use the Extra Support button to assist children who need additional instruction.

OPTIONAL: You may want to assign the Got It? Activity Worksheet for homework or have children complete it in class.

10 minutes ⊙

⊙ *Use the Lesson Steps marked with this icon to teach core content in less time!*

Begin to Read

- **MAKE CONNECTIONS** *Do you know your phone number and address?* If necessary, help children recite their phone number and address, including street address, city, and state.

Support English Language Learners

1. Content and Language
Paraphrase the lesson objectives and have children repeat them. Encourage children to restate the objectives in their own words.

2. Frontload the Lesson
Preview the lesson pictures. Invite children to describe activities they do at home, at school, and in the community.

3. Comprehensible Input
Point to each building. Role-play what children do in each place as you say simple sentences to describe it. Have children echo you and mime the actions.

Begin to Read

- ⦿ **CLASSIFY AND CATEGORIZE** *Where in your neighborhood would you go to mail a letter?* the post office

Differentiated Instruction

Use the following ideas to differentiate instruction when discussing places in a neighborhood.

L2 Extra Support: Encourage children to list five things they might find in each place pictured on the Flip Chart page.

L3 On-level: Have children say a sentence about what they do in each place. Record them on sentence strips and display them on a neighborhood bulletin board.

L4 Challenge: Fold a sheet of paper in thirds. Title the sections *home, school, community.* Invite children to draw a picture of items they might see in each place and then add sentences that describe them.

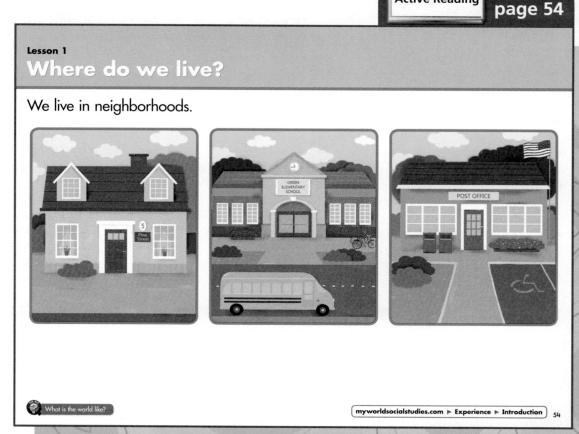

Lesson 1
Where do we live?

We live in neighborhoods.

What is the world like?   myworldsocialstudies.com ▶ Experience ▶ Introduction   54

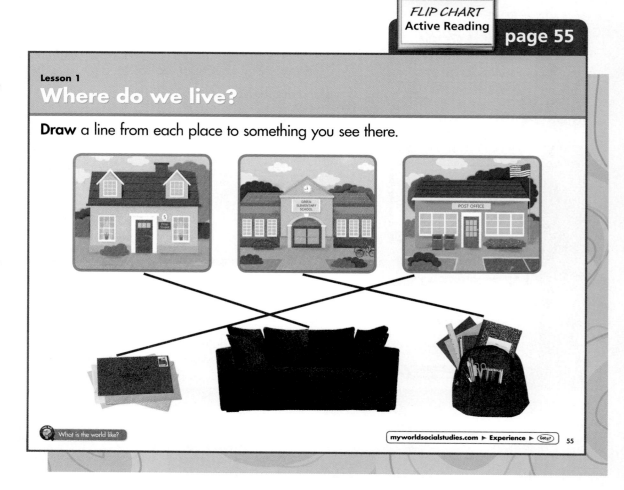

Lesson 1
Where do we live?

Draw a line from each place to something you see there.

What is the world like?   myworldsocialstudies.com ▶ Experience ▶ Got it?   55

Chapter 3 Lesson 2
Where are places located?
Lesson Plan Summary

Full Lesson Plan Online

To use or customize the full lesson plan for this lesson, log on to myWorldSocialStudies.com.

Objectives

- Describe the relative location of people, places, and things by using positional words.
- Use directions and positional words to describe the relative location of one place to another.
- Locate and describe places in the school and in the community.

⊙ **Target Reading Skill Objective:**
- Classify and categorize.

ELL Objective:
- Learn to talk about the location of places using position words.

---

1 **PRESENTATION**
Lesson 2 Introduction

myWorld and Me

Remind children of the discussion they had about the Big Question for this chapter: What is the world like?

- *What places are in your neighborhood?*

5 minutes ⏱

---

2 **FLIP CHART**
Student Activity Worksheets

Introduce the Lesson Vocabulary words: *behind, in front of, near, far, above,* and *below.* Point to objects on the lesson pages as you explain the meaning of each word. Then ask:

- *What places are near your home?* Possible answers: other homes, a park, a grocery store

Hand out the Vocabulary Worksheet, page 44. Help children complete it.

5 minutes ⏱

Not enough time for social studies? Teach this step during your reading block or as a center activity.

---

3 **FLIP CHART**
Active Reading

Model active reading by asking the questions and using the teaching strategies indicated next to this lesson's Flip Chart pages.

30 minutes

---

4 **PRESENTATION**
Got It?

Play the interactive Got It? activity to evaluate children's understanding of the key objectives in this lesson. Use the Extra Support button to assist children who need additional instruction.

OPTIONAL: You may want to assign the Got It? Activity Worksheet for homework or have children complete it in class.

10 minutes ⏱

⏱ *Use the Lesson Steps marked with this icon to teach core content in less time!*

Begin to Read

- ⊙ **CLASSIFY AND CATEGORIZE** *Where in the picture are houses located?* on the right

Support English Language Learners

1. Content and Language

Write position words on index cards; include all of the vocabulary terms. Point to the words as you paraphrase the objectives on page 55 of this guide. Encourage children to restate the objectives in their own words.

2. Frontload the Lesson

Draw a concept web with the words *Our School* in the center circle. Preview the lesson pictures and vocabulary words. Prompt children to describe their school's location. Record their responses in the web.

3. Comprehensible Input

Demonstrate how to play Simon Says using position words. Then encourage children to play the game.

Begin to Read

- **VISUALIZE** *What will you draw to the right of the library?* Accept reasonable responses.

Differentiated Instruction

Use the following ideas when discussing position words and location.

L2 Extra Support: Stand with children outside your school. Point to places and help children describe the location of these places in relationship to the school.

L3 On-level: Ask children to draw their home in the center of a piece of paper. Have them draw places that are located around their house. Then have them use position words to describe these locations.

L4 Challenge: Invite children to draw a simple map of their neighborhood. Have them use position words to describe the location of the places on the map.

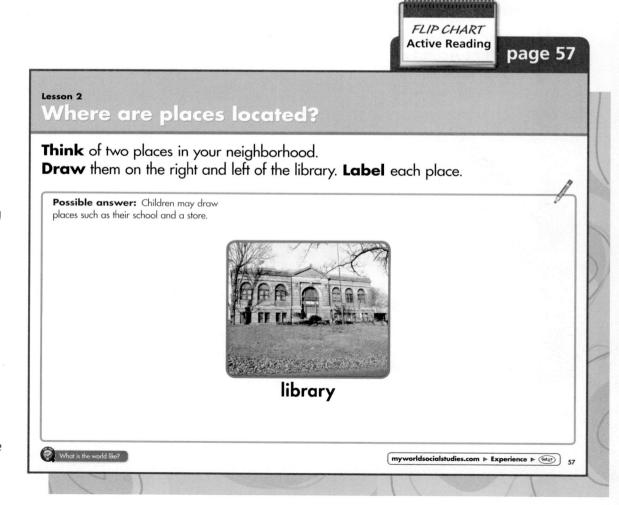

Lesson Plan Summary

Full Lesson Plan Online
To use or customize the full lesson plan for this lesson, log on to myWorldSocialStudies.com.

Objectives

- Explain that maps are simple, pictorial representations of large and small places on Earth.
- Explain that maps help to locate different places.
- Locate and distinguish between land and water on maps.

- Identify physical and human characteristics of a place on a map.
- Identify map symbols.

⊙ **Target Reading Skill Objective:**
- Classify and categorize.

ELL Objective:
- Learn strategies to access vocabulary about maps.

---

1 PRESENTATION
Lesson 3 Introduction

myWorld and Me
Remind children of the discussion they had about the Big Question for this chapter: What is the world like?
- *What do you think maps show?*
- *What would your house look like if you flew over it in a plane?*

5 minutes ⊙

---

2 FLIP CHART
Student Activity Worksheets

Introduce the Lesson Vocabulary words: *map, land,* and *water*. Point to pictures on the lesson pages as you explain the meaning of each word. Then ask:
- *Have you seen a map before? Where?* Possible answers: at the mall, in the car, at the bus station
- *If you draw a picture with water in it, how do you show the water?* Possible answers: color it blue, show waves

Hand out the Vocabulary Worksheet, page 46. Help children complete it.

5 minutes ⊙

Not enough time for social studies? Teach this step during your reading block or as a center activity.

---

3 PRESENTATION
Active Reading

Model active reading by asking the questions and using the teaching strategies indicated next to this lesson's Flip Chart pages.

30 minutes

---

4 PRESENTATION
Got It?

Play the interactive Got It? activity to evaluate children's understanding of the key objectives in this lesson. Use the Extra Support button to assist children who need additional instruction.

OPTIONAL: You may want to assign the Got It? Activity Worksheet for homework or have children complete it in class.

10 minutes ⊙

⊙ *Use the Lesson Steps marked with this icon to teach core content in less time!*

Begin to Read

- **⊙ CLASSIFY AND CATEGORIZE** *How can you tell the difference between land and water on a map?* Water is blue.

Support English Language Learners

1. Content and Language

Turn to the lesson page in the Flip Chart. Point to the map as you paraphrase the objectives for this lesson. Encourage children to restate them in their own words.

2. Frontload the Lesson

Draw a two-column chart with the headings *United States* and *neighborhood*. Have children look at the map and drawing on the Flip Chart page and tell what they know about each place. Write their responses on the chart.

3. Comprehensible Input

Ask questions about Flip Chart page 58. For example: *What does the big map show? What do the blue areas on this map stand for? Where is our state on the map?*

- **ANALYZE MAPS** *What does the large yellow circle stand for on the classroom map?* a round table

Differentiated Instruction

Use the following ideas to differentiate instruction when discussing maps.

L2 Extra Support: Point to a chair on the classroom map in the Flip Chart and then to a chair in the classroom. Explain that maps show where objects and places are in smaller form. Point to the U.S. map on the Flip Chart page and then ask: *Why is it helpful to show things in smaller form on maps?*

L3 On-level: Have children make a list of five items that could be included in a classroom map. Have them write each word and draw a symbol for each one.

L4 Challenge: Have children list five classroom items and decide on a symbol to represent each one. Then invite them to draw a map of their classroom that includes these items. Encourage them to share their maps with the class.

Lesson 3
What do maps show?

Maps show real places. They can show big places or small places. They can show land and water.

What is the world like?   myworldsocialstudies.com ▶ Experience ▶ Introduction   58

Lesson 3
What do maps show?

Circle the teacher's desk on the map.
Draw a place where children can read books.

Children should draw a mat, chair, or cushions near one of the bookcases.

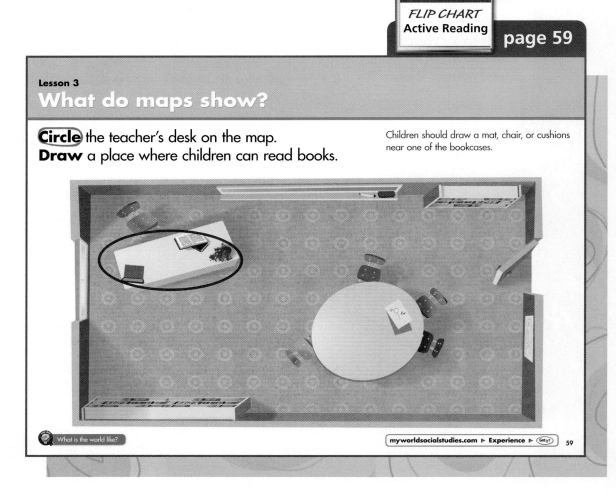

What is the world like?   myworldsocialstudies.com ▶ Experience ▶ Got it?   59

Full Lesson Plan Online

To use or customize the full lesson plan for this lesson, log on to myWorldSocialStudies.com.

Objectives

- Explain that maps help to locate different places.
- Identify cardinal directions (north, south, east, west).
- Locate and describe places in the school and community.

1

FLIP CHART
Teach the Skill

Cardinal Directions

Point to the arrow that says north. Encourage children to tell what they see in that location. Repeat the routine by pointing to the other directions. Then display signs in the classroom that say *north, south, east,* and *west*. Have children take turns walking to each sign and telling the direction in which they are walking.

20 minutes

2

FLIP CHART
Try It

Model active reading by asking the questions and using the teaching strategies indicated next to this lesson's Flip Chart pages.

15 minutes

3

PRESENTATION
Digital Presentation

Review the skill with children using the Digital Presentation.

Click on the Extra Support button for helpful hints and vocabulary help.

15 minutes

Map Skills: Cardinal Directions

21C

Directions tell us which way to go. Maps use **north**, **south**, **east**, and **west**. Look at the arrow that says north. The park is to the north.

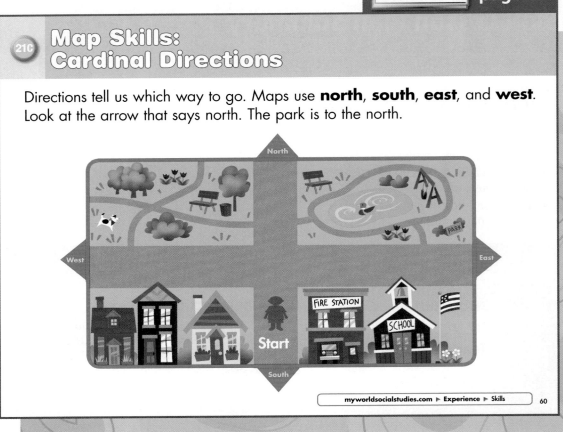

myworldsocialstudies.com ▶ Experience ▶ Skills   60

Map Skills: Cardinal Directions

21C

Try it!

Put your finger on Start. **Choose** a direction.
Draw a line in that direction. **Tell** what you see there.

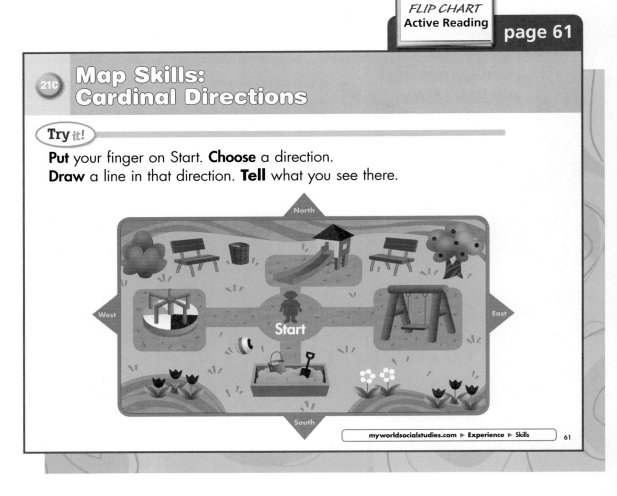

myworldsocialstudies.com ▶ Experience ▶ Skills   61

Differentiated Instruction

Use the following activities when discussing cardinal directions.

L1 Special Needs Point to each arrow, say the direction, and have children echo you. Have volunteers name the object on the Flip Chart page closest to each direction.

L2 Extra Support Invite children to take turns "walking" their fingers in a direction on the map. As they "walk" have them complete these sentences. *I am walking _____ (direction). I see a _____ (name of object).*

L3 On-level Have children play a guessing game with a partner. Start the game by saying the following: *I see a sandbox. Which way should I walk to get there?* <south>

L4 Challenge Ask children to draw a map of a park and include their favorite playground equipment. Remind them to put arrows on the map and label each direction. Then ask them to share their maps.

Full Lesson Plan Online

To use or customize the full lesson plan for this lesson, log on to myWorldSocialStudies.com.

Objectives

- Identify cardinal directions (north, south, east, west).
- Identify basic landforms.
- Differentiate between landforms and bodies of water on a map.

⊙ **Target Reading Skill Objective:**
- Classify and categorize.

ELL Objective:
- Learn strategies to access vocabulary about landforms.

---

1 PRESENTATION — Lesson 4 Introduction

myWorld and Me

Remind children of the discussion they had about the Big Question for this chapter: What is the world like?

- *Have you ever seen mountains? Were they near where you live?*

5 minutes ⏱

---

2 FLIP CHART — Student Activity Worksheets

Introduce the Lesson Vocabulary words: *mountain, hill, plain,* and *island*. Point to pictures on the lesson pages as you explain the meaning of each word. Then ask:

- *What kind of land has water all around it?* an island
- *What is the highest kind of land?* a mountain

Hand out the Vocabulary Worksheet, page 49. Help children complete it.

5 minutes ⏱

> *Not enough time for social studies? Teach this step during your reading block or as a center activity.*

---

3 FLIP CHART — Active Reading

Model active reading by asking the questions and using the teaching strategies indicated next to this lesson's Flip Chart pages.

30 minutes

---

4 PRESENTATION — Got It?

Play the interactive Got It? activity to evaluate children's understanding of the key objectives in this lesson. Use the Extra Support button to assist children who need additional instruction.

OPTIONAL: You may want to assign the Got It? Activity Worksheet for homework or have children complete it in class.

10 minutes ⏱

⏱ *Use the Lesson Steps marked with this icon to teach core content in less time!*

Begin to Read

• ⊙ CLASSIFY AND CATEGORIZE *What kind of land is colored green on the map?* plains

Support English Language Learners

1. Content and Language
Create illustrated flashcards for each vocabulary word. Point to the cards and to the Flip Chart page as you paraphrase the objectives for this lesson. Encourage children to restate them in their own words using the visuals as prompts.

2. Frontload the Lesson
Preview the lesson. Point to the title of the map and say it aloud. Point to each landform and say its name. Have children echo you. Invite them to tell what they know about each landform.

3. Comprehensible Input
While children look at the Flip Chart page, ask questions such as these: *What is the highest kind of land? What kind of land is flat?*

Begin to Read

• ANALYZE VISUALS *What kind of land is farthest from the water on this map?* mountains

Differentiated Instruction

Use the following ideas to differentiate instruction when discussing landforms.

L2 Extra Support: Display several photos of each kind of landform. Say the name of each one and point to it on the map: *These are mountains. These are the mountains on the map.*

L3 On-level: Give children cards with photographs of each kind of landform. Tell them to arrange the cards in the same order as the landforms are shown on the map. Then ask: *Which kind of land is highest? Which is next highest?*

L4 Challenge: Give children cards with photos and map symbols of different landforms. Have them sort the cards according to kind of landform.

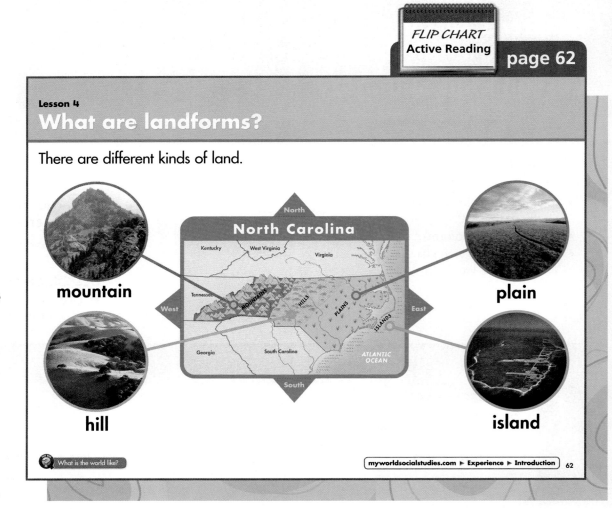

Lesson 4
What are landforms?

There are different kinds of land.

mountain

North Carolina

plain

hill

island

What is the world like?   myworldsocialstudies.com ▶ Experience ▶ Introduction 62

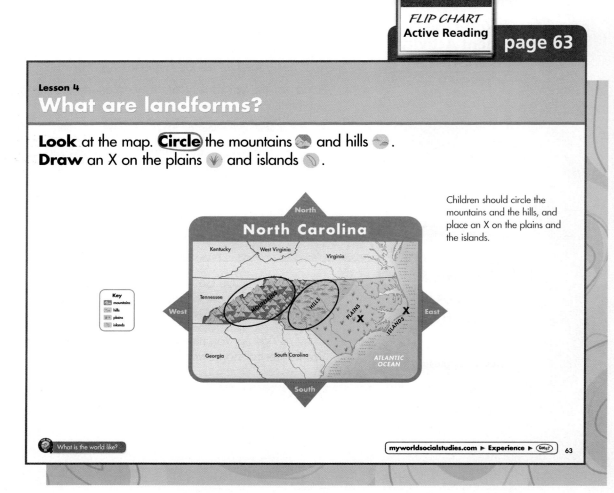

Lesson 4
What are landforms?

Look at the map. **Circle** the mountains 🟤 and hills 🟢.
Draw an X on the plains 🌱 and islands 🟠.

Children should circle the mountains and the hills, and place an X on the plains and the islands.

North Carolina

What is the world like?   myworldsocialstudies.com ▶ Experience ▶ Got it? 63

Full Lesson Plan Online

To use or customize the full lesson plan for this lesson, log on to myWorldSocialStudies.com.

Objectives

- Identify basic bodies of water (oceans, rivers, lakes).
- Differentiate between land and water on a map.

⦿ Target Reading Skill Objective:
- Classify and categorize.

ELL Objective:
- Use cooperative activities to learn about bodies of water.

---

1 PRESENTATION Lesson 5 Introduction

myWorld and Me

Remind children of the discussion they had about the Big Question for this chapter: What is the world like?

- *We saw a picture of people in a boat. Do you live near a place where people use boats?*

5 minutes ⓥ

---

2 FLIP CHART Student Activity Worksheets

Introduce the Lesson Vocabulary words: *ocean, river,* and *lake.* Point to pictures on the lesson pages as you explain the meaning of each word. Then ask:

- *What is a large body of salty water?* an ocean
- *What is a large stream of water that leads to an ocean?* a river

Hand out the Vocabulary Worksheet, page 52. Help children complete it.

5 minutes ⓥ

Not enough time for social studies? Teach this step during your reading block or as a center activity.

---

3 FLIP CHART Active Reading

Model active reading by asking the questions and using the teaching strategies indicated next to this lesson's Flip Chart pages.

30 minutes

---

4 PRESENTATION Got It?

Play the interactive Got It? activity to evaluate children's understanding of the key objectives in this lesson. Use the Extra Support button to assist children who need additional instruction.

OPTIONAL: You may want to assign the Got It? Activity Worksheet for homework or have children complete it in class.

10 minutes ⓥ

ⓥ *Use the Lesson Steps marked with this icon to teach core content in less time!*

Begin to Read

- ⊙ **CLASSIFY AND CATEGORIZE** *How can you identify rivers and lakes on a map?* They are shown in blue.

Support English Language Learners

1. Content and Language
Create illustrated word cards for each body of water. Paraphrase the objectives for this lesson. Have children restate the objectives in their own words as they point to each card.

2. Frontload the Lesson
Preview the lesson vocabulary and visuals. Then activate prior knowledge by asking children whether they have ever seen a river, lake, or ocean. Invite them to share any experiences they had with each body of water.

3. Comprehensible Input
Display photos of different bodies of water. Model using think-alouds to talk about each one, identifying its main characteristics and then naming the body of water.

Begin to Read

- **ANALYZE MAPS** *Identify different kinds of water shown on the map.* lake, river, ocean, gulf

Differentiated Instruction

Use the following ideas to differentiate instruction when discussing bodies of water.

L2 Extra Support: Point to the symbol of a river in the map key. Then encourage children to find and trace the river on the map. Repeat the routine for the word lake.

L3 On-level: Encourage children to tell what they know about different bodies of water. Display a physical map of the United States and have children find bodies of water.

L4 Challenge: Invite children to draw a map that includes land and different bodies of water. Have them label each body of water.

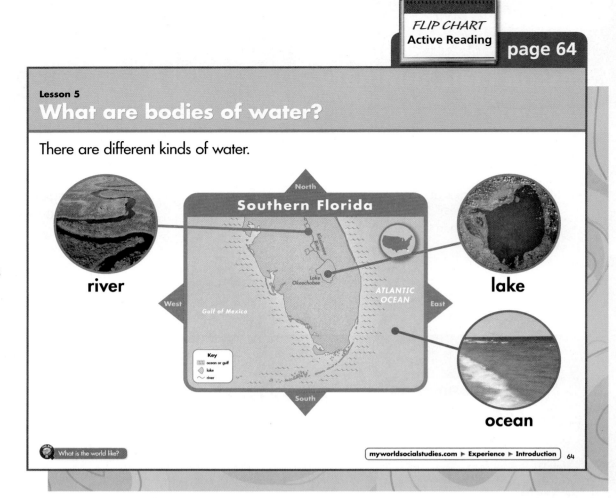

FLIP CHART
Active Reading
page 64

Lesson 5
What are bodies of water?

There are different kinds of water.

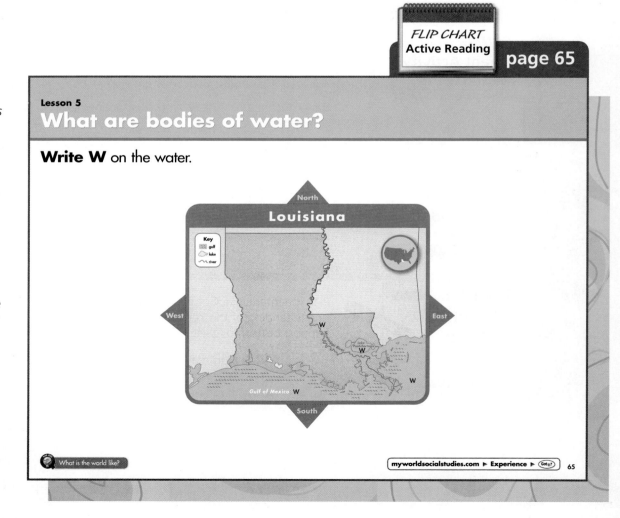

FLIP CHART
Active Reading
page 65

Lesson 5
What are bodies of water?

Write W on the water.

Chapter 3 Target Reading Skill
Classify and Categorize
Skill Lesson Plan Summary

Full Lesson Plan Online
To use or customize the full lesson plan for this lesson, log on to myWorldSocialStudies.com.

Objectives

- Identify and sort common words into basic categories.
- Describe the connection between two pieces of information in a text.
- Identify the differences between land and water.

1

FLIP CHART
Teach the Skill

Classify and Categorize
Before reading, invite children to describe what they see in each picture. Encourage them to point out the differences between them. Then explain that the land is either green or brown, while the water is blue. Afterwards, display pictures that show landforms and bodies of water. Have them sort the pictures into two piles.

20 minutes

2

FLIP CHART
Try It

Model active reading by asking the questions and using the teaching strategies indicated next to this lesson's Flip Chart pages.

15 minutes

3

PRESENTATION
Digital Presentation

Review the skill with children using the Digital Presentation.

Click on the Extra Support button for helpful hints and vocabulary help.

15 minutes

Reading Skills: Classify and Categorize

You can put things into groups when they are alike.

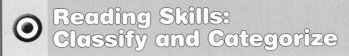

A hill and a mountain are landforms.

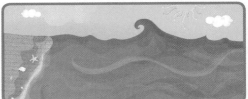
A river and an ocean are bodies of water.

Reading Skills: Classify and Categorize

Differentiated Instruction

Use the following ideas when classifying and categorizing the pictures.

L2 Extra Support Have children look closely at the pictures and identify whether they show land or water. Ask them to complete a sentence for each one. For example: *A river is a body of water. A mountain is a landform.*

L3 On-level Have children cut out magazine pictures of landforms and bodies of water. Have them glue each picture onto an oversized index card. On the back of each card, have them write a label that says *land* or *water*. Have children meet in small groups to sort collective pictures.

L4 Challenge Invite children to cut out magazine pictures of landforms and bodies of water. Have them make a collage of the images. Encourage them to include words that describe each one, such as *high peaks, salty water,* and include the location of each picture.

Try it!

Circle in brown the pictures that show kinds of land. Circle plain and mountain.

Circle in blue the pictures that show kinds of water. Circle ocean and river.

Chapter 3 Lesson 6
What do globes show?
Lesson Plan Summary

Full Lesson Plan Online
To use or customize the full lesson plan for this lesson, log on to myWorldSocialStudies.com.

Objectives

- Explain that a globe helps to locate different places and is a model of Earth.
- Differentiate between land and water features on globes.

⊙ **Target Reading Skill Objective:**
- Classify and categorize.

ELL Objective:
- Use different strategies to talk about land and water features on a globe.

1
PRESENTATION
Lesson 6
Introduction

myWorld and Me
Remind children of the discussion they had about the Big Question for this chapter: What is the world like?
- *What is Earth shaped like?*

5 minutes ⓥ

2
FLIP CHART
Student Activity
Worksheets

Introduce the Lesson Vocabulary words: *globe* and *Earth*. Point to pictures on the lesson pages as you explain the meaning of each word. Then ask:
- *How is a globe like Earth?* It is round and shaped like Earth.

Hand out the Vocabulary Worksheet, page 54. Help children complete it.

5 minutes ⓥ

Not enough time for social studies? Teach this step during your reading block or as a center activity.

3
FLIP CHART
Active Reading

Model active reading by asking the questions and using the teaching strategies indicated next to this lesson's Flip Chart pages.

30 minutes

4
PRESENTATION
Got It?

Play the interactive Got It? activity to evaluate children's understanding of the key objectives in this lesson. Use the Extra Support button to assist children who need additional instruction.

OPTIONAL: You may want to assign the Got It? Activity Worksheet for homework or have children complete it in class.

10 minutes ⓥ

ⓥ *Use the Lesson Steps marked with this icon to teach core content in less time!*

Begin to Read

- ⊙ **CLASSIFY AND CATEGORIZE** *What do the blue areas on a globe show?* water

Support English Language Learners

1. Content and Language

Display a globe. Point to it as you paraphrase the objectives on page 67 of this guide. Have children repeat each one. Then encourage them to restate the objectives in their own words.

2. Frontload the Lesson

Preview the lesson by reading the title and text aloud. Then invite children to point to the globe and tell what they know about different places, land, and water.

3. Comprehensible Input

Spin a globe as children point to it. When it stops spinning ask: *What are you pointing to? What color is it? How can you tell if it is land or water?* Explain that blue on a globe shows water. The other colors show land.

Begin to Read

- **DRAW CONCLUSIONS** *Why do we use globes?* to locate places on Earth

Differentiated Instruction

Use the following ideas to differentiate instruction when discussing globes.

L2 Extra Support: Use a toy car to show that a model is a small representation of a larger object. Explain that a globe is a model of Earth. Have children point to the blue areas. Tell them blue on a globe shows water.

L3 On-level: Use a toy car to show how a model represents a larger object. Discuss the relationship of a globe to Earth. Help children locate the United States and your state on the globe.

L4 Challenge: Display photographs of places shown on the globe and write their names on sticky notes. Have children locate the places on the globe and mark them with the sticky note.

FLIP CHART
Active Reading
page 68

Lesson 6
What do globes show?

A globe is a model of Earth. It shows land and water.

What is the world like?   myworldsocialstudies.com ▶ Experience ▶ Introduction 68

FLIP CHART
Active Reading
page 69

Lesson 6
What do globes show?

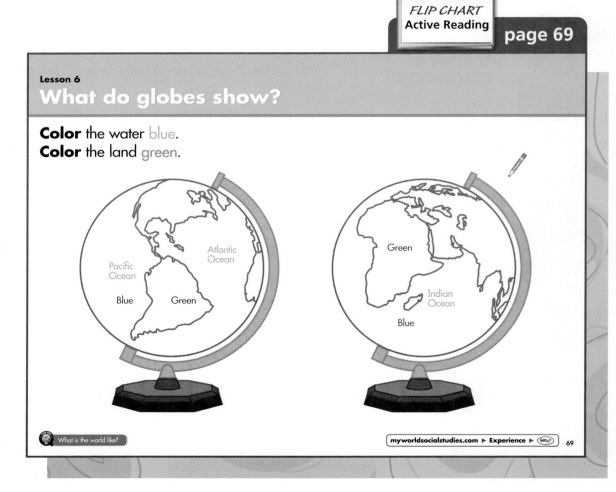

Color the water blue.
Color the land green.

What is the world like?   myworldsocialstudies.com ▶ Experience ▶ Get it? 69

Full Lesson Plan Online

To use or customize the full lesson plan for this lesson, log on to myWorldSocialStudies.com.

Objectives

- Identify weather as a physical characteristic of a place.
- Describe daily weather and its effects on people and places.

⊙ **Target Reading Skill Objective:**
- Classify and categorize.

ELL Objective:
- Use cooperative activities to learn about the weather.

---

1 PRESENTATION
Lesson 7 Introduction

myWorld and Me
Remind children of the discussion they had about the Big Question for this chapter: What is the world like?
- *What is the weather like today?*

5 minutes ⊘

---

2 FLIP CHART
Student Activity Worksheets

Introduce the Lesson Vocabulary words: *weather, rainy, cold,* and *hot.* Point to pictures on the lesson pages as you explain the meaning of each word. Then ask:
- *What would you wear to school if it was raining?* Children may say a raincoat, rain hat, and rubber boots.

Hand out the Vocabulary Worksheet, page 56. Help children complete it.

5 minutes ⊘

Not enough time for social studies? Teach this step during your reading block or as a center activity.

---

3 FLIP CHART
Active Reading

Model active reading by asking the questions and using the teaching strategies indicated next to this lesson's Flip Chart pages.

30 minutes

---

4 PRESENTATION
Got It?

Play the interactive Got It? activity to evaluate children's understanding of the key objectives in this lesson. Use the Extra Support button to assist children who need additional instruction.

OPTIONAL: You may want to assign the Got It? Activity Worksheet for homework or have children complete it in class.

10 minutes ⊘

⊘ *Use the Lesson Steps marked with this icon to teach core content in less time!*

Begin to Read

- **CAUSE AND EFFECT** *What might happen if you see dark clouds in the sky?* It might rain.

Support English Language Learners

1. Content and Language
Display pictures of different kinds of weather. Paraphrase the objectives for this lesson. Then ask children to restate them in their own words using the pictures as prompts.

2. Frontload the Lesson
Draw a word web and write *Weather* in the center circle. Have children look at the pictures and describe what they see as well as other weather they have experienced. Write these words in the surrounding circles.

3. Comprehensible Input
Point to each picture and describe the weather it shows. Act out how you would dress and the activities you would do in each kind of weather.

Begin to Read

- **⊙ CLASSIFY AND CATEGORIZE** *What would you wear on a cold and snowy day?* Possible answers: mittens, hat, gloves, a warm coat

Differentiated Instruction

Use the following ideas to differentiate instruction when discussing the weather.

L2 Extra Support: Write this sentence on the board: *I wear _____ when it is _____ outside.* Have children fill in the blanks with words that describe clothing and weather.

L3 On-level: Spread out pictures of clothing to wear in various kinds of weather. Announce different kinds of weather one at a time and have children collect the appropriate pictures. As a class, use interactive writing to create sentences after the activity.

L4 Challenge: Invite children to make a picture book of weather.

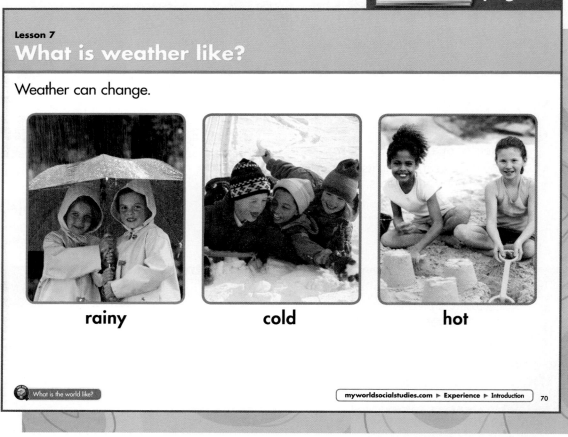

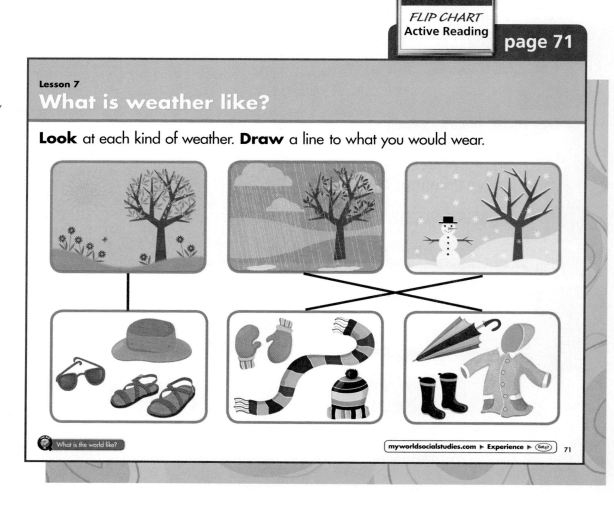

Full Lesson Plan Online

To use or customize the full lesson plan for this lesson, log on to myWorldSocialStudies.com.

Objectives

- Identify the four seasons.
- Describe patterns of weather and their effects on people and places.
- Describe how seasonal changes affect people.

⊙ **Target Reading Skill Objective:**
- Classify and categorize.

ELL Objective:
- Use cooperative activities to learn about the seasons.

---

1 PRESENTATION
Lesson 8 Introduction

myWorld and Me
Remind children of the discussion they had about the Big Question for this chapter: What is the world like?
- *Is the weather the same all year round? How does it change?*

5 minutes ⓥ

---

2 FLIP CHART
Student Activity Worksheets

Introduce the Lesson Vocabulary words: *season* and *change*. Point to pictures on the lesson pages as you explain the meaning of each word. Then ask:
- *How do you think the seasons are different?* Possible answer: It is warmer in summer than in winter.

Hand out the Vocabulary Worksheet, page 58. Help children complete it.

5 minutes ⓥ

Not enough time for social studies? Teach this step during your reading block or as a center activity.

---

3 FLIP CHART
Active Reading

Model active reading by asking the questions and using the teaching strategies indicated next to this lesson's Flip Chart pages.

30 minutes

---

4 PRESENTATION
Got It?

Play the interactive Got It? activity to evaluate children's understanding of the key objectives in this lesson. Use the Extra Support button to assist children who need additional instruction.

OPTIONAL: You may want to assign the Got It? Activity Worksheet for homework or have children complete it in class.

10 minutes ⓥ

ⓥ *Use the Lesson Steps marked with this icon to teach core content in less time!*

Begin to Read

- ⊙ **CLASSIFY AND CATEGORIZE** *In what season would you wear shorts and a t-shirt outside?* summer

Support English Language Learners

1. Content and Language

Display Flip Chart page 62. Point to the pictures as you paraphrase the objectives on page 71 of this guide. Encourage children to look at the pictures as they restate the objectives in their own words.

2. Frontload the Lesson

Preview the lesson title and visuals. Draw a KWL chart. Have children tell what they know about the seasons. Record their responses on the chart.

3. Comprehensible Input

Point to each picture and say the name of the season. Model an activity to do in each season. Then invite children to role-play activities they would like to do in each season.

Begin to Read

- **MAKE CONNECTIONS** *What is one seasonal weather change from fall to winter?* It gets colder outside.

Differentiated Instruction

Use the following ideas when discussing the seasons.

L2 Extra Support: Have children recall what the tree looks like in each season. Then have them complete this sentence. *In ____(name of season), the tree ____.*

L3 On-level: After children draw on page 73, ask them to write the name of the season. You may also show various picture cards representative of seasons (e.g., snowball, leaves, tulips). Have children sort the cards according to seasons.

L4 Challenge: Have children say a sentence that describes the tree in a particular season. Have them write it on a sentence strip. Offer help if necessary.

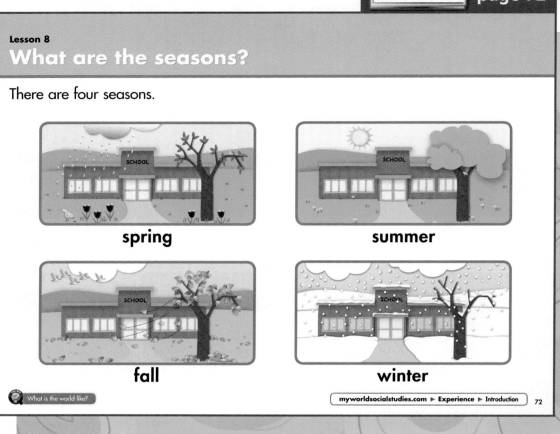

Lesson 8
What are the seasons?

There are four seasons.

spring   summer

fall   winter

What is the world like?   myworldsocialstudies.com ▶ Experience ▶ Introduction   72

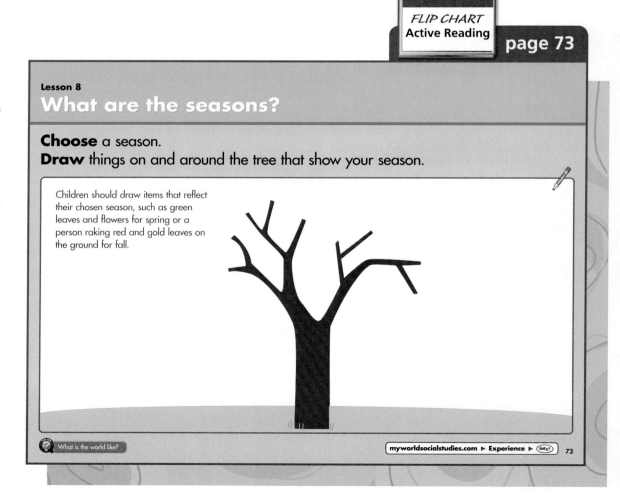

Lesson 8
What are the seasons?

Choose a season.
Draw things on and around the tree that show your season.

Children should draw items that reflect their chosen season, such as green leaves and flowers for spring or a person raking red and gold leaves on the ground for fall.

What is the world like?   myworldsocialstudies.com ▶ Experience ▶ Got it?   73

Full Lesson Plan Online

To use or customize the full lesson plan for this lesson, log on to myWorldSocialStudies.com.

Objectives

- Describe how human and physical characteristics of a place affect how and where people live.
- Identify ways people use natural resources to satisfy basic needs.
- Identify human-made and natural resources.

- Describe how people interact with and change their environment to satisfy basic needs.

⊙ **Target Reading Skill Objective:**
- Classify and categorize.

ELL Objective:
- Learn strategies to access vocabulary about natural resources.

---

1  *PRESENTATION* **Lesson 9 Introduction**

myWorld and Me
Remind children of the discussion they had about the Big Question for this chapter: What is the world like?
- *Where do you think water comes from?*

5 minutes ⊙

---

2 *FLIP CHART* **Student Activity Worksheets**

Introduce the Lesson Vocabulary words: *water, trees, plants,* and *food.* Point to pictures on the lesson pages as you explain the meaning of each word. Then ask:
- *What do we use that comes from Earth?* Children may say water and trees.

Hand out the Vocabulary Worksheet, page 60. Help children complete it.

5 minutes ⊙

Not enough time for social studies? Teach this step during your reading block or as a center activity.

---

3 *FLIP CHART* **Active Reading**

Model active reading by asking the questions and using the teaching strategies indicated next to this lesson's Flip Chart pages.

30 minutes

---

4  *PRESENTATION* **Got It?**

Play the interactive Got It? activity to evaluate children's understanding of the key objectives in this lesson. Use the Extra Support button to assist children who need additional instruction.

OPTIONAL: You may want to assign the Got It? Activity Worksheet for homework or have children complete it in class.

10 minutes ⊙

⊙ *Use the Lesson Steps marked with this icon to teach core content in less time!*

Begin to Read

- ⊙ **CLASSIFY AND CATEGORIZE** *What are things we make using wood from trees?* houses, furniture, pencils

Support English Language Learners

1. Content and Language

Display the Flip Chart page. Point to the visuals as you paraphrase the objectives for this lesson. Encourage children to use the visuals as prompts to restate the objectives in their own words.

2. Frontload the Lesson

Preview the lesson title, vocabulary, and visuals. Invite children to tell what they know about each of the resources pictured.

3. Comprehensible Input

Model using each of the resources pictured on the Flip Chart page. Then invite children to take turns acting out how they use each one while the rest of the class guesses the resource.

Begin to Read

- **MAKE CONNECTIONS** *How do we use water?* Possible answers: to drink, water plants, wash dishes

Differentiated Instruction

Use the following ideas to differentiate instruction when discussing Earth's resources.

L2 Extra Support: Have children look at the pictures and match the resource to the item that people use or make from it. Have them tell if the item is a *need* or a *want*.

L3 On-level: Invite children to draw a picture of three items they use, make, or eat from Earth's resources. Have them write a label for each picture. Have them tell if their picture is of a *need* or a *want*.

L4 Challenge: Have children make up clues about items they use, make, or eat that come from Earth's resources. Invite the class to guess the item.

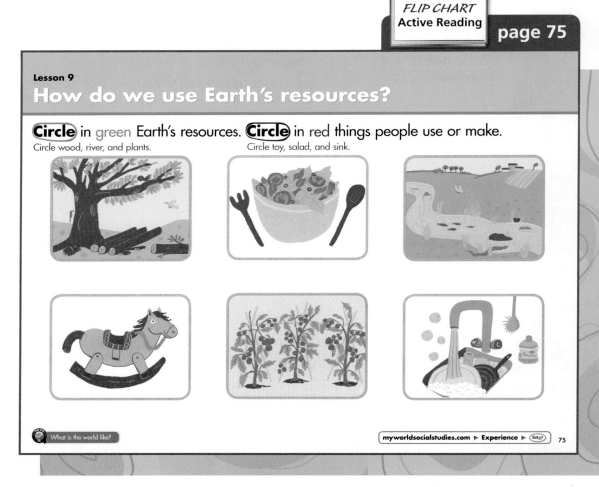

1 PRESENTATION
Vocabulary Review

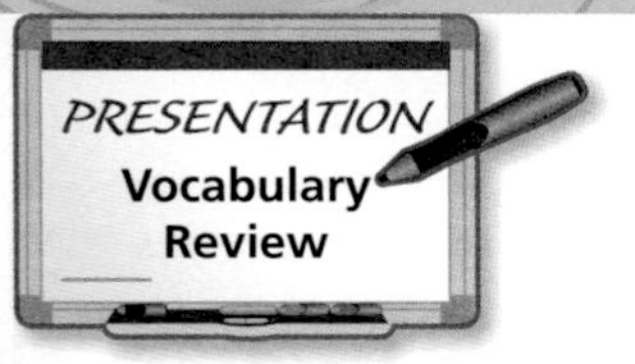

Use the Vocabulary Review game on the Digital Presentation for this lesson.

10 minutes ⓥ

2 *Performance Assessment*

Choice A
myStory Book

WRITING ACTIVITY Children will write and illustrate an eight-page booklet demonstrating their understanding of the key objectives, vocabulary, and Big Question for this chapter.

See the Online Lesson Plan for full instructions on how to complete the story together as a class, or have each child complete his or her own story. Make sure children's stories reflect what the chapter's content means to them.

30 minutes

Choice B
myWorld Activity

HANDS-ON ACTIVITY: Our World In this activity children play a game and demonstrate what they have learned about landforms, bodies of water, weather, and the seasons. See the Online Lesson Plan for full instructions for completing the activity. Use Activity Cards 11–15 for this activity.

30 minutes

3 *Formal Assessment*

OPTIONAL: You can assign the chapter Review and Assessment Student Activity Worksheets or use the Chapter Test and track scores online.

30 minutes ⓥ

ⓥ *Use the Lesson Steps marked with this icon to teach core content in less time!*

Notes

❓ Big Question

1. Ask children to think back to what they have learned about the world.
2. Call on children to share what they remember.
3. Discuss with children land, water, weather, and the seasons, and how we use Earth's resources to get what we need to live.

myWorld and Me

1. Have children think about places they would like to visit.
2. Encourage children to recall what different kinds of land and water look like and what they could do in each place.

myStory Book

1. Explain to children that they will now have the opportunity to create a story about what they learned in this chapter.
2. Have children choose their own words and select the images they think are best for the story.
3. Explain that prompts will guide them through the writing of the story.

my Story Book

Think of a place you would like to visit.
Draw a picture of what the place looks like.

What is the world like?   myworldsocialstudies.com ▶ Understand ▶ **my** Story Book   76

Chapter 4 Our Traditions
Planning With the End in Mind

**Ready, Set, Teach!**
For quick hints on how to teach this chapter, log on to myWorldSocialStudies.com.

Chapter Objectives
Begin With the End in Mind

 Big Question:
How is culture shared?

 Target Reading Skill:
Compare and Contrast

Children will demonstrate the following enduring understandings:

- People are alike and different.
- People celebrate in many ways.
- We learn about our country through stories and holidays.

- We are all part of a culture.
- There are many different cultures around the world.

Connect
Make Learning Meaningful

 Flip Chart
- Big Question
- myStory Spark
- Song
- Vocabulary Preview

 Digital Presentation
- Big Question
- myStory Spark
- myStory Video
- Song

Experience
Teach Knowledge and Skills

 Flip Chart
- Lessons 1–7
- Got It? Formative Assessments
- Target Reading Skill: Compare and Contrast
- 21C Skill Lesson: Distinguish Fact from Fiction

⭐ **myWorld Leveled Readers**

Digital Presentation
- Big Question
- Lesson Introduction
- Got It?

**21st Century Learning
Online Tutor**

Understand
Assess Understanding

 Flip Chart
- Review and Assessment
- myStory Book

⭐ **myWorld Activity**
- Celebration Vests
- Activity Cards #16–20

Chapter Assessment
- Chapter Test

 Digital Presentation
- Vocabulary Review
- myWorld Activity

myStory Book Online

Children write, illustrate, and publish a digital book.

Chapter Assessment

Administer online test.

Full Lesson Plan Online

To use or customize the full lesson plan for this lesson, log on to myWorldSocialStudies.com.

Objectives

- Establish meaning.
- Make meaningful connections to personal experiences.
- Use prior knowledge to gain understanding.

⊙ **Target Reading Skill Objective:**
- Compare and contrast.

ELL Objective:
- Use different strategies to explore new vocabulary.

1 PRESENTATION Chapter 4 Introduction

Use the Big Question Activity to introduce the chapter's main idea.
- myStory Spark
- myStory Video
- Song

🔲 Click on the Extra Support button for helpful hints and vocabulary help.

30 minutes ⊘

Introduce this chapter using the Digital Presentation or the Flip Chart.

2 FLIP CHART Active Reading

Use the Big Question to introduce the chapter's main idea.
- *How does your family celebrate special days?*

myStory Spark
- *What kind of food do you like to eat?*

Song
- *What does your family do on holidays?*

Vocabulary Preview
- *What is your favorite holiday?*

45 minutes

Not enough time for social studies? Teach these steps during your reading block or as center activities.

3  LEVELED READER

Use these Leveled Readers as you work through the chapter.
- On Level: *Jackie Robinson*
- Advanced: *Jackie Robinson Changes the Game*

⊘ *Use the lesson steps marked with this icon to teach core content in less time!*

The Big Question

- **ANALYZE VISUALS** *What are the people in the picture doing?* They are taking part in a parade for Chinese New Year.

- **MAKE CONNECTIONS** *How do you share your culture?* Children may say that their family cooks special kinds of foods on a holiday that they celebrate.

myStory Spark

- **SUMMARIZE** *What is your favorite food for breakfast, lunch, or dinner?* Answers will vary.

Differentiated Instruction

Use the following activities when discussing the Big Question.

L1 Special Needs: Have children brainstorm favorite foods that their families prepare on holidays or special days.

L2 Extra Support: Take a picture walk through the chapter and point out how people share their culture. Then have them think of a favorite food that is a part of their culture and complete this sentence: _____ (name of food) *is a part of my culture.*

L3 On-level: Have children write a simple label for the pictures they draw.

L4 Challenge: Ask children to write a sentence caption for the drawings of their favorite food pictures.

79

Song

- **ANALYZE VISUALS** *What are these families doing?* having a picnic and watching a parade

- **ANALYZE VISUALS** *What holiday do you think they are celebrating?* Possible answer: Independence Day

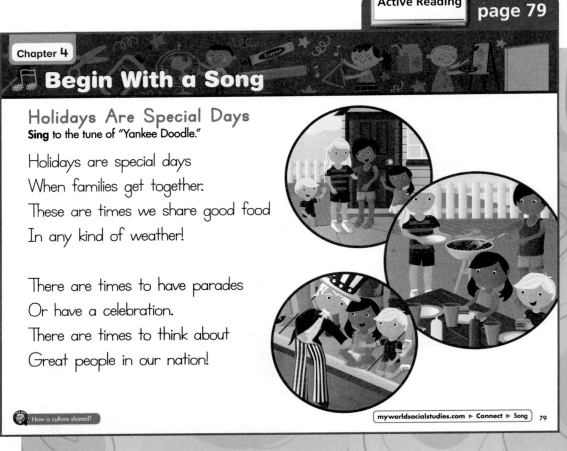

Chapter 4

Begin With a Song

Holidays Are Special Days
Sing to the tune of "Yankee Doodle."

Holidays are special days
When families get together.
These are times we share good food
In any kind of weather!

There are times to have parades
Or have a celebration.
There are times to think about
Great people in our nation!

How is culture shared?

myworldsocialstudies.com ▶ Connect ▶ Song   79

Vocabulary

- **ANALYZE VISUALS** *What foods do people celebrate with?* Possible answers: lemonade, hamburgers

Support English Language Learners

Beginning LOW/HIGH Display visual examples of the word *holiday.* Point to the pictures, say the word, and have children echo you. Repeat the routine with other vocabulary words.

Intermediate LOW/HIGH Point to a word and its corresponding picture and explain its meaning. Encourage children to use the word in a simple sentence.

Advanced LOW/HIGH Invite children to use each vocabulary word in a complete sentence. Encourage them to relate the word to themselves.

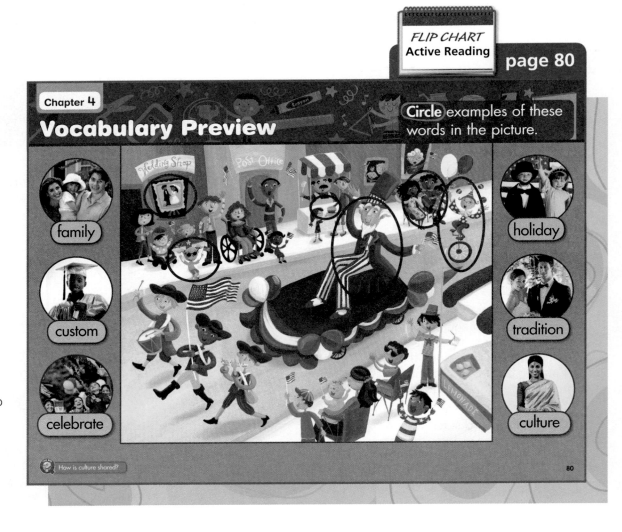

Chapter 4

Vocabulary Preview

Circle examples of these words in the picture.

family

custom

celebrate

holiday

tradition

culture

How is culture shared?   80

Chapter 4 Lesson 1
How are people alike and different?
Lesson Plan Summary

Full Lesson Plan Online

To use or customize the full lesson plan for this lesson, log on to myWorldSocialStudies.com.

Objectives

- Explain that people have both similarities and differences.
- Identify ways in which people are alike and different.

⊙ **Target Reading Skill Objective:**
- Compare and Contrast

ELL Objective:
- Respond to questions about how people are alike and different.

---

1  PRESENTATION
Lesson 1 Introduction

myWorld and Me
Remind children of the discussion they had about the Big Question for this chapter: How is culture shared?
- *How are you like your friends? How are you different?*

5 minutes ⓥ

---

2 FLIP CHART
Student Activity Worksheets

Introduce the Lesson Vocabulary words: *twins, alike, different,* and *same.* Point to pictures on the lesson pages as you explain the meaning of each word. Then ask:
- *How are people the same? How are they different?* Possible answers: alike—like to do fun thing, like to eat good food; different—play different games, eat different food

Hand out the Vocabulary Worksheet, page 66. Help children complete it.

5 minutes ⓥ

Not enough time for social studies? Teach this step during your reading block or as a center activity.

---

3 FLIP CHART
Active Reading

Model active reading by asking the questions and using the teaching strategies indicated next to this lesson's Flip Chart pages.

30 minutes

---

4 PRESENTATION
Got It?

Play the interactive Got It? activity to evaluate children's understanding of the key objectives in this lesson. Use the Extra Support button to assist children who need additional instruction.

OPTIONAL: You may want to assign the Got It? Activity Worksheet for homework or have children complete it in class.

10 minutes ⓥ

ⓥ *Use the Lesson Steps marked with this icon to teach core content in less time!*

Begin to Read

- ⊙ **COMPARE AND CONTRAST** *How are the children like each other?* Possible answers: They are both holding balls, they both have glasses.

Support English Language Learners

1. Content and Language
Create illustrated flashcards for *alike* and *different*. Point to each card as you paraphrase the objectives for this lesson. Have children restate them in their own words.

2. Frontload the Lesson
Preview the lesson title, text, and visuals. Have children predict what the lesson will be about.

3. Comprehensible Input
Ask questions to model active reading habits such as: *Who is pictured? How are they alike? What are they holding?*

Lesson 1
How are people alike and different?

The children are alike, or the same. They are different, too.

How is culture shared?   myworldsocialstudies.com ▶ Experience ▶ Introduction   81

Begin to Read

- **USE VISUALS** *How can you tell that these girls are twins?* They have the same facial features, hair color, and eye color; they are the same size.

Differentiated Instruction

Use the following activities to differentiate instruction when discussing how people are alike and different:

L2 Extra Support: Say a sentence using *alike* and *different*. Have children show thumbs up if the statement is true, thumbs down if the statement is false.

L3 On-level: Have children take turns pointing to similarities and differences in various pictures while stating what is the same and different.

L4 Challenge: Pair children and give them photos of people. Have them take turns telling how the people in the photos are alike and different.

Lesson 1
How are people alike and different?

Circle ways these sisters are alike.
Draw an X on ways they are different.

How is culture shared?   myworldsocialstudies.com ▶ Experience ▶ Got it?   82

Full Lesson Plan Online

To use or customize the full lesson plan for this lesson, log on to myWorldSocialStudies.com.

Objectives

- Identify basic similarities and differences between two photographs.
- Identify basic similarities and differences between two illustrations.

1
FLIP CHART
Teach the Skill

Compare and Contrast

Explain that when we compare two things, we tell how they are the same. Tell children that when we contrast two things, we tell how they are different. Then hold up two objects, such as two blocks. Be sure they are different in size, shape, or color. Ask children to tell how the blocks are alike and different. Repeat the routine with other classroom objects.

20 minutes

2
FLIP CHART
Try It

Model active reading by asking the questions and using the teaching strategies indicated next to this skill lesson's Flip Chart pages.

15 minutes

3
PRESENTATION
Digital Presentation

Review the skill with children using the Digital Presentation.

Click on the Extra Support button for helpful hints and vocabulary help.

15 minutes

Differentiated Instruction

Use the following activities to differentiate instruction when discussing comparing and contrasting:

L2 Extra Support: Have children look closely at the pictures and describe how they are the same and different. Have them complete these sentence frames: *The pictures are alike because _____. The pictures are different because _____.*

L3 On-level: Have children draw pictures of two things that show similarities and differences, such as two houses. Then have them take turns telling a partner how the items are alike and different. Ask partners to circle what is the same in the two pictures.

L4 Challenge: Have children work in pairs. Have each partner draw a house without showing it to the other. Have them compare and contrast the drawings and make a chart telling how the houses are alike and different.

⊙ Reading Skills: Compare and Contrast

Some things are alike, or the same.
Other things are different, or not the same.

myworldsocialstudies.com ▶ Experience ▶ Skills   83

⊙ Reading Skills: Compare and Contrast

Try it!

What do both pictures show?
Tell how they are alike and different.

Alike: ball games; played outside; played on grass playing fields; teams of players
Different: one shows soccer, one shows kickball; different kinds of balls; one game uses bases, the other a goal; kickball players in regular clothes, soccer players in uniforms; 3 players in one and 5 in the other.

myworldsocialstudies.com ▶ Experience ▶ Skills   84

Full Lesson Plan Online

To use or customize the full lesson plan for this lesson, log on to myWorldSocialStudies.com.

Objectives

- Describe how individuals and families grow and change.
- Recognize non-traditional families.
- Identify traditions and customs from their families, friends, school, and community.

- Identify different groups to which individuals belong.
- Describe how groups are made up of people who work, play, or learn together and share common interests.

⊙ **Target Reading Skill Objective:**
- Compare and contrast.

ELL Objective:
- Use full sentences to compare their family structure and makeup to those of other families.

1

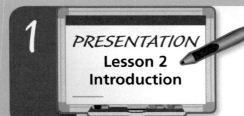

PRESENTATION
Lesson 2 Introduction

myWorld and Me   *5 minutes* ⊙

Remind children of the discussion they had about the Big Question for this chapter: How is culture shared?

- *What do the members of your family have in common?*

2

FLIP CHART
Student Activity Worksheets

Introduce the Lesson Vocabulary words: *family, parent, large,* and *small*. Point to pictures on the lesson pages as you explain the meaning of each word. Then ask: *5 minutes* ⊙

- *Which families are large? Which families are small?*

Hand out the Vocabulary Worksheet, page 69. Help children complete it.

Not enough time for social studies? Teach this step during your reading block or as a center activity.

3

FLIP CHART
Active Reading

Model active reading by asking the questions and using the teaching strategies indicated next to this lesson's Flip Chart pages.   *30 minutes*

4

PRESENTATION
Got It?

Play the interactive Got It? activity to evaluate children's understanding of the key objectives in this lesson. Use the Extra Support button to assist children who need additional instruction.   *10 minutes* ⊙

OPTIONAL: You may want to assign the Got It? Activity Worksheet for homework or have children complete it in class.

⊙ *Use the Lesson Steps marked with this icon to teach core content in less time!*

Begin to Read

- ⊙ **COMPARE AND CONTRAST** *How is your family like one of the families in the pictures?* Responses will vary.

Support English Language Learners

1. Content and Language

Display pictures of families sharing different traditions and customs. Point to the pictures and paraphrase the objectives for the lesson. Have children restate them in their own words.

2. Frontload the Lesson

Read the lesson title aloud. Ask children to predict what this lesson will be about.

3. Comprehensible Input

Compare families. For example, say *There are two people in this family.* As you say *two*, hold up two fingers. Then ask, *Who has two people in their family?* Encourage children to use full sentences in their responses.

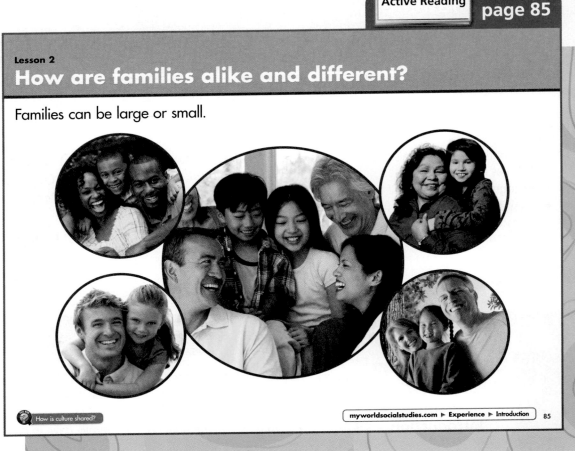

Lesson 2
How are families alike and different?

Families can be large or small.

How is culture shared?   myworldsocialstudies.com ▸ Experience ▸ Introduction 85

Begin to Read

- **COMPARE AND CONTRAST** *How will your drawing look different from other children's drawings?* Accept all responses.

Differentiated Instruction

Use the following activities to differentiate instruction when children draw their family pictures on page 86.

L2 Extra Support: Before children draw, have them identify the members of their family.

L3 On-level: Encourage children to write a label for each family member.

L4 Challenge: Share pictures of families from other places. Invite children to compare these families to the pictures they drew.

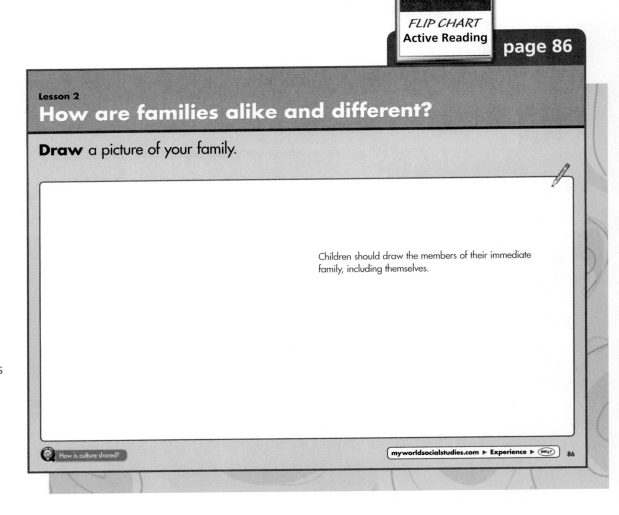

Lesson 2
How are families alike and different?

Draw a picture of your family.

Children should draw the members of their immediate family, including themselves.

How is culture shared?   myworldsocialstudies.com ▸ Experience ▸ Got it? 86

Chapter 4 Lesson 3
What is culture?
Lesson Plan Summary

Full Lesson Plan Online

To use or customize the full lesson plan for this lesson, log on to myWorldSocialStudies.com.

Objectives

- Recognize that there are many different cultures.
- Describe how culture is shared through art, music, customs, traditions, family celebrations, and language.

- Compare cultural similarities and differences in individuals, families, and communities.
- Compare our nation's holidays with holidays of other cultures.

⊙ **Target Reading Skill Objective:**
- Compare and contrast.

ELL Objective:
- Ask questions to identify and compare different cultures.

1

PRESENTATION
Lesson 3 Introduction

myWorld and Me

Remind children of the discussion they had about the Big Question for this chapter: How is culture shared?

- *What special things do you do with your family?*

5 minutes ⏱

2

FLIP CHART
Student Activity Worksheets

Introduce the Lesson Vocabulary words: *culture, share, eat,* and *dress*. Point to pictures on the lesson pages as you explain the meaning of each word. Then ask:

- *What kind of food does your family like to eat?* Sample response: My family likes to eat homemade tamales.

Hand out the Vocabulary Worksheet, page 71. Help children complete it.

5 minutes ⏱

Not enough time for social studies? Teach this step during your reading block or as a center activity.

3

FLIP CHART
Active Reading

Model active reading by asking the questions and using the teaching strategies indicated next to this lesson's Flip Chart pages.

30 minutes

4

PRESENTATION
Got It?

Play the interactive Got It? activity to evaluate children's understanding of the key objectives in this lesson. Use the Extra Support button to assist children who need additional instruction.

OPTIONAL: You may want to assign the Got it? Activity Worksheet for homework or have children complete it in class.

10 minutes ⏱

⏱ *Use the Lesson Steps marked with this icon to teach core content in less time!*

Begin to Read

- ⊙ **COMPARE AND CONTRAST** *How do people in our nation celebrate holidays like these families?* Possible answer: We eat special foods on holidays.

Support English Language Learners

1. Content and Language
Display pictures of customs, traditions, and celebrations. Point to the pictures and paraphrase the objectives for this lesson. Have children restate them in their own words.

2. Frontload the Lesson
Remind children that all families eat and have fun, but they may do them in different ways. Encourage children to describe or act out their own customs and traditions.

3. Comprehensible Input
Use a think-aloud to model asking questions as you point to the images: *Who is in this picture? Where are they? What are they doing?* Then have children ask questions of their own.

- **MAKE CONNECTIONS** *What is something you like to do that is part of your culture?* Possible answer: We wear colorful clothing and march in a parade during the Chinese New Year celebration.

Differentiated Instruction

Use the following ideas to differentiate instruction about different cultures.

L2 Extra Support: Encourage children to focus on an aspect of their culture, such as a special day. Have them describe it and then draw a picture that illustrates it.

L3 On-level: Invite children to draw a special food, item of clothing, or symbol that is part of their culture.

L4 Challenge: Have children draw a picture book that illustrates their culture. It should include pictures of special clothing, holidays, arts (such as dance), and food.

Lesson 3
What is culture?

We share ways to eat, dress, and have fun.

How is culture shared?   myworldsocialstudies.com ▶ Experience ▶ Introduction   87

Lesson 3
What is culture?

Draw something that is part of your culture.

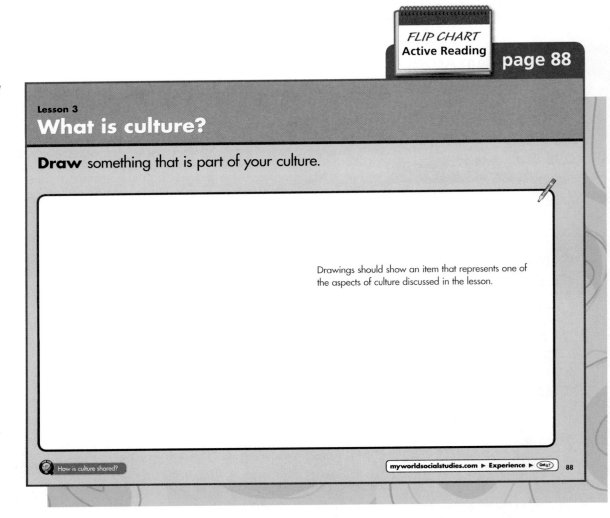

Drawings should show an item that represents one of the aspects of culture discussed in the lesson.

How is culture shared?   myworldsocialstudies.com ▶ Experience ▶ Got it?   88

Full Lesson Plan Online

To use or customize the full lesson plan for this lesson, log on to myWorldSocialStudies.com.

Objectives

- Identify celebrations as ways to show how we feel about special people and events.
- Explain that people celebrate in different ways.

- Compare family customs and traditions among cultures.
- Explain how people learn about others who are different from themselves.

⊙ **Target Reading Skill Objective:**
- Compare and contrast.

ELL Objective:
- Name special events and describe ways they are celebrated.

---

1 PRESENTATION
Lesson 4 Introduction

myWorld and Me
Remind children of the discussion they had about the Big Question for this chapter: How is culture shared?
- *How does your family celebrate special days?*

5 minutes ⓥ

---

2 FLIP CHART
Student Activity Worksheets

Introduce the Lesson Vocabulary words: *celebrate, special, tradition,* and *custom*. Point to pictures on the lesson pages as you explain the meaning of each word. Then ask:
- *What does the word* celebrate *mean?* to do something special
- *What special days do you celebrate?* Sample responses: Independence Day, Thanksgiving

Hand out the Vocabulary Worksheet, page 73. Help children complete it.

5 minutes ⓥ

Not enough time for social studies? Teach this step during your reading block or as a center activity.

---

3 FLIP CHART
Active Reading

Model active reading by asking the questions and using the teaching strategies indicated next to this lesson's Flip Chart pages.

30 minutes

---

4 PRESENTATION
Got It?

Play the interactive Got It? activity to evaluate children's understanding of the key objectives in this lesson. Use the Extra Support button to assist children who need additional instruction.

OPTIONAL: You may want to assign the Got It? Activity Worksheet for homework or have children complete it in class.

10 minutes ⓥ

ⓥ *Use the Lesson Steps marked with this icon to teach core content in less time!*

Begin to Read

- **ANALYZE VISUALS** *What special events are these people celebrating?* a girl's fifteenth birthday, a graduation, a wedding

Support English Language Learners

1. Content and Language

Display pictures of different celebrations. Point to the pictures as you paraphrase the objectives for this lesson. Have children restate the objectives in their own words.

2. Frontload the Lesson

Draw a concept web with the word *Celebrations* in the center circle. Invite children to share celebrations they have with their families and record these in the surrounding circles.

3. Comprehensible Input

As you show children pictures of different celebrations, invite them to act out what they do on these special days.

Begin to Read

- **◉ COMPARE AND CONTRAST** *Choose two of the items shown. Tell how they are used to celebrate.* Possible answers: We wave flags on national holidays. We have balloons at parties.

Differentiated Instruction

Use the following activities to differentiate instruction when discussing celebrations:

L2 Extra Support: Collect items or pictures used at different celebrations. Point to each item. Say a simple sentence and act out how to use it.

L3 On-level: Invite children to role-play or act out what they do to celebrate special days. Encourage the class to guess the celebration.

L4 Challenge: Invite children to make a picture book of celebrations. Encourage them to write captions for each picture.

Full Lesson Plan Online

To use or customize the full lesson plan for this lesson, log on to myWorldSocialStudies.com.

Objectives

- Explain that we celebrate special days to remember and honor people and events from our nation's past.
- Compare our nation's holidays with holidays of other cultures.

- Identify and discuss the contributions of individuals recognized on national holidays.
- Identify customs associated with national patriotic celebrations and holidays.

⊙ **Target Reading Skill Objective:**
- Compare and contrast.

ELL Objective:
- Use new vocabulary to role-play national holiday celebrations.

---

1 PRESENTATION — Lesson 5 Introduction

myWorld and Me

Remind children of the discussion they had about the Big Question for this chapter: How is culture shared?
- *What holidays do you celebrate?*

5 minutes ⊘

---

2 FLIP CHART — Student Activity Worksheets

Introduce the Lesson Vocabulary words: *remember, events,* and *holidays.* Point to pictures on the lesson pages and explain the meaning of each word. Then ask:
- *What does the word* holiday *mean?* a special day

Hand out the Vocabulary Worksheet, page 75. Help children complete it.

5 minutes ⊘

Not enough time for social studies? Teach this step during your reading block or as a center activity.

---

3 FLIP CHART — Active Reading

Model active reading by asking the questions and using the teaching strategies indicated next to this lesson's Flip Chart pages.

30 minutes

---

4 PRESENTATION — Got It?

Play the interactive Got It? activity to evaluate children's understanding of the key objectives in this lesson. Use the Extra Support button to assist children who need additional instruction.

10 minutes ⊘

OPTIONAL: You may want to assign the Got It? Activity Worksheet for homework or have children complete it in class.

⊘ *Use the Lesson Steps marked with this icon to teach core content in less time!*

91

Begin to Read

- ◉ COMPARE AND CONTRAST *How are Presidents' Day and Martin Luther King, Jr. Day alike?* Both are national holidays that remember important leaders.

Support English Language Learners

1. Content and Language
Display pictures that represent national holidays while you paraphrase the objectives from page 91 of this guide. Then have children restate the objectives in their own words.

2. Frontload the Lesson
Preview the lesson photos. Then display a KWL chart and ask children what they know about each national holiday. Fill in *K* and *W* before you explore the lesson.

3. Comprehensible Input
Have children role-play what they do to celebrate each national holiday. Encourage them to name the holiday using a complete sentence.

Begin to Read

- ANALYZE VISUALS *What important leader is pictured?* Abraham Lincoln

Differentiated Instruction

Use the following activities to differentiate instruction when discussing national holidays.

L2 Extra Support: Point to a picture on page 91 and name the holiday. Have children echo you. Then point to each picture and matching sentence on page 92, read it, and have children repeat it.

L3 On-level: Have children look at the lesson pictures and complete this sentence frame about each holiday: *We celebrate _____ (name of holiday) to _____ (reason for holiday).* Encourage them to complete the sentence frame with holidays from other cultures.

L4 Challenge: Display pictures of different holidays. Write sentence strips to describe each one. Have children match the pictures to the sentence strips.

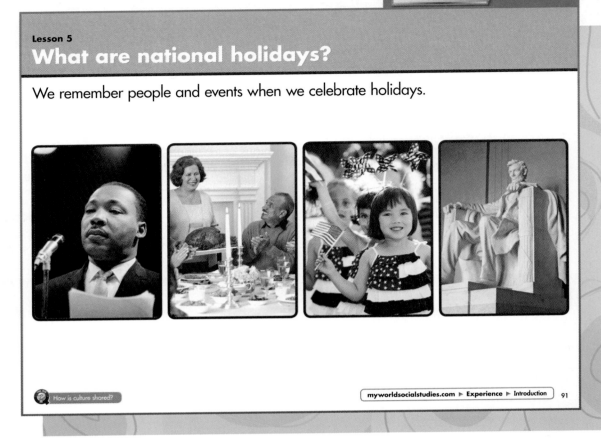

Lesson 5
What are national holidays?

We remember people and events when we celebrate holidays.

How is culture shared?   myworldsocialstudies.com ▶ Experience ▶ Introduction   91

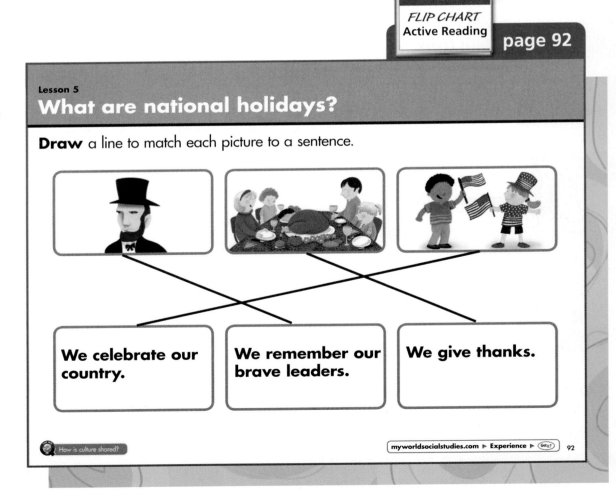

Lesson 5
What are national holidays?

Draw a line to match each picture to a sentence.

We celebrate our country.

We remember our brave leaders.

We give thanks.

How is culture shared?   myworldsocialstudies.com ▶ Experience ▶ Got it?   92

Chapter 4 Lesson 6
Who are American folk heroes?
Lesson Plan Summary

Full Lesson Plan Online

To use or customize the full lesson plan for this lesson, log on to myWorldSocialStudies.com.

Objectives

- Recognize that people use folk tales, legends, music, and oral histories to teach values, ideas, and traditions.
- Learn about America's past through stories about folk heroes.

- Listen to and retell stories about people in the past who have shown character ideals and principles including honesty, courage, and responsibility.

⊙ **Target Reading Skill Objective:**
- Compare and contrast.

ELL Objective:
- Use vocabulary and role-playing to retell stories about American folk heroes.

---

1 *PRESENTATION* **Lesson 6 Introduction**

myWorld and Me
Remind children of the discussion they had about the Big Question for this chapter: How is culture shared?
- *Do you know any stories about people from our nation's past?*

5 minutes ⏱

---

2 *FLIP CHART* **Student Activity Worksheets**

Introduce the Lesson Vocabulary words: *hero, folk, story,* and *retell.* Point to pictures on the lesson pages as you explain the meaning of each word. Then ask:
- *Have you heard a story about one of these characters? What was he or she like?* Answers will vary.

Hand out the Vocabulary Worksheet, page 77. Help children complete it.

5 minutes ⏱

Not enough time for social studies? Teach this step during your reading block or as a center activity.

---

3 *FLIP CHART* **Active Reading**

Model active reading by asking the questions and using the teaching strategies indicated next to this lesson's Flip Chart pages.

30 minutes

---

4 *PRESENTATION* **Got It?**

Play the interactive Got It? activity to evaluate children's understanding of the key objectives in this lesson. Use the Extra Support button to assist children who need additional instruction.

OPTIONAL: You may want to assign the Got It? Activity Worksheet for homework or have children complete it in class.

10 minutes ⏱

⏱ *Use the Lesson Steps marked with this icon to teach core content in less time!*

Begin to Read

- ⊙ **COMPARE AND CONTRAST** *How are the people in the pictures alike?* Possible answers: there are stories about all of them; they all worked hard

Support English Language Learners

1. Content and Language
Point to the Flip Chart pictures as you paraphrase the objectives for this lesson. Encourage children to restate them in their own words.

2. Frontload the Lesson
Display a KWL chart. Encourage children to tell what they know and want to know about each hero. Record their responses in the *K* and *W* columns.

3. Comprehensible Input
As you retell the story about each folk hero, use gestures to act out what the characters does. Then have children role-play the actions and story of each character.

Begin to Read

- **SUMMARIZE** *Which hero do you like best?* Responses will vary.

Differentiated Instruction

Use the following activities to differentiate instruction when discussing American folk heroes and their stories:

L2 Extra Support: Draw a chart with the following headings *Beginning, Middle,* and *End.* Read or tell the story about one of the folk heroes. Then help children fill in the chart with details from the story. Have them retell the story using sentence frames. *Once upon a time, ___ . Then ___ . In the end, ____.*

L3 On-level: Have children choose their favorite folk hero and retell the story.

L4 Challenge: Have children read or listen to a story about a folk hero who was not introduced in class. Then invite them to retell the story to classmates.

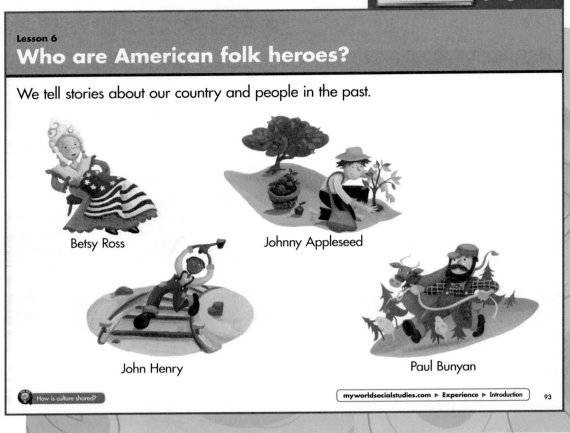

Lesson 6
Who are American folk heroes?

We tell stories about our country and people in the past.

Betsy Ross

Johnny Appleseed

John Henry

Paul Bunyan

myworldsocialstudies.com ► Experience ► Introduction   93

How is culture shared?

Lesson 6
Who are American folk heroes?

Circle the picture that stands for your favorite folk hero. Then **retell** the story.

Children will circle a picture and tell the story of the folk hero it stands for.

How is culture shared?

myworldsocialstudies.com ► Experience ► Got it?   94

Full Lesson Plan Online

To use or customize the full lesson plan for this lesson, log on to myWorldSocialStudies.com.

Objectives

- Identify similarities and differences among cultures.
- Recognize that various cultures enjoy different styles of music, art, dress, food, and languages.
- Identify contributions of different cultures.

- Compare our nation's holidays with those of other nations and communities around the world.
- Compare and contrast customs of families in communities around the world.
- Compare our nation's holidays with holidays of other cultures.

Target Reading Skill Objective:
- Compare and contrast.

ELL Objective:
- Use different kinds of media to talk about, compare, and appreciate different cultures.

---

1 PRESENTATION — Lesson 7 Introduction

myWorld and Me
Remind children of the discussion they had about the Big Question for this chapter: How is culture shared?
- *What kinds of music and dance do you enjoy?*

5 minutes ⏱

---

2 FLIP CHART — Student Activity Worksheets

Introduce the Lesson Vocabulary words: *many* and *world*. Point to pictures on the lesson pages as you explain the meaning of each word. Then ask:
- *Do you know where in the world spaghetti was first made?* Italy

Hand out the Vocabulary Worksheet, page 79. Help children complete it.

5 minutes ⏱

> *Not enough time for social studies? Teach this step during your reading block or as a center activity.*

---

3 FLIP CHART — Active Reading

Model active reading by asking the questions and using the teaching strategies indicated next to this lesson's Flip Chart pages.

30 minutes

---

4 PRESENTATION — Got It?

Play the interactive Got It? activity to evaluate children's understanding of the key objectives in this lesson. Use the Extra Support button to assist children who need additional instruction.

OPTIONAL: You may want to assign the Got It? Activity Worksheet for homework or have children complete it in class.

10 minutes ⏱

⏱ *Use the Lesson Steps marked with this icon to teach core content in less time!*

Begin to Read

- **ANALYZE VISUALS** *Which picture shows something you like to do?* Responses will vary.

Support English Language Learners

1. Content and Language
Show pictures of items and activities from different cultures. Point to them as you paraphrase the objectives for this lesson. Encourage children to restate them in their own words.

2. Frontload the Lesson
Preview the visuals with children. Invite children to share their own cultural practices. Then have children compare them with the ones pictured.

3. Comprehensible Input
Play audio clips of music and speech from different cultures as you talk about the text. If possible, model saying *Hello, my name is _____* in both English and another language. As appropriate, invite children to say the same thing in both English and another language.

Begin to Read

- ⊙ **COMPARE AND CONTRAST** *How are the items in the pictures like things you use? How are they different?* Possible answer: I eat noodles, but I use a fork, not chopsticks.

Differentiated Instruction

Use these ideas to differentiate instruction about other cultures.

L2 Extra Support: Point to each picture. Have children complete the sentence frame *This is a _____*. If necessary, say the word and have them repeat it.

L3 On-level: Have children draw pictures of familiar clothing, food, and musical instruments. Have children compare their pictures with a partner.

L4 Challenge: Ask children to describe each item pictured. Have them cut out magazine pictures and make a "Culture Collage" to display in the class.

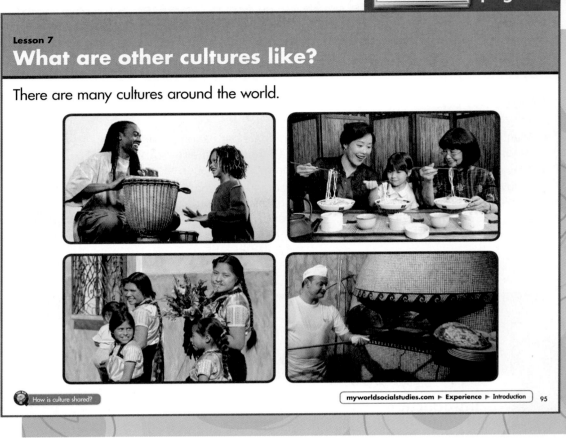

Lesson 7
What are other cultures like?

There are many cultures around the world.

How is culture shared? — myworldsocialstudies.com ▶ Experience ▶ Introduction   95

Lesson 7
What are other cultures like?

Color the things that you know.

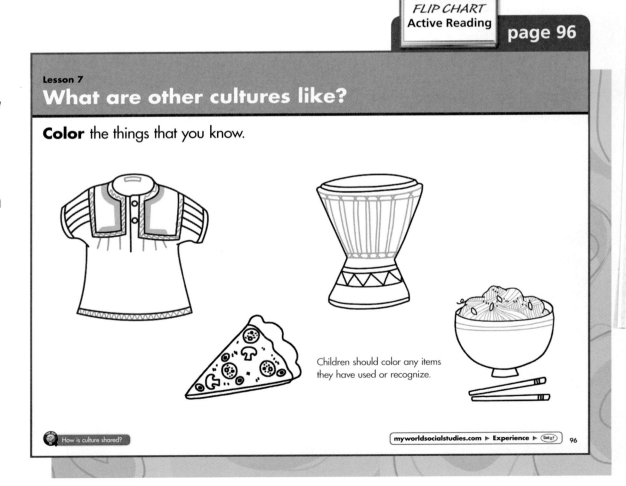

Children should color any items they have used or recognize.

How is culture shared? — myworldsocialstudies.com ▶ Experience ▶ Set 2   96

Full Lesson Plan Online

To use or customize the full lesson plan for this lesson, log on to myWorldSocialStudies.com.

Objectives

- Identify whether a text is fact or fiction.
- Use background knowledge, supporting details from the text, or another source to determine whether a reading selection is fact or fiction.

1

FLIP CHART
Teach the Skill

Distinguish Fact From Fiction
As children look at the picture of Abraham Lincoln, ask: *Is this person real or made up? What do you know about him?* Encourage children to share what they know about Lincoln to determine if the sentence is a fact. Repeat the routine with Jack from "Jack and the Beanstalk." Then display pictures of other real people and fictional characters. Have children sort the pictures into "fact" and "fiction" piles. Afterward, invite children to tell what they know about each person or character.

20 minutes

2

FLIP CHART
Try It

Model active reading by asking the questions and using the teaching strategies indicated next to this lesson's Flip Chart pages.

15 minutes

3

PRESENTATION
Digital Presentation

Review the skill with children using the Digital Presentation.

Click on the Extra Support button for helpful hints and vocabulary help.

15 minutes

Differentiated Instruction

Use the following questions to differentiate instruction for students when discussing fact and fiction on page 98.

L2 Extra Support: Be sure that children know the difference between fact and fiction. Practice by holding up objects in the classroom and making simple statements. Have children tell whether the statements are fact or fiction. For example, hold up a green ball and say: *This ball is red.* Point to yourself and say: *I am your teacher.*

L3 On-level: Play a game of "Thumbs Up/Thumbs Down." Say sentences about what children are learning in class. If they think the sentence is a fact, have them show "thumbs up." If they think it is fiction, have them show "thumbs down."

L4 Challenge: Invite volunteers to take turns saying a statement. Encourage the class to tell whether it is fact or fiction.

Critical Thinking: Distinguish Fact From Fiction

A fact is true. Fiction is made up.

Abraham Lincoln was a U.S. president.

fact

Jack climbed a giant beanstalk.

fiction

myworldsocialstudies.com ▶ Experience ▶ Skills   97

Critical Thinking: Distinguish Fact From Fiction

Try it!

Circle the picture that shows a fact.

Paul Bunyan was as tall as a tree.

George Washington was our first president.

myworldsocialstudies.com ▶ Experience ▶ Skills   98

Chapter 4
Review and Assessment
Lesson Plan Summary

1 PRESENTATION **Vocabulary Review**

Use the Vocabulary Review game on the Digital Presentation for this lesson.

10 minutes ⏱

2 *Performance Assessment*

Choice A
myStory Book

Writing Activity Children write and illustrate an eight-page booklet demonstrating their understanding of the key objectives, vocabulary, and Big Question for this chapter.

See the Online Lesson Plan for full instructions on how to complete the story together as a class, or have each child complete his or her own story. Make sure children's stories reflect what the chapter's content means to them.

30 minutes

Choice B
myWorld Activity

Hands-on Activity **Celebration Vests** In this activity children design a vest by drawing pictures of symbols that represent their favorite cultural celebration. See the Online Lesson Plan for full instructions for completing the activity. Use Activity Cards 11–15 for this activity.

30 minutes

3 *Formal Assessment*

OPTIONAL: You can assign the chapter Review and Assessment in the Student Activity Worksheets or use the Chapter Test and track scores online.

30 minutes ⏱

⏱ *Use the Lesson Steps marked with this icon to teach core content in less time!*

Notes

❓ Big Question

1. Ask children to recall what they learned about the ways people share culture.
2. Call on children to share what they remember.
3. Ask them to think about different customs, traditions, and celebrations they share with their families and those of other cultures. Guide them to see that different cultures have things in common.

myWorld and Me

1. Have children think about different celebrations they share throughout the year with friends and family.
2. Encourage children to recall how they prepare for each celebration and the activities they do with others on this special day.

myStory Book

1. Explain to children that they will now have the opportunity to create a story about what they learned in this chapter.
2. Have children choose their own words and select the images they think are best for the story.
3. Explain that prompts will guide them through the writing of the story.

my Story Book

Think of something you celebrate.
Draw a picture of what you do.

Children should draw themselves in a celebration.

How is culture shared?   myworldsocialstudies.com ▶ Understand ▶ my Story Book   99

Chapter 5 Life Then and Now
Planning With the End in Mind

Ready, Set, Teach!
For quick hints on how to teach this chapter, log on to myWorldSocialStudies.com.

Chapter Objectives
Begin With the End in Mind

 Big Question:
How does life change throughout history?

 **Target Reading Skill:**
Sequence

Children will demonstrate the following enduring understandings:

- Things change over time.
- Time can be measured.
- History is the story of our past.

- We learn about history from primary and secondary sources.

Connect
Make Learning Meaningful

 Flip Chart
- Big Question
- myStory Spark
- Song
- Vocabulary Preview

 Digital Presentation
- Big Question
- myStory Spark
- myStory Video
- Song

Experience
Teach Knowledge and Skills

 Flip Chart
- Lessons 1–10
- Got It? Formative Assessments
- Target Reading Skill: Sequence
- 21C Skill: Use Illustrations

 myWorld Leveled Readers

Digital Presentation
- Big Question
- Lesson Introduction
- Got It?

21st Century Learning Online Tutor

Understand
Assess Understanding

 Flip Chart
- Review and Assessment
- myStory Book

myWorld Activity
- Me in History
- Activity Cards #21–25

Chapter Assessment
- Chapter Test

 Digital Presentation
- Vocabulary Review
- myWorld Activity

myStory Book Online

Children write, illustrate, and publish a digital book.

Chapter Assessment

Administer online test.

Full Lesson Plan Online

To use or customize the full lesson plan for this lesson, log on to myWorldSocialStudies.com.

Objectives

- Establish meaning.
- Make meaningful connections to personal experiences.
- Use prior knowledge to gain understanding.

⊙ **Target Reading Skill Objective:**
- Identify sequence.

ELL Objective:
- Use different strategies to explore new vocabulary.

---

1 PRESENTATION
Chapter 5 Introduction

Use the Big Question Activity to introduce the chapter's main idea.
- myStory Spark
- myStory Video
- Song

⊞ Click on the Extra Support button for helpful hints and vocabulary help.

30 minutes ⏱

Introduce this chapter using the Digital Presentation or the Flip Chart.

---

2 FLIP CHART
Active Reading

Use the Big Question to introduce the chapter's main idea.
- *How has life changed from the past?*
- *How has school changed from the past?*

myStory Spark
- *What did you do when you were a baby?*

Song
- *What customs do you share with your family?*

Vocabulary Preview
- *What does a calendar show?*
- *What is your community like?*

45 minutes

Not enough time for social studies? Teach these steps during your reading block or as center activities.

---

3 LEVELED READER

Use these Leveled Readers as you work through the chapter.
- On Level: *Rosa Parks*
- Advanced: *Rosa Parks Stands Up for Freedom*

⏱ *Use the lesson steps marked with this icon to teach core content in less time!*

The Big Question

- **ANALYZE VISUALS** *How are the children in the pictures different from you?* Possible answers: different hair styles, different clothing

- **MAKE CONNECTIONS** *How are the children in the pictures like you?* Possible answers: They go to school.

myStory Spark

- ◉ **SEQUENCE** *When you were a baby, did you drink first from a bottle or from a cup?* a bottle

Differentiated Instruction

Use the following ideas to differentiate instruction.

L2 Extra Support: Have children describe what they were like as a baby or a toddler and make a list of their responses. Ask and record how they are different now.

L3 On-level: Have children write *Then* and *Now* labels for their pictures.

L4 Challenge: Encourage children to write a sentence caption for their pictures that describes how they have changed over time.

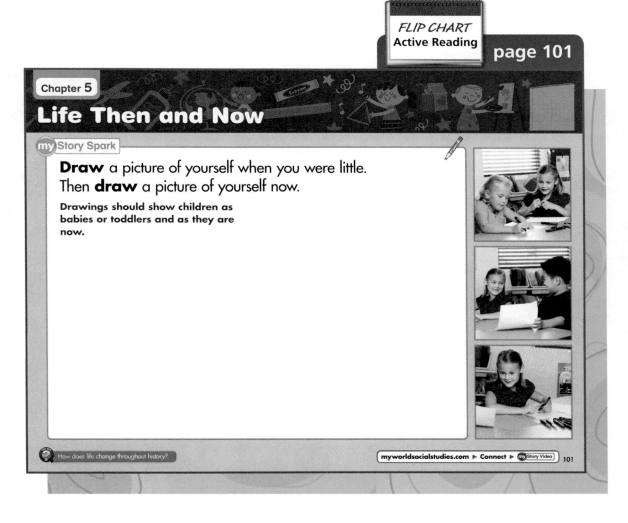

Song

- **ANALYZE VISUALS** *How does this family eat their food?* with chopsticks.
- **ANALYZE VISUALS** *What is the girl holding?* a toy horse

Vocabulary

- **ANALYZE VISUALS** *Point to the calendar in the classroom.* Children should point to the calendar.

Support English Language Learners

Beginning LOW Point to a vocabulary word such as *community*, and then to the picture of a community. Say the word slowly and have children echo you. Repeat the routine with other words.

Intermediate LOW Point to a word, say it, and have children echo you. Explain its meaning. Then have children find examples of the word in the picture. Repeat the routine with other words.

Advanced HIGH Have children point to a word and its corresponding picture in the scene. Then encourage them to use it in a sentence. Repeat with other words.

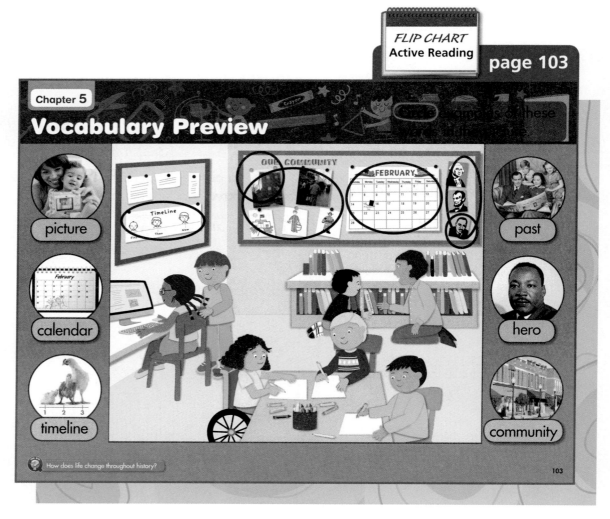

Full Lesson Plan Online

To use or customize the full lesson plan for this lesson, log on to myWorldSocialStudies.com.

Objectives

- Explain that history is the story of our past.
- Recognize that every child has a history.
- Use words and phrases related to chronology and time to explain how things change.

◉ **Target Reading Skill Objective:**
- Identify sequence.

ELL Objective:
- Use vocabulary to role-play activities children did in the past and activities they do today.

---

1 PRESENTATION
Lesson 1 Introduction

myWorld and Me
Remind children of the discussion they had about the Big Question for this chapter: How does life change throughout history?
- *What were you like when you were four years old?*

5 minutes ✓

---

2 FLIP CHART
Student Activity Worksheets

Introduce the Lesson Vocabulary words: *history, change, past,* and *present.* Point to pictures as you explain the meaning of each word. Then ask:
- *How have you changed since you were a baby?* Sample responses: I'm taller; I can walk and ride a bike.

Hand out the Vocabulary Worksheet, page 86. Help children complete it.

5 minutes ✓

Not enough time for social studies? Teach this step during your reading block or as a center activity.

---

3 FLIP CHART
Active Reading

Model active reading by asking the questions and using the teaching strategies indicated next to this lesson's Flip Chart pages.

30 minutes

---

4 PRESENTATION
Got It?

Play the interactive Got It? activity to evaluate children's understanding of the key objectives in this lesson. Use the Extra Support button to assist children who need additional instruction.

OPTIONAL: You may want to assign the Got It? Activity Worksheet for homework or have children complete it in class.

10 minutes ✓

✓ *Use the Lesson Steps marked with this icon to teach core content in less time!*

Begin to Read

- ◉ **SEQUENCE** *Describe how the girl changes as she grows.* First, she was very small. Then she got bigger. Now she can jump rope.

Support English Language Learners

1. Content and Language
Paraphrase the objectives for this lesson. Have children restate them in their own words.

2. Frontload the Lesson
Preview the lesson by looking at the pictures. Ask children to tell how they have changed since they were born.

3. Comprehensible Input
Model acting out activities children did in the past and activities they can do today. Then have children role-play the activities.

Lesson 1
What is my personal history?

History is the story of the past. We all have a history.

How does life change throughout history?   myworldsocialstudies.com ▶ Experience ▶ Introduction   104

Lesson 1
What is my personal history?

Circle in blue things you may have used as a baby.
Circle in red things you may use today.

Blue circle around the high chair and the key ring; red circle around the bike and the yo-yos

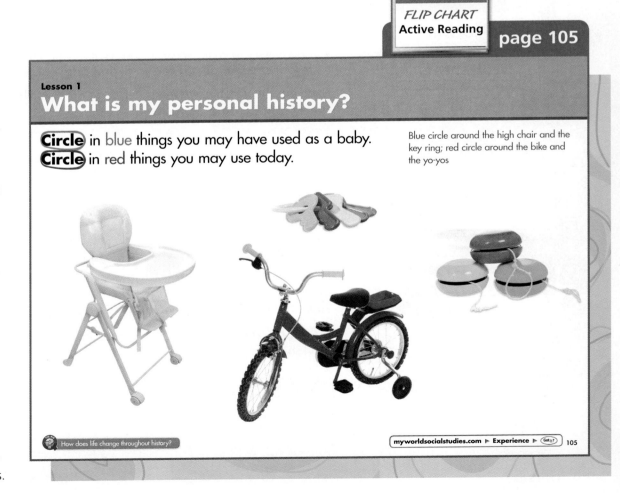

How does life change throughout history?   myworldsocialstudies.com ▶ Experience ▶ Got it?   105

Begin to Read

- **ASK QUESTIONS** *What other things did you use when you were a baby?* Possible answers: car seat, stroller, crib, bottle

Differentiated Instruction

Use the following activities when discussing personal history.

L2 Extra Support: Help children identify each picture on the activity page. Have them draw a picture of an item they used as a baby and one of something they use today. Or, have them cut out pictures from baby or toy store catalogs.

L3 On-level: Have children draw a picture showing themselves as a baby and what they are like now. Label the pictures *then* and *now*.

L4 Challenge: Invite children to draw three pictures in sequential order that show how they have changed since they were little. Have them label their pictures.

Full Lesson Plan Online

To use or customize the full lesson plan for this lesson, log on to <u>myWorldSocialStudies.com</u>.

Objectives

- Describe events of their day using sequence words.
- Arrange pictures and events in sequence.
- Use sequence words such as *first*, *next*, and *last*.

1

FLIP CHART
Teach the Skill

Sequence

Before reading, invite children to tell what is happening in each picture. Then have them describe the order of events again, beginning each sentence with the words *first, next,* and *last*. Afterwards, show children other pictures and have them put them in time order. Encourage children to use the words *first, next,* and *last* to begin each sentence.

20 minutes

2

FLIP CHART
Try It

Model active reading by asking the questions and using the teaching strategies indicated next to this lesson's Flip Chart page.

15 minutes

3

PRESENTATION
Digital Presentation

Review the skill with children using the Digital Presentation.

Click on the Extra Support button for helpful hints and vocabulary help.

15 minutes

Reading Skills: Sequence

You can use **first**, **next**, and **last** to show the order of when things happen.

first   **next**   **last**

myworldsocialstudies.com ► Experience ► Skills   106

Reading Skills: Sequence

Try it!

Look at the pictures.
Write first, next, or **last** under each picture to show the order.

first   next   last

myworldsocialstudies.com ► Experience ► Skills   107

Differentiated Instruction

Use the following activities to differentiate instruction for children when discussing sequence.

L1 Special Needs: Pretend to mix batter, then say: *First, I mix the batter for the muffins.* Encourage children to mime the action and repeat the sentence. Continue the routine with the other pictures.

L2 Extra Support: Point to each picture and have children describe the picture using these sentence frames: *First, he _____. Next, he _____. Last, he _____.*

L3 On-level: Ask children to draw three pictures of an activity they take part in. Have them label their pictures *first, next,* and *last*.

L4 Challenge: Have children draw three pictures of an activity they take part in. Have them write a sentence about each one, beginning with *first, next,* and *last*.

Full Lesson Plan Online

To use or customize the full lesson plan for this lesson, log on to myWorldSocialStudies.com.

Objectives

- Describe daily events in time order.
- Use words related to time and chronology, such as *before*, *after*, and *now*, to describe events of the school day in time order.

◉ **Target Reading Skill Objective:**
- Identify sequence.

ELL Objective:
- Learn vocabulary to tell the order in which they do things.

---

1 *PRESENTATION* **Lesson 2 Introduction**

myWorld and Me

Remind children of the discussion they had about the Big Question for this chapter: How does life change throughout history?

- *What do you do in the morning before school?*

5 minutes ⓥ

---

2 *FLIP CHART* **Student Activity Worksheets**

Introduce the Lesson Vocabulary words: *time, now, before,* and *after*. Point to pictures on the lesson pages as you explain the meaning of each word. Then ask:

- *What are you doing right now?* working and looking at the Flip Chart page
- *What do you do after school?* Sample responses: eat a snack, go to the park, do homework, play with a friend

Hand out the Vocabulary Worksheet, page 89. Help children complete it.

5 minutes ⓥ

Not enough time for social studies? Teach this step during your reading block or as a center activity.

---

3 *FLIP CHART* **Active Reading**

Model active reading by asking the questions and using the teaching strategies indicated next to this lesson's Flip Chart pages.

30 minutes

---

4 *PRESENTATION* **Got It?**

Play the interactive Got It? activity to evaluate children's understanding of the key objectives in this lesson. Use the Extra Support button to assist children who need additional instruction.

OPTIONAL: You may want to assign the Got It? Activity Worksheet for homework or have children complete it in class.

10 minutes ⓥ

ⓥ *Use the Lesson Steps marked with this icon to teach core content in less time!*

Begin to Read

- **PREDICT** *What do you think the children will do next?* Accept reasonable responses.

Support English Language Learners

1. Content and Language

Make vocabulary word cards for *before, now,* and *after.* Point to each card as you paraphrase the objectives for this lesson. Encourage children to restate the objectives in their own words, using the word cards as prompts.

2. Frontload the Lesson

Draw a chart with the headings *Before, Now,* and *After.* As children tell you what they do before, during, and after school, fill in the chart.

3. Comprehensible Input

Have volunteers act out something they do before, during, or after school and invite the class to guess the activity.

Lesson 2
How do we talk about time?

We can use **before**, **now**, and **after** to tell about time.

before   **now**   **after**

How does life change throughout history?

myworldsocialstudies.com ▶ Experience ▶ Introduction   108

Begin to Read

- ◉ **SEQUENCE** *What does the girl do after she paints?* She cleans up.

Differentiated Instruction

Use the following questions when discussing time.

L2 Extra Support: Ask children to look at the pictures on the Flip Chart pages and describe what the children are doing using the words *before, now,* and *after.* For "after" on the activity page, help them describe what the girl might do.

L3 On-level: Have children describe an activity they do in school. Have them use complete sentences beginning with the words *before, now,* and *after.*

L4 Challenge: In pairs, have one child act out a sequence of something he or she does in school. Then have the partner use the words *before, now,* and *after* to describe the sequence. Have partners switch roles and repeat the activity.

Lesson 2
How do we talk about time?

Look at each picture. **Draw** a picture to show what the girl would do after she paints.

Drawings may show child cleaning up or displaying the finished painting.

before   **now**   **after**

How does life change throughout history?

myworldsocialstudies.com ▶ Experience ▶ (Got it?)   109

110

Full Lesson Plan Online

To use or customize the full lesson plan for this lesson, log on to myWorldSocialStudies.com.

Objectives

- Recognize that time can be measured.
- Identify that time can be measured in days, weeks, months, and years.
- Explain that calendars represent days of the week and months of the year.
- Use terms related to time.

⊙ **Target Reading Skill Objective:**
- Identify sequence.

ELL Objective:
- Learn strategies to access vocabulary about time.

1

PRESENTATION
Lesson 3 Introduction

myWorld and Me

Remind children of the discussion they had about the Big Question for this chapter: How does life change throughout history?

- *What special activities are on the class calendar?*

5 minutes 🕐

2

FLIP CHART
Student Activity Worksheets

Introduce the Lesson Vocabulary words: *calendar, month,* and *year.* Point to pictures on the lesson pages and use gestures as you explain the meaning of each word. Then ask:

- *What month does the class calendar show?* Direct children's attention to the class calendar and point to the month.

Hand out the Vocabulary Worksheet, page 91. Help children complete it.

5 minutes 🕐

Not enough time for social studies? Teach this step during your reading block or as a center activity.

3

FLIP CHART
Active Reading

Model active reading by asking the questions and using the teaching strategies indicated next to this lesson's Flip Chart pages.

30 minutes

4

PRESENTATION
Got It?

Play the interactive Got It? activity to evaluate children's understanding of the key objectives in this lesson. Use the Extra Support button to assist children who need additional instruction.

OPTIONAL: You may want to assign the Got It? Activity Worksheet for homework or have children complete it in class.

10 minutes 🕐

🕐 *Use the Lesson Steps marked with this icon to teach core content in less time!*

Begin to Read

- **ANALYZE VISUALS** *Look at the calendar on the Flip Chart. What day of the week is November 5?* Friday

- ⊙ **SEQUENCE** *What day comes after Friday?* Saturday

Support English Language Learners

1. Content and Language
Display a calendar and paraphrase the objectives on page 111 of this guide. Have children use the calendar as they restate the objectives in their own words.

2. Frontload the Lesson
Display a calendar. As you turn to each month, have children name the month and describe what they do with their families to celebrate on special days.

3. Comprehensible Input
Point to each month of the year on a calendar. Have children role-play activities they do in each month.

- **ANALYZE VISUALS** *What months are the warmest?* Children may say the names of summer months.

Differentiated Instruction

Use the following activities when discussing how to measure time.

L2 Extra Support: Point to the class calendar. Talk about the weather, holidays, and special activities for the current month. Have children tell about an activity they do in this month. You may wish to have an adult record it.

L3 On-level: Have children draw an activity they do on a special day this month. Encourage them to write about it using this sentence frame: *I _____ (activity) in _____ (month).*

L4 Challenge: Provide a blank calendar for the month. Have children draw symbols of special days and words on it. Invite them to tell about what they will do on these days. Have them use terms, such as *day, week,* and *month.*

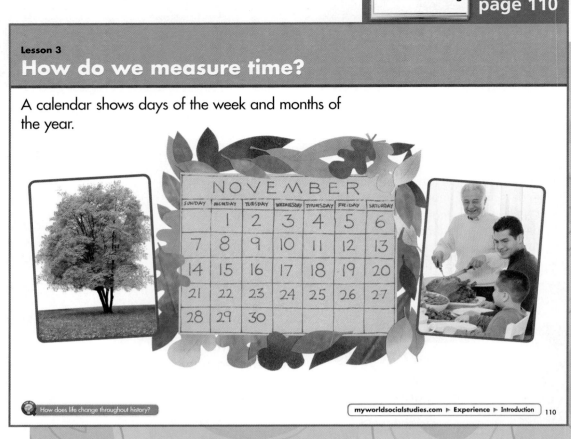

Lesson 3
How do we measure time?

A calendar shows days of the week and months of the year.

How does life change throughout history? myworldsocialstudies.com ▶ Experience ▶ Introduction 110

Lesson 3
How do we measure time?

Draw something you will do this month.

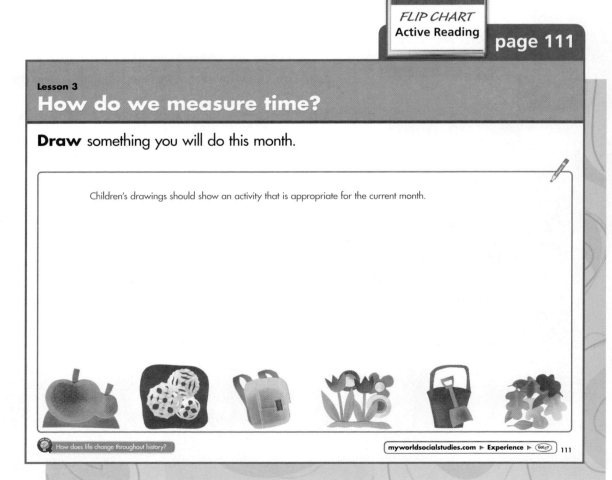

Children's drawings should show an activity that is appropriate for the current month.

How does life change throughout history? myworldsocialstudies.com ▶ Experience ▶ Got it? 111

Full Lesson Plan Online

To use or customize the full lesson plan for this lesson, log on to myWorldSocialStudies.com.

Objectives

- Recognize that change occurs over time.
- Explain what a timeline shows.
- Describe how to place key events on a timeline.
- Explain how to read timelines.

Target Reading Skill Objective:
- Identify sequence.

ELL Objective:
- Learn strategies to access vocabulary about sequence.

---

1 PRESENTATION
Lesson 4 Introduction

myWorld and Me
Remind children of the discussion they had about the Big Question for this chapter: How does life change throughout history.
- *What did you do yesterday? What are you doing today?*

5 minutes ⏱

---

2 FLIP CHART
Student Activity Worksheets

Introduce the Lesson Vocabulary words: *timeline, order, first,* and *next*. Point to pictures on the lesson pages and use gestures as you explain the meaning of each word. Then ask:
- *What did you do first in class today? What did you do next?*
  Possible answers: put coats away, sat down

Hand out the Vocabulary Worksheet, page 93. Help children complete it.

5 minutes ⏱

Not enough time for social studies? Teach this step during your reading block or as a center activity.

---

3 FLIP CHART
Active Reading

Model active reading by asking the questions and using the teaching strategies indicated next to this lesson's Flip Chart pages.

30 minutes

---

4 PRESENTATION
Got It?

Play the interactive Got It? activity to evaluate children's understanding of the key objectives in this lesson. Use the Extra Support button to assist children who need additional instruction.

OPTIONAL: You may want to assign the Got It? Activity Worksheet for homework or have children complete it in class.

10 minutes ⏱

⏱ *Use the Lesson Steps marked with this icon to teach core content in less time!*

Begin to Read

- ⊙ **SEQUENCE** *What does the first picture on the timeline show?*
  a chick hatching out of an egg

Support English Language Learners

1. Content and Language

Draw or display pictures of seeds, a seedling, and a tree. Point to the pictures as you paraphrase the objectives on page 113 of this guide. Encourage children to use the pictures as prompts to restate the objectives in their own words.

2. Frontload the Lesson

Draw a three-column chart with the headings *First*, *Next*, and *Last*. Preview the lesson pictures. Then have children describe what they could do as a baby, as a toddler, and now. Record the information on the chart.

3. Comprehensible Input

Ask think-aloud questions such as these: *What is the name of a baby hen? Which animal is smaller: a hen or a chick? Which animal is the youngest? How can I tell?*

Begin to Read

- **ACADEMIC VOCABULARY** *What is a timeline?* a line that shows the order of when things happen

Differentiated Instruction

Use the following activities when discussing timelines.

L2 Extra Support: Have children use pre-made sequence cards and put them in the correct order. Have them tell about the pictures.

L3 On-level: Have children bring in photographs of themselves at different ages. Encourage them to order the pictures to create a visual timeline of their lives. Have children describe the pictures using time order words.

L4 Challenge: Provide children with a blank timeline. Have them draw three events that happened this month and add words. Ask them to describe each event, beginning the sentences with words such as *first, next,* and *last.*

114

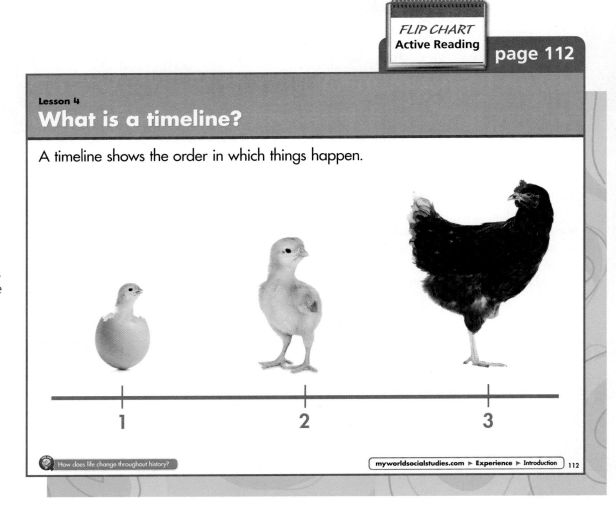

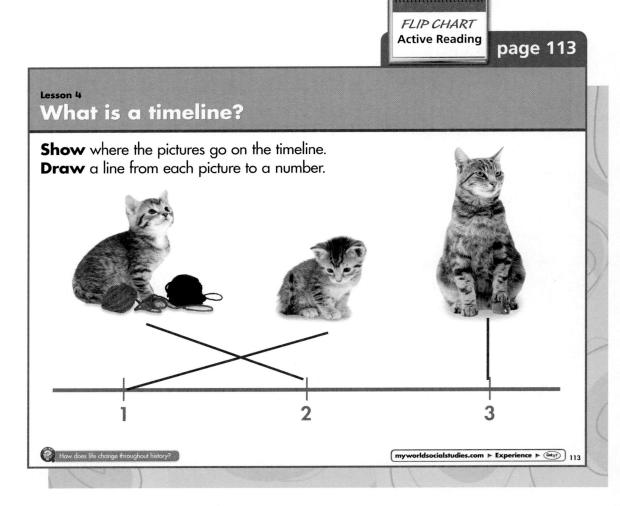

Lesson Plan Summary

Full Lesson Plan Online

To use or customize the full lesson plan for this lesson, log on to myWorldSocialStudies.com.

Objectives

- Describe ways people learn about the past.
- Identify ways we can learn about history.
- Compare information from different types of sources.
- Develop an awareness of a primary source.

⊙ Target Reading Skill Objective:
- Identify sequence.

ELL Objective:
- Use vocabulary to compare and contrast different sources from the past and present.

1
PRESENTATION
Lesson 5 Introduction

myWorld and Me

Remind children of the discussion they had about the Big Question for this chapter: How does life change throughout history?

- *How can you find out what you were like as a baby?*

5 minutes ⏱

---

2 FLIP CHART
Student Activity Worksheets

Introduce the Lesson Vocabulary words: *stories, past*, and *photograph*. Point to pictures on the lesson pages as you explain the meaning of each word. Then ask:

- *How can we learn about the past from photographs?* We can see what people looked like.

Hand out the Vocabulary Worksheet, page 95. Help children complete it.

5 minutes ⏱

Not enough time for social studies? Teach this step during your reading block or as a center activity.

---

3 FLIP CHART
Active Reading

Model active reading by asking the questions and using the teaching strategies indicated next to this lesson's Flip Chart pages.

30 minutes

4
PRESENTATION
Got It?

Play the interactive Got It? activity to evaluate children's understanding of the key objectives in this lesson. Use the Extra Support button to assist children who need additional instruction.

OPTIONAL: You may want to assign the Got It? Activity Worksheet for homework or have children complete it in class.

10 minutes ⏱

⏱ *Use the Lesson Steps marked with this icon to teach core content in less time!*

Begin to Read

- ⊙ **SEQUENCE** *Which family photograph is older, the one in black and white or the one in color?* the black and white photo

Support English Language Learners

1. Content and Language
Display the Flip Chart page. Point to the visuals as you paraphrase the objectives for this lesson. Encourage children to restate the objectives in their own words.

2. Frontload the Lesson
Take a picture walk through the lesson. Have children describe what they see and name the ways we can learn about the past.

3. Comprehensible Input
Point to each picture. Use gestures as you describe ways we can learn about the past. For example, point to the toy truck and say: *This is a toy truck from long ago.* Hold up a contemporary toy truck. *This is a toy truck you play with now. How are they alike? How are they different?* Encourage children to compare them. Offer help when necessary.

Begin to Read

- **ANALYZE PRIMARY SOURCES** *Is the black and white photograph a primary source?* yes

Differentiated Instruction

Use the following ideas when discussing how we can learn about history.

L2 Extra Support: Have groups participate in the On-level activity using appropriately challenging items, pictures, songs, or stories.

L3 On-level: Share various items, pictures, songs, and stories with children. Ask them to describe how they learned about the past from each one.

L4 Challenge: Display pictures of items that are obsolete. Ask children to draw a picture of something used for the same purpose today. Have them write a sentence about the picture. Ask them to tell how the item has changed.

Lesson 5
How can we learn about history?

We can listen to stories about the past.
We can look at pictures and things from the past.

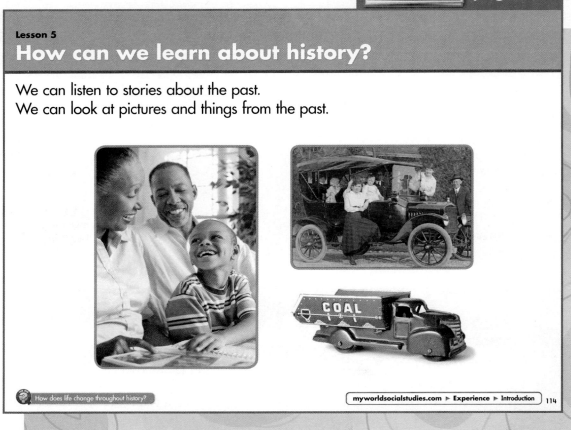

How does life change throughout history?   myworldsocialstudies.com ▶ Experience ▶ Introduction 114

Lesson 5
How can we learn about history?

Circle ways we can learn about history.

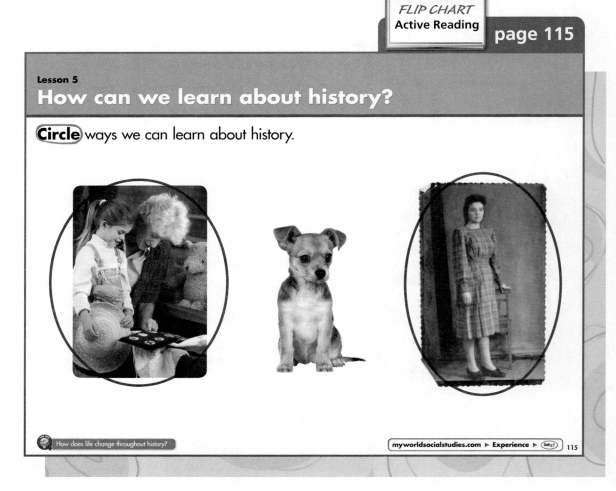

How does life change throughout history?   myworldsocialstudies.com ▶ Experience ▶ Got it? 115

Full Lesson Plan Online

To use or customize the full lesson plan for this lesson, log on to myWorldSocialStudies.com.

Objectives

- Use photographs to make predictions.
- Match photographs to text content.

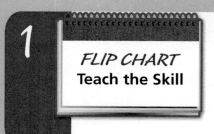

1 FLIP CHART
Teach the Skill

Use Illustrations

Have children look at the picture and describe what is happening. Then read the text aloud as you track the print with your finger or a pointer. Explain that pictures can show what a sentence tells. Then display other pictures with captions. Encourage children to look at the picture and predict what the caption says. Then read it aloud so children can confirm their predictions.

20 minutes

2 FLIP CHART
Try It

Model active reading by asking the questions and using the teaching strategies indicated next to this lesson's Flip Chart page.

15 minutes

3 PRESENTATION
Digital Presentation

Review the skill with children using the Digital Presentation.

Click on the Extra Support button for helpful hints and vocabulary help.

15 minutes

Differentiated Instruction

Use the following activities to differentiate instruction for the activity.

L1 Special Needs: Point to each picture and say a short sentence that describes it. For the picture that has a sentence, track the print as you speak. Next, point to a picture and help children repeat the sentence you said that matches.

L2 Extra Support: Say a sentence that describes one of the pictures and have children point to it. For example: *The boy blows bubbles.*

L3 On-level: Have children take turns acting out each picture. Invite children to say a sentence that describes the action.

L4 Challenge: Invite children to draw a picture of a simple action. On the back of the paper, ask them to write a sentence about it. Then have children take turns showing their pictures to the class. Ask them to predict what the sentences say.

Critical Thinking: Use Illustrations

Pictures can show what a sentence tells.

Jen washes her dog.

myworldsocialstudies.com ▶ Experience ▶ Skills 116

Critical Thinking: Use Illustrations

Try *it!*

Circle the picture that shows what the sentence says.

Matt feeds his fish.

myworldsocialstudies.com ▶ Experience ▶ Skills 117

Full Lesson Plan Online

To use or customize the full lesson plan for this lesson, log on to myWorldSocialStudies.com.

Objectives

- Identify important people in U.S. history and their contributions.
- Describe actions of important individuals and how their actions affected the nation.

- Listen to and retell stories about people in the past who have shown honesty, courage, and responsibility.

⊙ **Target Reading Skill Objective:**
- Identify sequence.

ELL Objective:
- Use vocabulary to role-play the contributions of important people in U.S. history.

---

1 PRESENTATION
Lesson 6
Introduction

myWorld and Me
Remind children of the discussion they had about the Big Question for this chapter: How does life change throughout history?
- *Do you know someone who helps other people?*

5 minutes ⊘

---

2 FLIP CHART
Student Activity
Worksheets

Introduce the Lesson Vocabulary words: *hero* and *courage*. Point to pictures on the lesson pages as you explain the meaning of each word. Then ask:
- *Can you name an American hero from long ago?* Responses will vary; record them to discuss further.

Hand out the Vocabulary Worksheet, page 98. Help children complete it.

5 minutes ⊘

Not enough time for social studies? Teach this step during your reading block or as a center activity.

---

3 FLIP CHART
Active Reading

Model active reading by asking the questions and using the teaching strategies indicated next to this lesson's Flip Chart pages.

30 minutes

---

4 PRESENTATION
Got It?

Play the interactive Got It? activity to evaluate children's understanding of the key objectives in this lesson. Use the Extra Support button to assist children who need additional instruction.

OPTIONAL: You may want to assign the Got It? Activity Worksheet for homework or have children complete it in class.

10 minutes ⊘

⊘ *Use the Lesson Steps marked with this icon to teach core content in less time!*

Begin to Read

- ⊙ **SEQUENCE** *Who was America's first president?* George Washington

Support English Language Learners

1. Content and Language
Point to the American heroes on the Flip Chart page as you paraphrase the objectives on page 119 of this guide. Encourage children to restate the objectives in their own words.

2. Frontload the Lesson
Draw a KWL chart. Have children tell what they know about the American heroes on the Flip Chart page. Record this information and any questions children have on the chart. After completing the lesson, invite children to tell what they learned about each hero. Record this information and use it to complete the chart.

3. Comprehensible Input
Show paintings or photographs of each American hero engaged in different activities. Have children retell their stories by acting out what each hero did.

Begin to Read

- **MAKE CONNECTIONS** *How did Martin Luther King Jr. show courage?* He spoke out against unfair laws.

Differentiated Instruction

Use the following activities to differentiate instruction for children.

L2 Extra Support: Have children use sentence frames to describe the people and their contributions. _____ (name of person) *was* _____ (character ideal). *He/she* _____ (accomplishment).

L3 On-level: Invite children to say a sentence about each American hero. Record their responses on sentence strips and display them in the class.

L4 Challenge: Play a "Who Am I" game. Have children take turns saying a clue about an American hero. The child who guesses correctly can say the next clue. You may also read about another hero not mentioned in the lesson and share this information with the class.

Lesson 6
Who are American heroes from the past?

A hero works to help others.

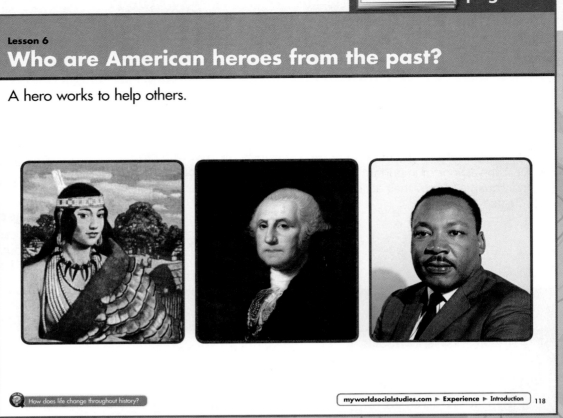

How does life change throughout history?   myworldsocialstudies.com ▶ Experience ▶ Introduction   118

Lesson 6
Who are American heroes from the past?

Circle a picture of an American hero from the past. **Tell** the hero's story.

Children tell the story of the person they circle.

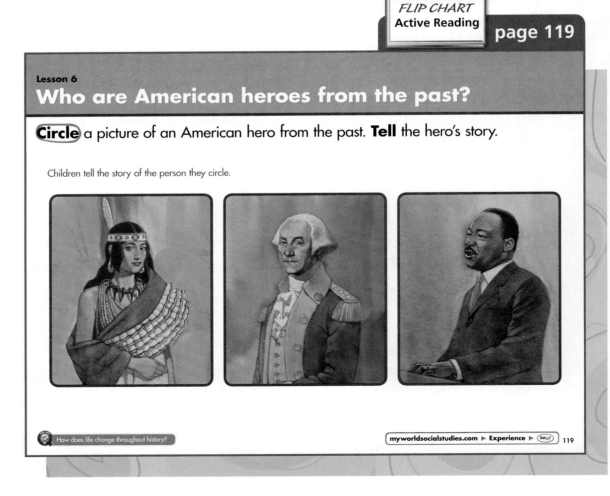

How does life change throughout history?   myworldsocialstudies.com ▶ Experience ▶ Got it?   119

Full Lesson Plan Online

To use or customize the full lesson plan for this lesson, log on to myWorldSocialStudies.com.

Objectives

- Compare family life in the past and family life today.
- Compare objects from the past and objects of today.
- Compare photographs of families in the past and families today.

◉ **Target Reading Skill Objective:**
- Identify sequence.

ELL Objective:
- Use vocabulary to talk about how family life has changed over time.

---

1 PRESENTATION
Lesson 7 Introduction

myWorld and Me

Remind children of the discussion they had about the Big Question for this chapter: How does life change throughout history?

- *What activities do you do with your family?*

5 minutes ⊙

---

2 FLIP CHART
Student Activity Worksheets

Introduce the Lesson Vocabulary words: *family, then, now, clothing, travel,* and *toys.* Point to pictures on the lesson pages as you explain the meaning of each word. Then ask:

- *How are the clothes in each picture different?* Sample response: The family in the older photo look more dressed up. The family in the newer photo are wearing t-shirts and jeans.

Hand out the Vocabulary Worksheet, page 100. Help children complete it.

5 minutes ⊙

Not enough time for social studies? Teach this step during your reading block or as a center activity.

---

3 FLIP CHART
Active Reading

Model active reading by asking the questions and using the teaching strategies indicated next to this lesson's Flip Chart pages.

30 minutes

---

4 PRESENTATION
Got It?

Play the interactive Got It? activity to evaluate children's understanding of the key objectives in this lesson. Use the Extra Support button to assist children who need additional instruction.

OPTIONAL: You may want to assign the Got It? Activity Worksheet for homework or have children complete it in class.

10 minutes ⊙

⊙ *Use the Lesson Steps marked with this icon to teach core content in less time!*

121

Begin to Read

- **ANALYZE VISUALS** *Name two ways the people in the two photographs look different.* clothing, hairstyles

Support English Language Learners

1. Content and Language

Show pictures of family life from the past and the present. Point to the pictures as you paraphrase the objectives on page 121 of this guide. Have children restate the objectives in their own words, using the pictures as prompts.

2. Frontload the Lesson

Have children bring in family photos from the past as well the present. Encourage children to compare the pictures and talk about how family life has changed over time. Also discuss how it has remained the same.

3. Comprehensible Input

Ask think-aloud questions: *Which family lived in the past? How are the families alike? How has family life changed from the past? How is it still the same?*

Begin to Read

- ⊙ **SEQUENCE** *Which came first: the shoes on the left or the sneakers on the right?* the shoes on the left

Differentiated Instruction

Use the following activities to differentiate instruction for children.

L2 Extra Support: Point to the shoes and say *then*. Point to the sneakers and say *now*. Repeat the routine with the other items. Have children take turns saying a sentence about each item.

L3 On-level: Using pictures from magazines, have children make "then and now" flashcards, pairing items from the past and similar items used today. Place the flash cards face down on a table. Invite children to take turns matching pairs of objects.

L4 Challenge: Invite children to make a "then and now" collage of pictures that show family life and everyday objects from long ago and today.

Lesson 7
How have families changed?

Some things about families change. Some things stay the same. Families wear different clothes. They do the same things in a new way.

then   **now**

How does life change throughout history?   myworldsocialstudies.com ▸ Experience ▸ Introduction 120

Lesson 7
How have families changed?

Draw lines from things used long ago to things we use today.

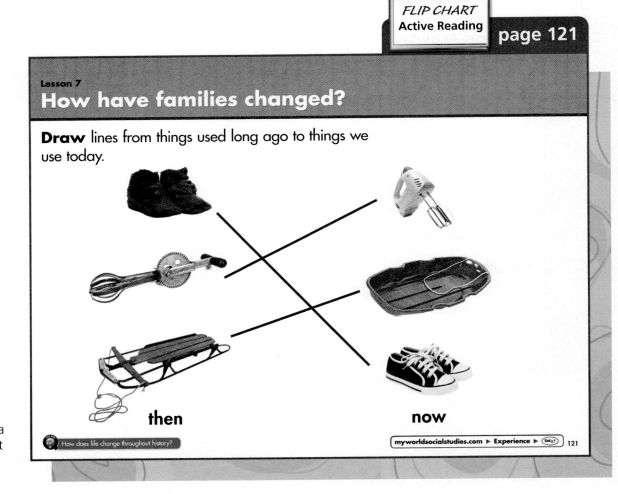

then   **now**

How does life change throughout history?   myworldsocialstudies.com ▸ Experience ▸ Got it? 121

Full Lesson Plan Online

To use or customize the full lesson plan for this lesson, log on to myWorldSocialStudies.com.

Objectives

- Describe how school today is the same as and different from school in the past.
- Compare photographs of schools today and schools in the past.

◉ **Target Reading Skill Objective:**
- Identify sequence.

ELL Objective:
- Learn different strategies to access vocabulary about how school today is similar to and different from school in the past.

---

1 PRESENTATION
Lesson 8 Introduction

myWorld and Me
Remind children of the discussion they had about the Big Question for this chapter: How does life change throughout history?
- *What do you think school was like when your parents were in Kindergarten?*

5 minutes ⊘

---

2 FLIP CHART
Student Activity Worksheets

Introduce the Lesson Vocabulary words: *computer, long ago, same,* and *different.* Point to pictures as you explain the meaning of each word. Then ask:
- *Did schools have computers long ago?* no

Hand out the Vocabulary Worksheet, page 102. Help children complete it.

5 minutes ⊘

Not enough time for social studies? Teach this step during your reading block or as a center activity.

---

3 FLIP CHART
Active Reading

Model active reading by asking the questions and using the teaching strategies indicated next to this lesson's Flip Chart pages.

30 minutes

---

4 PRESENTATION
Got It?

Play the interactive Got It? activity to evaluate children's understanding of the key objectives in this lesson. Use the Extra Support button to assist children who need additional instruction.

OPTIONAL: You may want to assign the Got It? Activity Worksheet for homework or have children complete it in class.

10 minutes ⊘

⊘ *Use the Lesson Steps marked with this icon to teach core content in less time!*

Begin to Read

- ⊙ **Sequence** *Which came first: books or computers?* books

Support English Language Learners

1. Content and Language
Paraphrase the objectives on page 123 of this guide. Then encourage children to restate the objectives in their own words.

2. Frontload the Lesson
Draw a two-column chart with the headings *Then* and *Now.* Ask children what they think school was like long ago. Record their responses under *Then.* Ask children what school is like today. Record this information in the second column.

3. Comprehensible Input
Display pictures of classroom tools from the past and present. Have children role-play how to use the tools, then compare the tools using simple sentences.

Begin to Read

- **Analyze Visuals** *What did children write on long ago?* a slate

Differentiated Instruction

Use the following activities to differentiate instruction for children.

L1 Special Needs: Point to each item in the lesson, say its name, and have children repeat the word. Use the word in a sentence. Encourage children to make up their own sentences.

L2 Extra Support: Show children pictures of classroom tools used long ago. Then have them complete these sentences: *Long ago, children used ____. in school. Today we use ____.*

L3 On-level: Have children compare classroom tools and games from the past and present.

L4 Challenge: Have children participate in the On-level activity. After discussion, encourage them to write sentence strips explaining the comparisons.

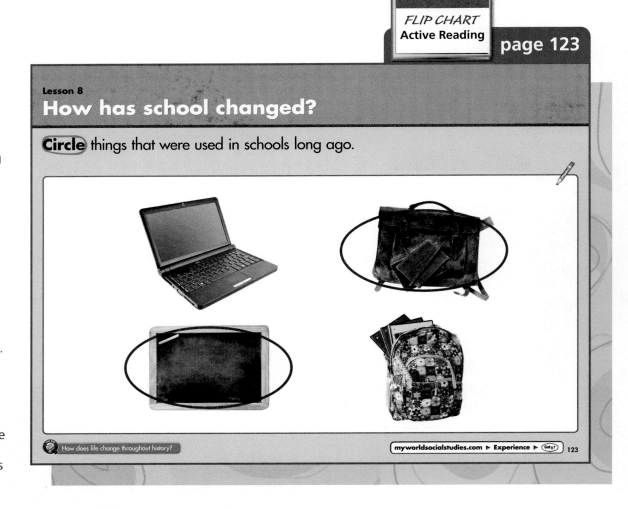

Lesson 8
How has school changed?

Some things about school change. Some things stay the same. Children now sit in groups to read. They still put up a hand to speak.

then

now

How does life change throughout history?

myworldsocialstudies.com ▸ Experience ▸ Introduction 122

Lesson 8
How has school changed?

Circle things that were used in schools long ago.

How does life change throughout history?

myworldsocialstudies.com ▸ Experience ▸ Got it? 123

Full Lesson Plan Online

To use or customize the full lesson plan for this lesson, log on to myWorldSocialStudies.com.

Objectives

- Describe people and places in the school and in the community.
- Examine photographs of communities today and in the past and summarize changes.

- Explain how communities today and in the past are alike and different.
- Identify ways everyday life has both changed and remained the same.

⊙ **Target Reading Skill Objective:**
- Identify sequence.

ELL Objective:
- Use vocabulary and role-play to describe life in communities of the past and of the present.

---

1 PRESENTATION
Lesson 9 Introduction

myWorld and Me
Remind children of the discussion they had about the Big Question for this chapter: How does life change throughout history?
- *What is your community like today?*

5 minutes ⊙

---

2 FLIP CHART
Student Activity Worksheets

Introduce the Lesson Vocabulary words: *community*, *before*, and *after*. Point to pictures on the lesson pages as you explain the meaning of each word. Then ask:
- *What buildings are in your community?* Record children's responses for discussion later.

Hand out the Vocabulary Worksheet, page 104. Help children complete it.

5 minutes ⊙

Not enough time for social studies? Teach this step during your reading block or as a center activity.

---

3 FLIP CHART
Active Reading

Model active reading by asking the questions and using the teaching strategies indicated next to this lesson's Flip Chart pages.

30 minutes

---

4 PRESENTATION
Got It?

Play the interactive Got It? activity to evaluate children's understanding of the key objectives in this lesson. Use the Extra Support button to assist children who need additional instruction.

OPTIONAL: You may want to assign the Got It? Activity Worksheet for homework or have children complete it in class.

10 minutes ⊙

⊙ *Use the Lesson Steps marked with this icon to teach core content in less time!*

Begin to Read

- ◉ **SEQUENCE** *What picture would come first on a timeline: a car or a horse and wagon?* a horse and wagon

Support English Language Learners

1. Content and Language
Point to the community pictures on the Flip Chart page as you paraphrase the objectives for this lesson. Then invite children to restate the objectives in their own words.

2. Frontload the Lesson
Take a picture walk through the lesson. Encourage children to share their predictions about the lesson content.

3. Comprehensible Input
Have children role-play living in a community from the past and today. Use the Flip Chart page as a prompt for acting out and describing each scene.

Lesson 9
How have communities changed?

Some things about communities change. Some things stay the same. There are new buildings. Today people use cars.

then   **now**

How does life change throughout history?   myworldsocialstudies.com ▸ Experience ▸ Introduction   124

Begin to Read

- **MAKE CONNECTIONS** *List three things that are the same in both pictures.* children, school bus, fire hydrant

Differentiated Instruction

Use the following activities to differentiate instruction for children.

L2 Extra Support: Model comparing the pictures. Have children take turns telling how they are alike and different.

L3 On-level: Have children look at pictures of the community in the past. Make a list of the differences. Discuss if these changes are helpful or not.

L4 Challenge: Display pictures of your community at different periods. Invite children to write words or sentences that show how the community has changed over time.

Lesson 9
How have communities changed?

Look at the pictures of the same place then and now.
Circle what is different in the picture that shows now.

then   **now**

How does life change throughout history?   myworldsocialstudies.com ▸ Experience ▸ Got it?   125

Full Lesson Plan Online
To use or customize the full lesson plan for this lesson, log on to myWorldSocialStudies.com.

Objectives

- Explain how technology meets people's needs.
- Identify ways we use tools and technology today.
- Identify ways everyday life has both changed and remained the same.

- Explain how changes in communication have changed the way families live and work.
- Compare photographs of tools and technology today and tools and technology in the past.

⊙ Target Reading Skill Objective:
- Identify sequence.

ELL Objective:
- Use vocabulary and cooperative activities to explore changes in tools for communication.

---

1 PRESENTATION
Lesson 10 Introduction

myWorld and Me
Remind children of the discussion they had about the Big Question for this chapter: How does life change throughout history?
- *How do you think people could stay in touch without telephones?*

5 minutes ⊙

---

2 FLIP CHART
Student Activity Worksheets

Introduce the Lesson Vocabulary words: *typewriter, telephone,* and *television.* Point to pictures on the lesson pages and use gestures as you explain the meaning of each word. Then ask:
- *How are a computer and a typewriter similar?* They are both used to create documents.

Hand out the Vocabulary Worksheet, page 106. Help children complete it.

5 minutes ⊙

Not enough time for social studies? Teach this step during your reading block or as a center activity.

---

3 FLIP CHART
Active Reading

Model active reading by asking the questions and using the teaching strategies indicated next to this lesson's Flip Chart pages.

30 minutes

---

4 PRESENTATION
Got It?

Play the interactive Got It? activity to evaluate children's understanding of the key objectives in this lesson. Use the Extra Support button to assist children who need additional instruction.

OPTIONAL: You may want to assign the Got It? Activity Worksheet for homework or have children complete it in class.

10 minutes ⊙

⊙ *Use the Lesson Steps marked with this icon to teach core content in less time!*

Begin to Read

- ⊙ **SEQUENCE** *What tool would come last on a timeline: a typewriter or a computer?* a computer

Support English Language Learners

1. Content and Language

Point to the pictures on the Flip Chart page. Paraphrase the objectives on page 127 of this guide. Have children restate them in their own words.

2. Frontload the Lesson

Display pictures of tools used in the past. Invite children to tell what they know about each one. Record this information on a KWL chart.

3. Comprehensible Input

Display pictures of different technologies from the past and the tools that have replaced them today. Act out how each one is used, and tell how it has changed over time.

Lesson 10
How has technology changed?

The tools and machines we use have changed from the past.

then   **now**

How does life change throughout history?   myworldsocialstudies.com ▶ Experience ▶ Introduction   126

Begin to Read

- **ANALYZE VISUALS** *How have telephones changed?* They are smaller now than in the past.

Differentiated Instruction

Use the following activities to differentiate instruction for children.

L1 Special Needs: Point to each tool, say its name, and have children echo you. Act out how to use each one.

L2 Extra Support: Invite children to take turns acting out how to use each tool. Have volunteers guess the tool.

L3 On-level: Make a "then and now" chart. Have children draw tools that people use to communicate.

L4 Challenge: Display materials about communication tools. Have children use pictures and words to make a timeline of communication tools.

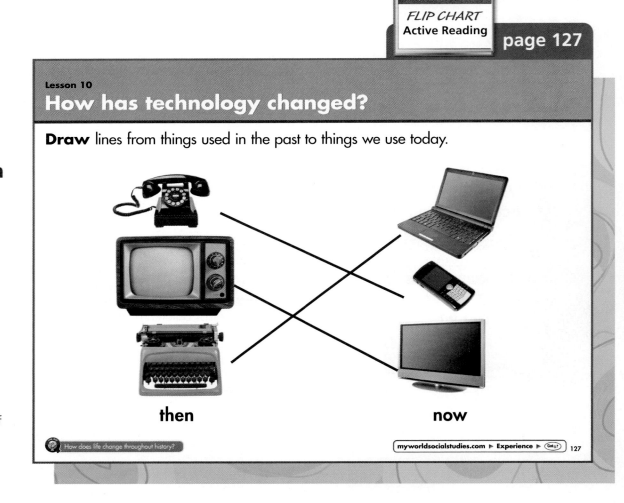

Lesson 10
How has technology changed?

Draw lines from things used in the past to things we use today.

then   **now**

How does life change throughout history?   myworldsocialstudies.com ▶ Experience ▶ GotIt?   127

1 **PRESENTATION** Vocabulary Review | Use the Vocabulary Review activity on the Digital Presentation for this lesson. | *10 minutes* 🕐

2 *Performance Assessment*

| Choice A **myStory Book** | **WRITING ACTIVITY** Children write and illustrate an eight-page booklet demonstrating their understanding of the key objectives, vocabulary, and Big Question for this chapter. | *30 minutes* |

See the Online Lesson Plan for full instructions on how to complete the story together as a class, or have each child complete his or her own story. Make sure children's stories reflect what the chapter's content means to them.

| Choice B **myWorld Activity** | **HANDS-ON ACTIVITY: Me in History** In this activity children demonstrate what they learned by creating a timeline that shows them in the past and present. See the Online Lesson Plan for full instructions for completing the activity. Use Activity Cards 21–25 for this activity. | *30 minutes* |

3 *Formal Assessment* | **OPTIONAL:** You can assign the chapter Review and Assessment Student Activity Worksheet or use the Chapter Test and track scores online. | *30 minutes* 🕐

🕐 *Use the Lesson Steps marked with this icon to teach core content in less time!*

Notes

? Big Question

1. Ask children to recall what they have learned about the different ways life changes throughout history.
2. Call on children to share what they remember.
3. Discuss with children how family, school, and community life have changed, and how different kinds of transportation and communication make life easier for people.

myWorld and Me

1. Have children think about the ways people traveled in the past and the ways they travel today.
2. Encourage children to discuss how life has been made easier by changes in the ways people travel from place to place.

myStory Book

1. Explain to children that they will now have the opportunity to create a story about what they learned in this chapter.
2. Have children choose their own words and select the images they think are best for the story.
3. Explain that prompts will guide them through the writing of the story.

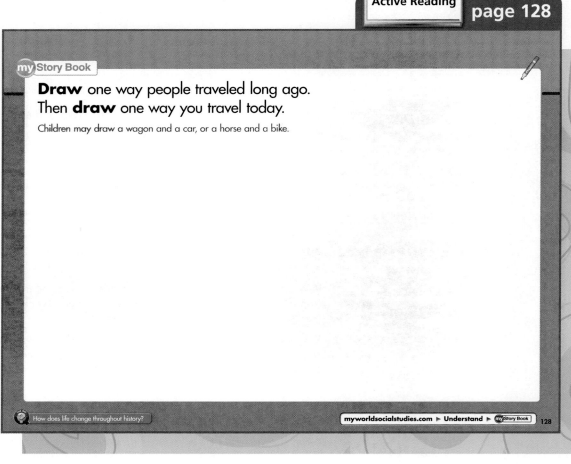

my Story Book

Draw one way people traveled long ago.
Then **draw** one way you travel today.

Children may draw a wagon and a car, or a horse and a bike.

How does life change throughout history?   myworldsocialstudies.com ▶ Understand ▶ my Story Book   128